Life in Custer's Cavalry

Life in Custer's Cavalry

Diaries and Letters of Albert and Jennie Barnitz
1867–1868

Edited by

ROBERT M. UTLEY

University of Nebraska Press
Lincoln and London

Copyright © 1977 by Robert M. Utley
Manufactured in the United States of America

First Bison Book printing: 1987

Library of Congress Cataloging-in-Publication Data

Barnitz, Albert Trovillo Siders.
    Life in Custer's cavalry.

    Reprint. Originally published: New Haven:
Yale University Press, 1977. Originally published
in the series: Yale Western Americana series.
    "Bison book."
    Bibliography: p.
    Includes index.
    1. Indians of North America — Wars — 1868 – 1869 —
Personal narratives. 2. Barnitz, Albert Trovillo Siders
— Diaries. 3. Barnitz, Jennie — Diaries.
4. United States. Army. Cavalry, 7th — Biography.
5. Soldiers — United States — Diaries. 6. Indians of
North America — Kansas — Wars. I. Barnitz, Jennie.
II. Utley, Robert Marshall, 1929–   . III. Title.
[E83.869.B37 1987]   973.8'1'0922   86-25104
ISBN 0-8032-9553-7 (pbk.)

Reprinted by arrangement with Robert M. Utley

∞

Contents

Illustrations

Preface

As an intermittent Custer buff, I have known *of* Albert Barnitz for nearly three decades, for all accounts of the Battle of the Washita note the fearful wound he suffered in that memorable attack on Black Kettle's Cheyenne village. But I did not actually *know* Albert Barnitz until my good friend Archibald Hanna introduced me. Archie had been alerted to the existence of a body of Barnitz Papers by William H. Goetzmann, then of Yale, now of the University of Texas, and set out in pursuit of them with the courtly tenacity that marks his stewardship of Yale's Beinecke Library and contributes so greatly to its distinction as an institution incredibly rich in basic sources of western American history.

Through Archie I gained access to the Barnitz Papers, and through them I came to know Albert and Jennie intimately. From them I have learned much of frontier army life; of the attitudes of officers and their wives toward Indians, settlers, and themselves; and of particular characters and events in the story of Indian warfare in Kansas after the Civil War. I have also come to appreciate Albert and Jennie, and many of their associates, as human beings rather than as wooden figures in dry official records and old wet-plate photographs. I hope that readers of this volume will experience a similar pleasure and gratitude that Albert and Jennie left so rich a record, in diaries and letters, of their brief life on the frontier.

Archie Hanna found the Barnitz Papers in the custody of a truly remarkable woman. She is the Marquesa de Zahara, formerly Betty Byrne, granddaughter of Albert and Jennie, daughter of an Irish officer of the United States Army, and widow of a Spanish diplomat. I have come to appreciate the Marquesa greatly through her colorful letters. I would like to meet her, but some years ago, after collaborating with Archie Hanna in gathering all the historically valuable papers from the attic of the family homestead in Ohio, she packed up and moved to Ireland, where she seemingly leads a quiet pastoral life. I am immensely indebted to her, not only for presenting the Barnitz Papers to Yale and making available to me some of the photographs that appear in this book, but also for sharing with me her memories of Albert and Jennie.

The Barnitz Papers are voluminous. The diaries, for example, intermittently span the years 1860 to 1912. Those for the Civil War years contain much of historical value; those for the years after 1869 are chiefly of family interest. I have focused only on the two years of frontier military service. Even for this brief period, the biggest challenge was selection. The passages presented in the following pages represent probably less than half of what Albert and Jennie recorded in these two years, and I have been forced to omit important material that I would like to have included.

Some of my more scholarly friends may quarrel with my basic approach, which dispenses with the conventional apparatus of scholarly editing. I adopted this approach because it seemed to me that digressive footnotes would unduly burden the narrative flow established by the combination of diaries and letters and because they seemed so alien to the distinctively human flavor of the Barnitzes' writings. Thus, recognizing that this is the story of Albert and Jennie and not a display of the scholarly attainments of the editor, I have kept my own intervention to a minimum. What I have to say is said in brief connective passages and in appendixes that further describe the people and places marked in the text with an asterisk. If some of the Barnitzes' statements seem to call for a correction, elaboration, or discussion that I have not provided, I can only hope that the deficiency may be more than offset by a textual flow uninterrupted by lengthy footnote digressions.

In addition to the help of people already acknowledged in this preface, I wish to record my appreciation for the aid and counsel of the following: Melody Webb Grauman of the National Park Service in Fairbanks, Alaska; Nyle H. Miller of the Kansas State Historical Society; Minnie Dubbs Millbrook of Topeka, Kansas; Mildred Eide of the Fort Leavenworth Museum; Michael Musick of the National Archives in Washington, D.C.; Lawrence Frost of Monroe, Michigan; Henry Judd and Franklin G. Smith, also National Park Service associates; Gary Roberts of Abraham Baldwin Agricultural College, Georgia; Harry Kelsey of the Los Angeles

County Natural History Museum; and Mrs. F. Michael Trevitt of Fountain Valley, California, niece of the Marquesa de Zahara.

A final word about brevet rank, which the uninitiated will find constantly confusing. Many of the officers who wander in and out of these pages held both regular and brevet rank. The first was actual rank in line or staff, the second that which had been bestowed in recognition of notable services. Although officers might occasionally be assigned to duty in their brevet rank, most served in their regular grades. Thus Barnitz, a captain and company commander,· held brevets of major and lieutenant colonel for combat achievements in the Civil War. Custer, a lieutenant colonel, was a brevet major general. Sometimes officers were addressed or identified by their regular rank, other times by their brevet rank. Similarly, sometimes they wore insignia of their brevet rank, sometimes not, and sometimes both. I have tried throughout to lessen the confusion, but there is no wholly satisfactory way to do it. Capt. Arthur T. Lee, like Barnitz a soldier-poet, perhaps said of brevets all that needs saying:

What is a Brevet?

As Captain Forbes walked off parade,
Sam Green inquiringly said:
"Pray tell me, Cap.,—and tell me true,
Why all those officers in blue
Walk up and touch their caps to you;
They've leaves and eagles, them 'ere chaps,
Whilst you've but bars upon your straps."

"Why, Sam," says Forbes, "you *must* be green;
The reason's plainly to be seen:—
My straps, so humble in their place,
Are worth the symbol on their face,
Whilst leaves and eagles pay no debts:—
Those officers are all brevets."

  Says Green, "that puzzles me,—you bet;—
Cap, tell me,—what is a brevet?"

  "Well, Sam,—to put it through your pate,
You listen, whilst I illustrate.
You see yon turkey on the fence:—

That's turkey, Sam, in every sense;
Yon turkey-buzzard on the tree:—
He's *brevet* turkey:—do you see?"

Moral

A Turkey has some value, Sam,
A Buzzard isn't worth a damn!

1. Albert and Jennie

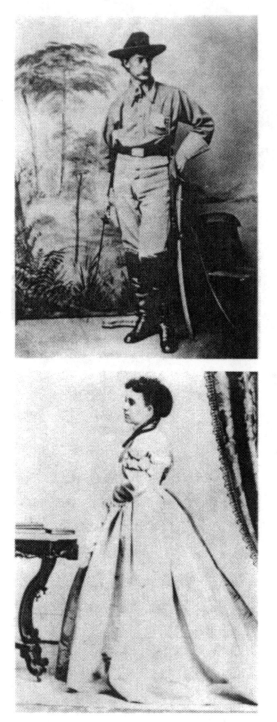

Albert, equipped with saber, pistol, and riding crop, is attired for the field. The shirt is almost certainly one made by Jennie after a pattern obtained from Elizabeth Custer. The portrait was probably made by a Leavenworth City photographer early in 1868.

Jennie wears her wedding dress, a dove-gray fabric trimmed in pink and ornamented with pink and crystal dangles. Curls are artificial hairpiece known as a frisette.

Albert and Jennie met at the end of the Civil War. He was thirty-one and a soldier-poet, veteran of several score combat actions and author of numerous verses that commanded no more than a modest readership. She was twenty-five or thereabouts (one cannot be certain because she never disclosed her age—even to Albert) and much sought after by Cleveland's bachelors. She was very beautiful and very conscious of it. He was beautiful too, in his blue uniform with brass buttons and gold shoulder straps and his head overflowing with unruly blond curls. She was the product of a stable, close-knit, staunchly religious, and comfortably situated though frugal middle-class family; he of a youth of hard work to aid a widowed mother with three children. She, for all her preoccupation with feminine attractions, was something of a prude; he, with his poet's disdain of convention, boldly made fun of the canons of Victorian society. The shared, however, an affinity for the romantic clichés of that same society and, not altogether consistently, an ambition for intellectual freedom and enrichment.

Albert and Jennie were married and went west with the army to serve on the Indian frontier. The military interlude occupied only three of their forty-six years of marriage. But because they saw and lived some important history, because they were literate, and because they kept diaries and, when apart, wrote long and uninhibited letters, they left to posterity a body of papers that contains both a contribution to history and a warm human story.

Albert was born on March 10, 1835, at Bloody Run, in Bedford County, Pennsylvania. His parents named him Albert Trorillo Siders Barnitz. Although his middle names seem fitting for one of the literary and romantic inclinations that marked his adult character, he never used them. Perhaps this was because there was also in his adulthood a balancing practicality and resourcefulness shaped by a hard and demanding youth. His father, a physician, died when Albert was thirteen. But somehow, in addition to helping to care for the family, he found time to read widely and deeply and to begin framing the romantic verses, brimming with Victorian sentiment, that he turned out for the rest of his life.

In Ohio, where the family had moved shortly after his birth, Albert Barnitz grew up to be a genial young man with intense eyes, handsome face, and a mountain of curly blond hair. Possessed of a good intellect, a sense of humor, and inextinguishable cheerfulness, he made friends easily.

3

His formal education was limited—a year at Kenyon College in 1851 and two years, 1858–59, of intermittent study at the Cleveland Law College—but he read voraciously and made of himself an educated man. Articulate, literate, something of a showman, he toured Ohio, Kentucky, and Indiana giving dramatic readings and conducting classes in elocution. In 1857 in Cincinnati he published a 288-page volume of original poetry entitled, appropriately, The Mystic Delvings. *It was locally well received but financially unsuccessful.*

A frayed handbill testifies to the variety of Barnitz's youthful attainments, at least as he viewed them, and also to nineteenth-century America's tastes in entertainment. The year was 1858, and prospective customers were informed that for twenty-five cents they could hear "The Young American Poet Albert Barnitz of Cincinnati, Author of 'The Mystic Delvings!'" present "Readings and Recitations! From our Standard Authors and Poets, interspersed with remarks and instruction upon the cultivation of the Voice; Amusing Imitations of Eccentric Characters, and various styles of Stump Oratory; Examples of faulty Pulpit Elocution, and common defects in the Oratory of the Bar; Illustrations of the Passions: Love, Hate, Despair, Joy &c., Fear, Courage, Sorrow, Hope, &c., As denoted by the tone of the voice, the expression of the features, and gestures of the body, together with numerous Personations of Character." He offered all this and more—readings from Shakespeare, Tennyson, and Poe—and "The Whole to conclude with Imitations of the Great Tragedians."

While at Cleveland Law College, Barnitz paid passionate court to "Little Eva" Prouty, a red-haired beauty who lived at nearby Mentor. Late in 1859 they were married. It seems to have been a blissful union, unmarred by the slightest friction—at least so Albert assured sister Rucy in a May 1860 letter and so the surviving poems proclaiming his devotion tend to confirm. That summer the couple moved to St. Paul, Minnesota, where Eva had relatives. And there she died in childbirth, along with the infant daughter. Inconsolable—indeed, he never wholly shook off his grief—the husband placed the bodies in a casket and brought them back to Mentor.

Fort Sumter fell in April 1861 and Lincoln called for three-month volunteers. To one of the three-month regiments, the 13th Ohio Infantry, Barnitz offered his services without actually enlisting. He functioned, as he later explained, "as Drill-Master, Clerk at Hd. Qrs., and factotum generally, without compensation, and for the 'mere love of the thing.'" The suppression of the rebellion, of course, turned out to be more than a three-month undertaking, and on August 18, 1861, he enlisted in Com-

pany G, 2d Ohio Volunteer Cavalry. He was mustered as a sergeant and quickly found himself a man of consequence. Drill of the unit usually fell to him because "the officers of that day (who subsequently resigned on getting into actual service) did not seem to possess the faculty of acquiring knowledge from books."

After training at Camp Dennison, near Cincinnati, the 2d Ohio went to Missouri in January 1862 and for the next year operated along the turbulent frontier of Kansas and Indian Territory against the "Jayhawker" bands of Quantrill and other guerrilla chieftains. In June 1862 Barnitz proudly sewed on the shoulder straps of a second lieutenant: "the first one commissioned from the ranks in my regiment, and this without effort or solicitation on my part."

In December 1862 the 2d Ohio returned home for refitting. At Camp Chase a new colonel, August V. Kautz, set out to whip the regiment into fighting trim. A crusty veteran of the regular army, Kautz began by purging the companies of incompetent officers. In this process, in February 1863, Barnitz became the junior first lieutenant and, a week later, the senior captain.

Eastern Kentucky and Tennessee provided Barnitz his next field of service. Here, in the spring of 1863, the newly commissioned captain conceived and urged a daring raid by his company on enemy transportation lines. "The design of the expedition," he later wrote, "was to enter East Tennessee through one of the unguarded passes, and destroying bridges, depots, &c. along the great railroad connecting Chattanooga and Lynchburg." Overcoming the reluctance of his superiors, Barnitz successfully carried out this mission. In the course of the raid, however, his horse fell on him and caused severe injuries, including a broken jaw, that brought him near death. During his convalescence he served as judge advocate on the staff of the Provost Marshal General of East Tennessee. He was thus in Knoxville during the weeks in which Gen. Ambrose E. Burnside held out against the besieging Confederate army of Gen. James Longstreet.

Early in 1864 General Burnside returned to the Army of the Potomac, taking the 2d Ohio Cavalry with him. With great difficulty Barnitz secured his release from staff duty in order to go east with his comrades. In Virginia the regiment became part of the Cavalry Corps, Army of the Potomac, newly energized by a scrappy little general from the West, Philip H. Sheridan.* Barnitz fought with the First Brigade, Third Division, through the series of murderous battles by which, in the spring of 1864, Gen. Ulysses S. Grant pushed from the Wilderness through Spottsylvania to Cold Harbor, in the vicinity of Richmond. These operations also fea-

tured several big cavalry actions, as Grant allowed Sheridan to try his hand against the invincible Jeb Stuart. In one, at Ashland Station on June 1, Captain Barnitz had his horse shot from under him, and then, while leading his men on foot, carbine in hand, took a minié ball in the right thigh. Five days later, from a hospital bed at White House Landing, he wrote exuberantly to brother Mack, a Cincinnati clergyman: "The army is in fine condition. It is the grandest thing in all the universe, and is heroically driving the infuriated secesh right along down every day. I would not have missed this campaign for a dozen bullet holes."

In a Philadelphia hospital for officers, Barnitz recovered from his wound while also serving on a general court-martial that sat all summer. In the autumn he returned to his regiment, now fighting Gen. Jubal Early in the Shenandoah Valley. The Third Division had a new commander, a daredevil youth four years Barnitz's junior, who had become a general at twenty-three and who boasted golden curls even more impressive than Barnitz's. Under George Armstrong Custer,* the Ohio troopers fought in the succession of engagements that turned back Early's army and so thoroughly devastated the Shenandoah Valley that it no longer afforded the Confederates an avenue for menacing Washington.

March 1865 found Sheridan's cavalry back with the Army of the Potomac, poised for the final pursuit of the war as Lee made ready to break loose from the Petersburg defenses. In the absence of field officers, Barnitz as senior captain commanded the 2d Ohio. Actually, he had been promoted to major the previous summer, but the regiment had fallen so much below strength that it was judged not to be entitled to a major. In the battles that marked the death throes of Lee's army, Barnitz and the 2d Ohio played a conspicuous part. Under Custer's vigorous direction, they fought with distinction at Dinwiddie Court House, Five Forks, Namozine Church, Saylor's Creek, Appomattox Station, and finally, on April 9, Appomattox Court House. At Saylor's Creek on the sixth the Ohioans captured 12 cannon, 68 officers (including 3 generals), 891 enlisted men, 4 battle flags, and a wagon train three miles long. In a headlong charge on Appomattox Station on the eighth, they seized 53 cannon, several railroad supply trains, and hordes of prisoners. The regiment was the last under fire and had the last man killed before the surrender of Lee. Later, Barnitz immortalized these adventures in an epic poem of twenty-five stanzas, entitled "With Custer at Appomattox," which he read at veterans' reunions. In recognition of this record, General Sheridan placed the 2d Ohio in the lead as his Cavalry Corps joined the Army of the Potomac in the grand

A beardless Albert as he appeared at the age of twenty. This picture appeared in his book, *The Mystic Delvings,* in 1857.

Albert as a captain in the 2d Ohio Cavalry about 1864.

Jennie, from a tiny locket portrait.

review down Pennsylvania Avenue in Washington, D.C., on May 23, 1865.

After Lee's surrender the 2d Ohio filled out its ranks, boated down the Ohio River to St. Louis, and took station at Springfield, Missouri. Barnitz, at last wearing major's shoulder straps, commanded the post and regiment in summer-long police operations along the still-troubled Kansas border. In September 1865 the order came to muster out the regiment, and he returned to civilian life a veteran of countless adventures and almost a hundred combat actions.

Exactly when Albert Barnitz met Jennie Platt is not certain. There is a family tradition that Jennie spied the handsome, curly headed officer, accompanied by his dead wife's mother, in a horsecar plying between Cleveland and East Cleveland and promptly set out to conquer him. She had been betrothed to a young lawyer who failed to return from the war and in 1866, when she was about twenty-five, began to feel desperate about marriage—or so says tradition. As Albert later explained to his family, "I looked so beautiful to Jennie, that she put on her biggest hoop skirts, with which she couldn't get through the door, and came right around to call on Mrs. Prouty."

Reading Jennie's diary for 1866, one suspects that Albert or the family may have embellished the story in later years. He first appears in her diary in February 1866 and thereafter is a frequent, sometimes daily suitor. He quickly saw Jennie for what she was: a beautiful girl with straight black hair, flawless teeth, and tiny bones and features, and of imperious, comfort-loving, and somewhat lazy disposition. A "willful and selfish little mortal," he called her, only partly in jest. She lavished great care on her appearance and constantly compared herself, advantageously, to others. She disapproved of alcohol and tobacco, both of which Albert used in moderation. She subscribed to Victorian morality, which Albert constantly and irreverently belittled. And she was devoutly religious, which Albert assuredly was not; he rarely concealed his skepticism or his acid contempt for the pretense of organized religion. But Jennie was warm, vivacious, fun-loving, and stimulating. He quickly fell in love with her and paid her assiduous court.

On March 19, 1866, Albert proposed. Family tradition or no, Jennie did not accept. "Ah I think I shall never understand my heart," she wrote, adding "Sick all day"—as she was so often and would be all her life. The truth is, Jennie had two other suitors in 1866, both of whom declared their love and pleaded for acceptance. Albert's bold defiance of convention may have frightened her a bit. The competitors gained headway during the summer as Barnitz traveled in Missouri seeking business opportunities and, in the autumn, established a business partnership in Michigan. As late as November, Jennie wrote in her diary: "How strongly I am situated! Three young men waiting now *for my answer—yes or no. May I do right."*

The civilian world did not promise to be kind to Barnitz. In the summer of 1866, as the bill providing for a peacetime army neared passage in Congress, he wrote to his congressman, Representative Rufus P. Spalding, expressing a desire to enter the regular army. He sought this help, he said, reluctantly and with misgivings but upon the presumption "that merit, unaided by political influence, would scarcely secure an appointment and confirmation." Recounting his wartime services, he concluded on a light note: "If the fact that I served so long under Sheridan be not a sufficient passport to some modest position in the Army, let it be further remembered that I was in Custer's Division, *and that* ought *to settle the matter, and favorably too!" Representative Spalding endorsed his young constituent to the attention of the War Department, but one is led to conclude, in view of the immense political support other applicants brought to the cause, that merit did indeed play a part in Barnitz's appointment. In November 1866 he received notice of his appointment as a captain in the 7th U.S. Cavalry. One of the four new mounted regiments authorized by the Army Act of July 28, 1866, it was even then organizing at Fort Riley,* Kansas.*

As 1867 opened, Barnitz renewed his assault on Jennie's affections. He also boarded a train for Washington, D.C., to appear before an army examining board, a formality for all newly appointed officers.

Albert to Jennie, Washington, D.C., Jan. 15, 1867:

I saw a Sergeant of Cavalry on the train. Accosting him, I found that he belonged to the 2nd Cavalry, and had formerly been stationed at Fort Riley. Said it is a pleasant and flourishing place, the fort built of stone, officers quarters &c. in good style. Says the R.R. is completed to within a few miles of the fort, and trains running daily, that the 7th Cavalry is there organizing, that *Custer* is Lieutenant Colonel of the Reg't (by appointment, same as myself) and in command! Then of course his amiable little wife, whom you would love, I think, will be there. Isn't that pleasant! I hope it will prove to be true.

Albert to Jennie, Washington, D.C., Jan. 17, 1867:

Jennie, not for one moment have I ceased to think of you, since I have been here. When I visit places of historic interest, or go to the "receptions" given by distinguished persons, the notables of the nation, I desire only that you could be with me. And yet I would not wish you to do more than take one look at society, as it exists here. I would not be willing that you should breathe the contaminating atmosphere of this famed metropolis for more than a very brief period. I have just come from the White House, the President's Mansion, where I was presented to and shook hands with the President [Andrew Johnson]. He holds a levee to night. The Green Room, the Red Room, the East Room, and all the other celebrated apartments of the mansion are brilliantly illuminated, one hundred ushers and members of the police are in attendance, and in one of the smaller rooms stands the President, with his anxious and care-worn face, while beyond him, in the back-ground of the picture, as Artists would say, are grouped various members of his household, and cabinet. Carriages and pedestrians are constantly arriving, and already the visitors throng the halls and corridors, and fill most of the space in the rooms and antechambers. The Marine Band, gorgeous in scarlet and gold lace, discourses music. It is a sad pageant, with all its brilliance, and I was glad to escape from it, to the scarcely less multitudinous gathering at Willard's Hotel, in one of the rooms of which I am now writing, while all around me are people discoursing of the weather, and various topics of kindred interest, writing, reading papers, smoking cigars, and making themselves generally agreeable. . . .

I have reported to the President of the Examining Board [Maj. Gen. David Hunter] and am to pass an examination tomorrow. I do not apprehend any difficulty at all, either as regards the examination or confirmation by the Senate. The chief difficulty has already been overcome, in obtaining the appointment. I have been highly honored. Congress only authorized the raising of four additional regiments of cavalry, two of which (the 9th & 10th) were to be composed of colored troops. The [Army] Act [of 1866] provides that one third of the captains are to be selected

from the line of the Regular Army, and the remaining two thirds
from officers of Volunteers "who have distinguished themselves
for meritorious service" &c. &c. Inasmuch as there were but 16
vacancies, in all, to which I was eligible, (in the two white regiments), and about a thousand applicants, and . . . as I was
placed high up in the list, in the 7*th* Cavalry, which, as I am told by
Genl. Hunter, and officers of the War Department, is to be the
finest regiment in the service, and "far superior to any of the old
regiments," I ought to feel considerably honored. Don't you think
so? Maj. Genl. (of Vols.) A.J. Smith,* who commanded a corps
under Grant, at Vicksburg, and under Sherman, afterwards, is
Colonel of the Reg't, and all the other officers are proportionately
distinguished.

Albert to Jennie, Washington, D.C., Jan. 18, 1867:

I appeared before the Examining Board to day, passed through
the ordeal successfully, and received the required certificate, to
that effect, from Genl. Hunter, the President of the Board. Several others who presented themselves for examination were not so.
fortunate!—I could only sympathize with them. As to my confirmation by the Senate, I regard it as absolutely certain. And
now what do you say Jennie? What *do* you say! "tell me, quick!" I
do believe that you love me, and *may I never see you again if I do not
love you dearer than all the world besides!* There, that's equivalent to a
vow, and may the "Good Man" cause the cars to run off the tracks,
for my especial benefit, or be otherwise unamiable, at my expense,
if I do not utter it "without any mental reservation or evasion
whatsoever!"

But I am coming home soon, and then we will conclude what is
to be done. I will apply to the Secretary of War tomorrow for
permission to delay joining my regiment for 20 days. In the mean
time, Jennie, do be right industrious!

*The couple did indeed conclude what would be done. Jennie had decided
in favor of Albert. They were married in East Cleveland on February 11,
1867, and that very night they boarded a train for the frontier.*

2. Forts Riley and Harker, February–March 1867

Fort Riley in 1867.

The newlyweds arrived at Fort Riley, Kansas, on February 21, 1867. Here they found the headquarters and four troops of the 7th Cavalry. In the absence on leave of Col. A. J. Smith, the lieutenant colonel of the regiment commanded. He was Albert's old division commander, Bvt. Maj. Gen. George A. Custer. The other eight troops of the 7th occupied stations along the Smoky Hill and Arkansas River roads to Colorado and New Mexico: Forts Harker,* Hays,* Dodge,* and Wallace* (Kansas) and Lyon* and Morgan* (Colorado).

Jennie to her mother, Mary Platt, Fort Riley, Kan., Feb. 26, 1867:

We came here Thursday evening. We were at once invited to Gen Custers—who is nicely established here, & were his guests until yesterday—(Monday). Mrs. Custer* is a charming woman, very gay. We were constantly receiving calls from officers, some times a half dozen at a time. They are splendid—I should think all all of them are from the best class of society, & were all officers of high rank in our war. The Colonels in Volunteer service are only Lieutenants in Regular Army. How Albert came to be appointed Captain I dont know. I dined on Friday with Mrs. Gen. Gibbs [wife of the senior major of the 7th, Bvt. Maj. Gen. Alfred Gibbs*] who puts on an immense amount of style. I was relieved when dinner was over. The officers assume a great deal here. The poor privates are perfect slaves. I do pity them from the bottom of my heart. We are now boarding with the Chaplain [Rev. Charles Reynolds], an Episcopal clergyman, who has a very pleasant family. . . .

The Army life is delightful & is eminently suited for me, as I do love so much to be waited upon, you know. No one is expected to do anything here. It is not at all *military*, & almost disgraceful. It is an exciting time here now. Supplies being prepared & sent for 10,000 men etc. This is a beautiful Fort. The buildings cost a million of dollars.

16 FORTS RILEY AND HARKER

Albert to Mr. and Mrs. Andrew Platt and Hattie (Jennie's sister), Fort Riley, Kan., Feb. 27, 1867:

Indian depredations have quite unsettled things for a time. It appears to be an understood thing that all the troops on the western frontier are to unite in an expedition against the Indians at a very early date. Probably within a couple of weeks, or even earlier. General Hancock,* now in command of the Department [of the Missouri], (Hd Qrs. at Fort Leavenworth*) is coming on in person to take command. His ambulance has already arrived. A battery of artillery is expected here daily. I do not much believe myself that any serious fighting with the Indians is likely to take place on *our* front, though I think that an expedition which has started, or *is* to start westward from Omaha will be likely to wage a war of extermination, or something of the kind, against the Sioux.

On the northern plains, the Teton Sioux and Northern Cheyennes had united to cut off travel on the Bozeman Trail to the Montana goldfields, and on December 21, 1866, they had wiped out a detachment of eighty men under Capt. William J. Fetterman. On the southern plains, the chiefs of the buffalo-hunting tribes—Southern Sioux and Cheyenne, Arapaho, Kiowa, Comanche, and Plains Apache—probably desired peace but could not restrain their young men from committing occasional depredations on settlers, travelers, and railroad builders. Lt. Gen. William T. Sherman, commanding the Division of the Missouri, planned two major campaigns in the spring of 1867. The one against the Sioux, alluded to above by Barnitz, did not materialize. The one against the southern tribes, led by Maj. Gen. Winfield S. Hancock, had an ambiguous purpose that reflected the ambiguous disposition of the Indians: "to confer with them to ascertain if they want to fight, in which case he will indulge them."*

Barnitz had been assigned to command Troop G of the 7th, stationed at Fort Harker, fifty miles west of Riley. He was to lead a detachment of 160 recruits and 4 officers as far as Harker, then participate in the Hancock Expedition.

Albert to Mr. and Mrs. Platt, Fort Riley, Kan., March 11, 1867:

I expected certainly to have got started this morning, and in anticipation of this, I placed Jennie under the charge of a surgeon, who was going as far as St. Louis on leave of absence, and started her *en route* for home, at 5 o'clock this morning. I had almost concluded to take her with me to Fort Harker, and she was very willing, indeed quite *anxious* to go, not because she desired to make the trip, I apprehend, as that she desired to be with me, until the very moment of my starting on the much-talked-of Indian Expedition, but when it came to the test I could scarcely gain the consent of my heart to let her undertake the journey, as the officer's quarters at Harker are not quite completed yet, and from present indications I could only expect to remain there for a very short time after my arrival there. I think Jennie is about perfect, and you must all love her a great deal for my sake. I do not much expect to see her again before Fall, we all expect to be on the war-path for five or six months this season, but of course all is uncertainty as yet. For myself, I do not understand distinctly what Indians we are expected to operate against. It may be after all that we are only going out to hold "big talks," and distribute beads! I am very, very lonesome to day, since Jennie's departure. I think she scarcely closed her eyes last night, she was very sad at parting. You must all try to console her, and make her cheerful.

A snowstorm and freezing temperatures delayed Barnitz's departure. In a letter to Jennie on March 15, he alluded to Anna Darrah, an attractive young friend of Elizabeth Custer who had come west to enjoy the adventures of the frontier and the attentions of dashing cavalry officers:

Saw a good pen-and-ink sketch of Miss Darrow yesterday. She is represented standing with a bird-cage by her side, and small net, with a long handle, in her hand, fishing for *straps*! a strap thus ![sketch]—to represent a 1st Lieutenant of Cavalry, is seen flying through the air, while she is making every effort to capture it, with her net—having just dropped one which she had already caught—one without the bars—obviously a 2nd Lieutenant!

Despite continuing bad weather, Barnitz's command left Fort Riley on March 17, as he informed Jennie in a letter from "Abilena" on March 18, 1867:

We got under way at last—crossed on a pontoon bridge, and went into camp on the other side of the river—night very cold, and windy. Yesterday morning we started early, passed through that beautiful little village known as Junction City, where, in spite of all precautions some of the recruits managed to get whiskey, and were under the necessity of doing a little "extra duty" in the transportation line as soon as they were sufficiently recuperated! We encamped last night in the vicinity of a *ranch* known as "the hay ricks" where the good man, the proprietor thereof, expected to do a lively business in the whiskey line, but I had him walked up to camp behind a couple of loaded carbines, and arranged with him to discontinue the whiskey business for one evening at all events!

The command reached Fort Harker on March 22. Here Barnitz found his own troop, G, together with F, commanded by 2d Lt. Henry J. Nowlan.* Commanding the post and garrison was Maj. Alfred Gibbs, whom Albert and Jennie had already met at Fort Riley.

Albert to Jennie, Fort Harker, Kan., March 23, 1867:

Well, I am much pleased with Fort Harker, in spite of all disagreeable surroundings. The horses are all in good stables, the men in temporary barracks, and only the officers in tents—which are floored and have board doors &c. The officers' quarters are progressing finely, and they will be indeed handsome—even more pleasant and cozy than those at Fort Riley—and they are beautifully situated. I am also *very much* pleased with the officer whom I found in charge of my company [2d Lt. Henry Jackson*]. He is very much of a gentleman, and a thorough soldier. My horses look very well—and I now have two excellent ones for myself. I am hurrying up the preparations for our "expedition!"—as Genl. Gibbs thinks we will certainly move as soon as Genl. Smith arrives—*probably* as soon as the last of next week! Genl. Hancock is at Fort Riley hurrying things.

. . . Am very well pleased with Genl. Gibbs.

Albert to Jennie, Fort Harker, Kan., March 26, 1867:

Last night . . . just before tattoo Genl. Gibbs sent his compliments, and requested to see me at his residence—the same invitation being extended to the other officers—and of course I could not well excuse myself from complying, knowing from previous invitations that the order of business for the evening was a "coallation" [collation]—that's the word to express pound-cake and wine isn't it?—well then a coallation and a dance were in contemplation. Twelve officers were present, and four ladies Mrs. Genl. Penrose,

A Sandhurst graduate and Crimean War veteran, Henry J. Nowlan immigrated in 1862 and received a 7th Cavalry appointment in 1866. He served the regiment continuously until, a major, he died of a heart attack in 1898. This picture was made in 1876.

Miss Penrose, and the wives of two Infantry officers of this Post. One of the officers played the flute and another a guitar, in admirable style, and the whole affair was a complete success. Having been on duty as Officer of the Day, and up nearly all the previous night, visiting the outposts, I quietly departed about 12 o'clock, and betook myself to the remote corner of a double wall tent, where my cozy bunk was situated, and soon fell asleep, thinking of "the darlingest little girl!"

General Penrose was Capt. William H. Penrose of the 3d Infantry, a brigadier by brevet. He had been with another column, commanded by Maj. Wickliffe Cooper* of the 7th Cavalry, that had also marched from Fort Riley and was destined for posts farther west.

I did not see much of either Major Cooper or the Penrose outfit on the march from Fort Riley. They generally encamped with the Infantry, and I always endeavored to encamp the cavalry across some stream half a mile off, to avoid details. Genl. Penrose and Major Cooper however had jolly times on the march, as you may suppose—having plenty of old rye along—and each of them used up a horse or two on the way, chasing wolves through the prairie-dog villages! I think Genl. Gibbs must have given Major Cooper a little good advice, on his arrival here, for he has become remarkably temperate of late! *I* am the "goodest child" of course. I don't use any liquor at all. I still have the square bottle which was presented to me in Cincinnati and which I am keeping for the campaign, to cure snake bites! . . .

. . . I am fast getting every thing in proper shape. Indeed I found things in fine order here, and had only the recruits to put in train. I have now a fine troop—or company—("Troop" is the word used here—to distinguish it from an Infantry Company) of 91 men and horses present for duty. The horses are in stables and doing well. I just wish that you could be here for a day, to witness the order and regularity with which every thing is done. Having a good orderly sergeant, and other non-commissioned officers, and a first class Lieutenant, I have little to do except sign my name, and give orders. *All* officers attend roll calls however, and Genl. Gibbs is always present in the centre of the Parade ground to receive the reports.

Albert to Jennie, Fort Harker, Kan., March 28, 1867:

Did I tell you how comfortably my troop is situated? The men are all in one building—not at all crowded—and the building is well floored, and fitted up with comfortable bunks—each of which is provided with a straw mattress, a "bed tick" rather, the building is well lighted (with glass windows) and is heated with three large stoves. We have an abundance of fuel—more than we can use. In rear of the building occupied by the men is another for a mess room, and, at the end of it, a room partitioned off as a kitchen. The mess room has a long table, at which the whole Troop can sit down, and is warmed by two large stoves. In the kitchen is a very large cooking stove. I inspect the barracks and kitchen daily, and see that the cooking is properly done—and indeed the soup, baked beans, roast meat &c. will compare *very* favorably with the same class of fare provided by many hotels.

Albert to Hattie (Jennie's sister), Fort Harker, Kan., March 29, 1867:

I received an order to turn in all surplus property to the Ordnance and Quartermaster's Departments, and hold myself in readiness to march with my command at one hour's notice! Since then I have had my Farrier & Blacksmiths busy—have had all the shoes that were at all worn removed from my horses, heel and toe corks sharpened, and shoes reset—all the horse equipments inspected, and broken or defective parts mended or re-supplied— all the sabres ground as sharp as butcher's knives, carbines and revolvers put in the best possible order, new cartridge pouches, blankets and ponchioes [ponchos] issued, and ammunition got in readiness, a pair of buffalo overshoes drawn for every man, surplus stores boxed and invoiced, unserviceable horses turned in, &c. &c.—*ad infinitum*! I now have every thing in fine shape, and so am measurably at ease, and will "hold myself in readiness" &c, until the final order comes to move, but I do not much expect that it will be received until after the arrival of General Hancock—he is expected here, with the advance of the column from Forts Leavenworth and Riley tomorrow evening. I have no idea where we are going! During the war, military movements used to be conducted with great secrecy, for fear that the rebels would gain some information, and now I suppose that they are conducted with equal secrecy for fear that the Indians will take alarm. For my part, I am unable to arrive at any fair conclusion as to the real object of the expedition, and am half inclined to believe that General Hancock wishes to go on a reconnoissance through his Department, visit the Indian tribes, and the Rocky Mountains, and hunt buffalo, on a big scale, and so has hit upon this plan of doing it! Well, in any event, we will be in readiness for war. I have now twenty eight thousand rounds of ammunition on hands for the Spencer's (seven-shooting) carbines, and requisitions approved and sent in for as much more! I am not going to be caught away out on the plains without ammunition, at all events.

3. The Hancock Expedition, April 1867

The Hancock Expedition at Fort Harker, as sketched by Theodore Davis for *Harper's Weekly* and as photographed by Alexander Gardner. In the foreground of the photograph is Parsons's Battery B, 4th Artillery, whose smart appearance impressed Barnitz.

Albert to Jennie, Fort Harker, Kan., April 2, 1867:

Genls. Hancock, Smith, Custer and [John W.] Davidson, arrived yesterday, and went into camp in sight of the Post. — They brought with them four companies of the 7th Cavalry (all that were at Fort Riley) eight companies of the 37th Inf [under Capt. John Rziha], a Battery of Artillery [B of the 4th, Capt. Charles C. Parsons*], and supply trains—and to day I went into camp along side of them, with my squadron. The day is very pleasant—or rather unpleasantly warm! I am very busy, of course, but had to write you a line before going! Tomorrow we all move out on the expedition on the plains!

The Hancock Expedition broke camp at Fort Harker on April 3, 1867, and marched southeast by way of Fort Zarah* to Fort Larned,* a distance of about sixty-five miles, and the troops went into camp on April 7. Here two more troops of the 7th joined, giving the command a strength of about 1,400. In addition, there was a contingent of Delaware Indian scouts and some white guides and scouts, including James B. "Wild Bill" Hickok.* Colonel Smith had returned from leave but had been assigned to command the District of the Upper Arkansas. Custer, therefore, continued to command the 7th Cavalry.

Albert to Jennie, camp near Fort Larned, Kan., April 8, 1867:

[Fort Larned] consists of a couple of stone buildings, one of which is the Suttler's Store, and the other the Commissary building—a few low uncouth looking *adobe* structures, occupied by two companies of the 3d Infantry, and the commandant of the Post—Post Quartermasters Offices and den of the Post Bakery (We have soft bread by the way!)—a few stables dug out of the river bank, and covered with poles, straw and mud, and some *houses* dug out in the same manner!—they are only distinguishable from the stables by the chimnies, which are little piles of sod, or sun dried bricks, or else barrels, daubed with mud on the inside!

We have been drilling all the way here—under Genl. Custer. We had a fine field for maneuvering; the open, rolling prairies.

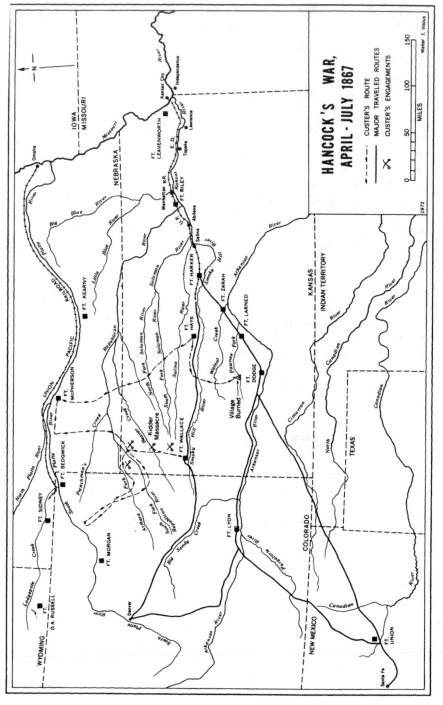

MAP 1. Hancock's War, April–July 1867.

The Artillery usually forming one column, the Infantry and wagon train another, and the Cavalry away off on the flank moving in squadron (or close) column (two companies abreast)— or in column of fours, or platoons, and occasionally forming in line at the gallop—sabres drawn, guidons fluttering, and bugles repeating the signals. Occasionally we would pass over a prairie dog village, and then the troopers had to look out, or the horses would sink into the holes up to their knees, and be likely to fall down. The prairie dogs are very jolly little fellows! . . .

Capt's [Robert M.] West* & [Albert P.] Morrow 7th Cav. joined us yesterday, from Forts Hayes & Dodge, with their two companies, Lieut. [David W.] Wallingford* is with Capt Morrow (Co. "E".) About ten thousand Indians are within a radius of 40 miles of this Fort, and have been sent for, and are expected to come here (a few are about here now—fine looking men)—at least the principal men among them,—to a council. They are reported to be in favor of peace. I suppose they always are when troops approach their hunting grounds in any force! The result is uncertain but we will see. Genl. Hancock has a band of Indians—noted scouts &c along. "Wild Bill" is along.

Albert to Jennie, camp near Fort Larned, Kan., April 9, 1867:

It is snowing furiously, with three inches in depth already on the ground, and wind from the North West. Not a soul is stirring in camp except the sentinels. As fuel is not to be had, except a little for cooking, and stoves were left with the tradition girls—"behind us" [a reference to the traditional cavalry air, "The Girl I Left Behind Me"]—of course fires are out of the question, and all the men—yes and officers too (except your Albert!) are wrapped up in their blankets and sound asleep! Lieut. Jackson, of my company is in bed, and entirely oblivious, (owing to the reduction of transportation we share a tent together) and his big dog "Kioway"— reared by the Kioway Indians, and about two thirds wolf, sleeps beside him. "Lula" [Barnitz's dog] is with Frank [his striker, or servant], in his little tent, fat and hearty—a great pet. It is under such circumstances, and with such surroundings that I seat myself to write to you. . . .

. . . A circular was sent around to the officers last ev'g from Regimental Hd. Qrs. informing them that "officers' call" would be sounded at 9:45 this morning, when all the officers of the regiment would assemble at the Adjutant's quarters, and go up in a body to the Hd. Qrs. Department of the Missouri—300 paces from here to pay their respects to Genl. Hancock—one of the 5 Major Generals of the U.S. Army, and commander of this Department. Well, at the appointed time, having made my toilette to the best advantage,—having shaved under great *dis*advantage!— and put on my blackest pair of boots, and brightest spurs, dress coat, sash and sabre—(by the way, I "imported" a very handsome sash from St. Louis) I was about to leave the tent, when an orderly came around with a circular notification that owing to the inclemency of the weather the contemplated visit would be postponed! Well, I thereupon went up and called on Genl. Custer. I found Genl. Smith there—and also Genl. Gibbs, who has been very much under the weather for the past two or three days— quite ill in fact—not able to "stand grief" like some of the younger ones of the party. Well, we all had a social talk for half an hour or so, when Genl. Smith left. (He stays at Department Hd. Qrs., with Genl. Hancock—Genl. Custer being in command of the Regiment,) and Genl. Gibbs retired, and was comfortably tucked up under half a dozen blankets (in Genl. Custer's tent,) Genl. Custer then told me that the programme is about as follows: Genl. Hancock is to hold a pow-wow with the Kioway & Cheyenne (Shyenne) Indians—the Hd Chiefs are expected here tomorrow—and endeavor to make a treaty with them to go south, and remain at least 100 miles south of the Smoky Hill route to Denver City—(the road which we have followed up to this point) none of their hunting parties or braves are to come further north. Should they accede to these terms and *keep* the treaty, we will go back to Harker or close to Hayes (45 miles N. of here) where we will remain until about the middle of May, or later, and all the officers who are named and wish to take their wives west with them will be allowed to go to Fort Riley for them, plenty of transportation being allowed— about all that the officers wish—the regiment will then go west— part to Puebla 175 miles (or so) [120] S. of Denver City, into a beautiful country, and part to Fort Morgan about 70 miles N. of Denver City, where permanent buildings (of stone) will be erected by the soldiers, aided by employees of the Q.M. Dept. and we will be allowed to remain there and do about as we please, fishing, hunting and cultivating gardens indeffinitely! (A brilliant pros-

Heavy with Civil War honors, General Winfield Scott Hancock proved unequal to the task of fighting Indians. His campaign of 1867, Barnitz's introduction to frontier service, was a dismal failure.

pect, truly!) Genl. Custer seems very much pleased with the idea—expects to take his wife.—If, however, the Indians will not accept the terms offered them, then we are to commence hostilities, and make them do so—and finally, if they break the treaty (provided they agree to one) then *of course* we will have to ride about and "expend" a few thousand of them! Which horn of the dilemma do you prefer? . . .

. . . Capt. Morrow of the 7th Cav. has been promoted Major of the 9th Cav. (colored)—he is now here, and has been temporarily assigned to duty as Major. I am much pleased with Capt. West of the 7th Cav. (now here)—he was colonel of Art. during the war, and commanded a brigade in the Army of the Potomac—he is a thorough soldier, and a polished gentleman—of the *reliable* type. . . .

What do you think I have had for dinner? Why a big plumb pudding!—fact—and "soft bread" & butter and meat (boiled tongue & ham) and "hard tack" and baked beans. (I have a bake kettle—"Dutch oven") and coffee, canned peaches &c—cooked out in the "big field" in the driving snow!—I have an excellent cook, but how he manages to get along to day is more than I can tell. We have a little mess chest exactly like Lt. Wallingford's, *white* plates cups & saucers, glass drinking goblets &c. We still have about 10 pounds of butter left. Genl. Custer has a barrel of apples along. I have six big blankets, two rubber "talmas" [cloaks] an over coat, and saddle blanket, and straw tick, stuffed with hay, besides a pair of buffalo overshoes—small ones, which I wear in place of slippers. So I manage to endure the "winter's cold" with as good grace as possible—though seriously I do not find it very pleasant sitting here by my little camp table, (which, as well as camp stools, I managed to bring along) writing to my own dear little wife! . . .

Did I tell you what sport we had on the march chasing Antelope, with Genl. Custer's Greyhounds? It was quite exciting, but they always ran away from the dogs. The chase would be kept up for two or three miles, and then abandoned as useless.

Albert to Jennie, camp near Fort Larned, Kan., April 12, 1867:

Have just returned from pow wow with the Cheyennes. Genl. Hancock made a couple of speeches to them, and they replied. We

march at 7 o'clock tomorrow morning to the Cheyenne camps—
without invitation!—to visit them at home, and talk war or peace
to them, as they may elect. Their camps are 20 miles from here
towards Fort Dodge. We expect to return here in two or three
weeks. . . . Recd your 2d & 5th letters this ev'g—while on my way
to the Pow-wow, and read them midst of the "Big Chiefs"—greasy
fellows! . . . The Big war Chiefs did not talk altogether pleasantly
to night I thought—they used some "circumlocution!" Yet I think
they will not dare to fight. So don't feel any anxiety about me.

The chiefs were Tall Bull, Bull Bear,* White Horse,* and Little
Robe* of the Southern Cheyennes. They were from a village of both
Cheyennes and Southern Oglala Sioux located on Pawnee Fork about
thirty miles upstream from Fort Larned. At Tall Bull's behest, privately
conveyed, Indian Agent Edward W. Wynkoop* tried to talk Hancock out
of marching to the village. The Sand Creek Massacre of 1864, in which
Colorado volunteers almost obliterated Black Kettle's band of Cheyennes,
remained fresh in the minds of the Indians, and the approach of soldiers
might so frighten them that they would flee.*

Albert's journal, April 13, 1867:

Camp near the "Shyennes." The command broke camp at 7
o'clock this morning and marched in the direction of the Pawnee
Camps [i.e., the camps on Pawnee Fork] said to be 25 miles from
Fort Larned, somewhat in the direction of Dodge. Weather warm,
wind from the S.W. Crossed the Pawnee Fork at 3 p.m. Crossing
good. Pontoons put down for the Infantry. After crossing
marched about 3 miles, and encamped on the left bank of (as I
suppose) the Pawnee Fork. . . . After crossing Pawnee Fork we
saw a great smoke ahead in the direction, as we suppose, of the
Cheyenne camps, and soon small parties of Indians were seen
reconnoitering us from the distance of two or three miles, and
fled on our approach. An Indian, a Cheyenne, I suppose—and a
big chief, doubtless, from his dress, or make up rather—he had 20
or 30 silver dollars, flattened out to the size of saucers, fastened
"flatwise" on a thong about a yard and a half long, one end of
which was attached to the crown of his head and the other end
floated out behind him as he rode. His moccasins were embroidered with small beads, and he was enveloped in a dark blanket.

His poney was quite respectable looking. Well, the Indian thus attired whoever he was, was sent forward to communicate with the Cheyennes, and set off at a canter, digging his heels into the sides of his poney at every jump, dollars flying, and whip going, and doubtless considered himself an object worthy of considerable interest, his figure was seen bobbing up and down until lost in the distance—(up the valley of the Pawnee)—moving in the direction of the smoke—vivid and repeated flashes of lightning (the first we have had this spring) being seen meanwhile in the same direction—the sound of the thunder only occasionally reaching us. About this time we turned off to the left and went into camp. Our train did not arrive until about dusk, and in consequence the horses had to be held, as we had no picket rope, until the wagons came up. The mules were nearly exhausted. I feel very tired and hungry and am anxious for supper. I hear nothing further about the Indians. A picket guard is to go out (mounted) tonight, and a dismounted guard is also to be reported.

The Indian described by Barnitz may have been one of the delegation that conferred with Hancock the night before. A letter from Barnitz to the Cleveland Herald *of May 1, published in the May 10 edition, describes Tall Bull as wearing such a necklace during the council of April 12. In the afternoon White Horse of the Cheyennes and Pawnee Killer* of the Southern Oglala Sioux met with Hancock and assured him that all the chiefs would gather at his camp the next morning for a conference.*

Albert to Jennie, camp on Pawnee Fork, near the Cheyenne camps, Kan., April 14, 1867:

We moved from our camp this morning in order of battle—Infantry in line, cavalry in "close column" on the flanks, and trains in three columns in the centre, my squadron (having been in advance yesterday) acting as rear guard, when about a mile from our camp Indians to the number of 3 or 400 appeared in our front and on the flanks, mostly mounted on ponies, some of them gaily dressed, with flaming red toggery and scarlet blankets, displaying their burnished lances &c. &c.—but they kept at a very respectful distance, until a big white flag was hoisted in the centre of our line, when a couple of them ventured near enough to hold a parley. Our force then advanced and the Indians disappeared, except small parties that were seen passing over the hills on our front, flanks and rear. In this clear air objects are sharply defined against the sky at a great distance. An Indian's head can easily be seen above the hills at the distance of 3 or 4 miles. Well, we are finely encamped on the Pawnee Fork, on a beautiful terrace—on our left the wooded stream, beyond which at the distance of a mile or two are the bluffs—on our right a mile or two off, rolling swells of the prairie, and on our right front, by a little belt of timber, is the Indian (Cheyenne) encampment. Their teepes, or tents are plainly visible—said to number 3 or 400 (teepes or "lodges")— each of which represents 2 or 3 Indians. It is reported that the Cheyennes have sent off all their women & children and old men, and are in shape for the war path! Wouldn't you like to be here? Seriously, it is right pleasant this ev'g—and I do not apprehend any great trouble from the Indians now here—I think we are a match for them and all the allies they can collect at this season of the year provided they even *mean* war, which is not yet established. At all events the *big* pow-wow is to come off tomorrow, and I will then write you the first opportunity.

The confrontation was more ominous than Barnitz suspected. The chiefs did not appear, as promised, on the morning of April 14. Bull Bear came in to explain that they were delayed by a buffalo hunt. Hancock therefore took up the march toward their village. As described by Barnitz, Indian and military forces faced each other uncertainly for a time, with a clash of arms apparently a distinct possibility. Then Hancock, through Agent Wynkoop, invited a parley between the lines. The Cheyenne Roman Nose* acted as spokesman for the dozen or so chiefs. Arrangements were made for still another conference, and the military column resumed its march to the vicinity of the village, which later was found to number 111 Cheyenne lodges and 140 Sioux lodges.

Albert to Jennie, camp near Downer's Station, on Smoky Hill route to Denver City, April 17, 1867:

We are regularly on the war path, and no mistake! I wrote you a very hasty letter from our camp near the Cheyenne village, or encampment, on Sunday ev'g last [April 14]. Just after I had sent Frank to Genl. Smith's Hd. Quarters with the letter, and had "turned in," . . . I heard Genl. Custer ride up, and inquire for me. I knew very well, from his tone of voice, that something was to be done, which required haste and secrecy, and so I got up at once, drew on my boots, and reported for orders. Was directed to have my command saddled as quickly as possible and provided with 45 rounds of ammunition to the man, and to send him word when I was in readiness to move. Well the upshot of the whole affair was this. The Indians had all along (in their intercourse with Genl. Hancock) evinced any thing but a pacific spirit. It was obvious that they were not at all satisfied with the prospect of being forced into making a treaty, (and I noticed that one of their principal chiefs, "Tall Bull," while making a speech, at the council of Larned,—or rather while the interpreter was translating a not very concilliatory portion of it—stood tapping the ground with his foot, in a very defiant manner—) and so while being careful to post a proper guard on the evening alluded to, Genl. Hancock was equally careful to watch the movement going on in the Indian encampment, and at length it was reported that the Indians were about leaving, and the Genl. determined, if possible to frustrate their intentions, so as soon as the command was in readiness it moved out (all the cavalry) over the prairie and deploying formed a cordon entirely around the Indian encampment, which proved to be upon a series of Islands in the north fork of the Pawnee—a lovely site—and then we all closed in on it, with carbines advanced, and when within a suitable distance a party was sent forward to reconnoiter, and soon returned and reported the camp deserted!—The Indians had just left, as noiselessly as wolves! I was sent in with my squadron to take possession and hold the camp until daylight, and the remainder of the command returned to our own camp. On entering the camp I was astonished at its magnitude and magnificence! The "teepes" or tents were all left standing, just as they were—the Indians being evidently in too great haste, or else too poorly supplied with transportation to take them along. Each tent would contain 20 or 30 persons—and they were very numerous. I counted 150 or 60 through the vistas among the tall trees . . . and there were many that I did not see. As soon as I had established my outposts, to guard against surprise, and made arrangements for picketing the horses of the remainder of the squadron, I took a party, and started to look through the tents—at first view the tents very much resemble our "Sibley" tents, being conical and open at the top, to give an outlet for the smoke, but on closer inspection one is surprised to find that they are all made of dressed buffalo hides—almost as white and soft as kid gloves. They are very costly, and much valued by the Indians, I am told, as it costs a great deal of labor (on the part of their squaws!) to prepare the robes, and on their own part to obtain the poles, (which are transported from the mountains) the latter are perfectly round and smooth—generally of hickory—and about 20 feet in length. It requires about 30 for each tent—They are almost invaluable to the Indians. Well, I found the tents filled with buffalo robes, Indian saddles, camp kettles of iron, brass and copper, iron pots, axes and other tools, "tom-toms" or Indian drums, papoose baskets &c. &c. &c. *ad infinitum*, some of which I took away with me. A little girl supposed to be a white girl about 10 or 12 years old was found in one of the tents apparently in great distress—the surgeon after examination reported that she had been violated and most shamefully abused by the Indians just previous to their departure. She could not speak English and there is some doubt as to whether she is a captive from some other tribe or a white child captured while very young. Well, I will have to stop writing presently and I may as well say that I was ordered back to camp before day light that morning, and marched with the command—the cavalry only—(the Infantry, Artillery, tents and horses &c. &c. being left behind to go elsewhere)—in pursuit, we have been going day and night ever since—with scarcely any time for rest. Last night we marched 30 miles across a tractless waste from Walnut Creek to the Smoky. We are now 90 miles N.W. of Ft. Larned, and 110 miles west of Harker. My light is finally out and I must close—It is 12 o'clock and we march in two hours—We are now on the trail of the Indians—They killed four white men, scalped and partially burned their bodies at a place near here—and we have captured some of their ponies which they were forced to abandon—the horses are much fatigued—and the whole command entirely worn out but we will get "them Indians" if the thing is possible.

The command followed the Smoky Hill road eastward to Fort Hays, where on April 20 Barnitz brought his journal up to date:

Broke camp on North Fork of the Pawnee, near deserted Indian villages on Monday morning, April 15, leaving Head quarters Dept Mo., and Dist. Upr. Ark., in the Field, the Infantry and Artillery, and all the led horses, and about 80 men of the 7th Cav., the most of our baggage wagons, (3 from each company) tents, company desks, &c &c, behind, in charge of Lieut. Jackson. Marched all day in North & N.W. direction crossing and recrossing North Fork of Walnut Creek, finding many traces of Indians, and encamped in the evening on high ground on right bank of same stream. Saw Indian trail several times during the day— tracks of teepe poles, and unshod ponies, &c &c, repeated smokes, &c but no Indians, but strong evidences that Indians were not far ahead. . . . Day very warm.

On Tuesday morning, April 16, we broke camp at 2 a.m., crossed Walnut Creek, and proceeded 8 or 10 miles over high, rolling ground, often broken, but generally prairie, covered with the usual dry, buffalo grass. Discovered large droves of buffalo, and Elk, which we at first mistook for Indians, and made preparations for battle. Discovered our error, and sent detail to shoot some, and an ambulance was sent over and brought in the game. . . . We now retraced our way to Walnut Creek, and encamped on left bank, in order to cook, with notification that we were to march again at 6 p.m. Day especially hot. Marched at 6 p.m. and continued 30 miles in North Westerly direction 'till 4 o'clock on the morning of—

Wednesday, April 17. When we crossed the Great Smoky at Sand Hills, west of Monument Creek, where we went into camp, and remained during prevalance of strong S.E. wind, until 10 a.m., when we marched in eastwardly direction and went into camp in evening on Great Smoky Hill Route to Denver City, at a Stage Station known as Downer's Station, where we found that the occupants, two men, had been in a state of siege for several days, shut up in a little "Fort" of about the size and appearance of a potato hill! Some of my men very successful in shooting buffalo today. No indications of grass yet. A prairie-fire broke out in camp tonight. Wrote a long letter to Jennie tonight. Learned that the Indians of whom we are in pursuit killed the four occupants of a Ranche or Stage Station on this route about 20 or 30 miles East of here yesterday—scalped two of them, and burned the bodies of all, partially.

Thursday, April 18. We broke camp at 4 a.m., and continued

the march toward Fort Hayes. Passed two Ranches, (or Stage Stations rather) and the bodies of many prairie wolves, which had been poisoned for their skins. Were overtaken in the afternoon by a severe "Nor' Wester" or hurricane of wind with hail and rain, which gave me quite a chill, as I had no overcoat with me and my talma would persist in blowing away from my shoulders. Wagons nearly upset by the wind. We encamped at night at Ranche where the men were killed & burned by the Indians—disinterred and re-buried the charred remains. Some of my men on detail sent out to shoot game, captured a young buffalo bull today, and gave him to me. He is quite a curiosity. They brought him in to camp in one of the wagons. Surgeon [Henry] Lippincott* loaned me a pair of blankets for the night.

Friday, April 19. We broke camp at daylight, and marched to Fort Hayes, a distance of 17 or 18 miles, passing Big Creek Stage Station on the way, and encamped on left bank of Big Creek, about half a mile south by west from the Post. Day warm. [Thomas H.] Kincaid the scout came in with dispatches from Genl. Hancock, who is still at Indian Encampment on North Fork of the Pawnee. The scout was pursued by the Indians (he says) and had a narrow escape. He was scarcely able to speak on his arrival, having ridden nearly 300 miles within 72 hours, and that on broken down, or jaded horses—at that he had necessarily been on the move all the time. He was once driven back across the Smoky, by the Indians. He returns tonight. We found no forage here. Had expected to find a 20 day supply for 3000 animals. Wild Bill going to Fort Harker tonight, as bearer of dispatches. He will ride a mule and expects to reach Harker by daylight.

Albert to Jennie, Fort Hays, Kan., April 20, 1867:

We arrived here last evening—very much worn out, and the horses especially quite exhausted, expecting to find here 20 days supply of forage for 3000 horses—but instead of that, we found only *one* day's supply for the animals already at the post, and Genl. Custer ordered that taken for *our* horses. We expected to leave here again to day, but as it is, we will have to await supplies, which can not possibly reach us before tomorrow evening. Wild Bill was started as Courier to Fort Harker last evening at dusk, mounted on a mule, and was sanguine that he could make the trip (60 miles) by daylight this morning, unless driven out of his course by the Indians. He was armed with two revolvers (and a carbine which I loaned him for the trip,) and thought that he was good for a dozen Indians at all events. A scout whom we sent back from our camp on the "Big Smoky" the morning of the 17th to communicate with Genl. Hancock, . . . was pursued by the Indians nearly all the way—and once driven back across the Smoky—was fired upon repeatedly—shot one Indian, and a pony, and arrived here on his return last ev'g, having ridden constantly for near 300 miles. He was so exhausted that he could hardly talk—but after four hours rest was supplied with a fresh horse—not *so very* fresh either:—and started back with dispatches.

. . . I have a young buffalo calf which we caught a few days ago. I thought I would try to get it to Cleved. but fear it will be difficult to rear it without milk—and there is not a cow at this post. However I will leave it here, in charge of some of the Infantry, and if it does well, I may be able to send it through. We live mostly on buffalo meat. The soldiers here have a great variety of pets, gophers, prairie dogs, owls, wolves, buffalo, &c. &c. This post is beautifully situated, in a pleasant valley on Big Creek, a well timbered stream of good water—but the post is not equal to Riley or Harker so far as the appearance goes. The buildings are mostly small, one story high and built of logs—except two or three of stone. We raised a great scare here on our approach—they supposing us to be Indians! They had run out the artillery on the heights, and were preparing to give us a warm reception.

Albert to Jennie, camp near Fort Hays, Kan., April 23, 1867:

Did I forget to tell you in my last letter that we had marched without tents—with only one wagon to a company—leaving behind everything which was not absolutely indispensible? Well, it was ever so. I was thoughtful enough to bring along one small common tent, which is the only one in the company, and I was equally fortunate in bringing along a little stationery—a not very select assortment however, as you will have observed!—and a pocket inkstand. I write on my knee, having no other desk than a few sheets of paper. I left all my bedding except a pair of blankets and talma, and such a thing as a campstool is unknown in the command! The fact is, we are very poorly provided with the comforts of life, and had no idea when we started from our camp on the Pawnee that we should be so long separated from our wagons, company desks &c. &c. or we should have made serious efforts to bring along a few extra things. The worst of all, however, was that the evening after we started my cook made the discovery that my box of provisions—canned fruit, butter, baker's bread, ham &c. &c. had, by mistake, been put into the wrong wagon, and was left behind! The result was that I did not fare sumptuously every day, although I was fortunate enough to be invited to mess with a brother officer of the squadron—whose bill of fare however, was not very choice—consisting mainly of hard bread and bacon, with an occasional can of preserved meats (chicken or turkey) and green peas. However, we managed to subsist in some fashion on buffalo meat and such other game as the country afforded. We expected on our arrival here to find the commissary well provided, but in this we were disappointed. With the exception of a little canned fruit he had scarcely anything, and the Post Bakery is not able to furnish bread up to the full demand.

We have no late news here. The latest paper that has reached this post, so far as I am aware, is a copy of the *Washington Chronicle* of March 22, over a month old!—and it has been read by every body in the regiment I suppose, as, when I last saw it, it had the appearance of an old spelling book where little thumbs have worn through its pages! . . .

Guard mounting is just taking place. The music (of our eight buglers, or "trumpeters" rather) is really very fine. They are improving daily. The *Band*, as I have written you, has been sent back to Fort Riley for instruction and practice—they will join us by the time the officers' wives come on.

Thus paralyzed by want of forage, Hancock's much-heralded "Expedition to the Plains" ground to an embarrassing halt. The general had remained uncertainly on Pawnee Fork until a courier brought word from Custer of the outrages on the Smoky Hill. Although Agent Wynkoop argued forcefully (and correctly) that the Sioux and Cheyennes had fled out of fear of another Sand Creek Massacre, and although there was some doubt of their complicity in the Smoky Hill depredations, Hancock on April 19 put their village to the torch. After parleying with Arapaho and Kiowa chiefs at Forts Dodge and Larned, he reached Fort Hays on May 3, ordered Custer to take the field as soon as possible, then retreated to his Fort Leavenworth headquarters. For him the war was over. For the Sioux and Cheyennes, infuriated by the destruction of the village, it had scarcely begun.

4. *Camp on Big Creek, April–June 1867*

Old Fort Hays in 1867, shortly after its abandonment in the wake of the Big Creek flood of June. It was re-established fifteen miles to the west.

For more than a month the 7th Cavalry remained in camp on Big Creek, near Fort Hays, stockpiling supplies and forage and rebuilding the strength of the horses. For Barnitz, it was a time of uncertainty, indecision over whether to send for Jennie, and growing disenchantment with Custer.

Albert to Jennie, camp near Fort Hays, Kan., April 25, 1867:

The present whereabouts of the Indians cannot be ascertained. Last evening a poor Irishman came in minus everything but half a pair of trousers, and reported, as soon as he had recovered breath sufficiently to do so, that the Indians were all around his shanty, or ranche—that there were thousands of them—that the whole plains were black with them, and that he had barely escaped with his life down a ravine, and had run all the way to the Fort, never stopping to look back, for fear of being scalped! He had come direct through bogs and swamps, and was covered with mud from head to foot! A reconnoissance was at once made, and not an Indian was to be seen—nor any trace of Indians! If they had really been there, they avoided leaving any indications behind them.

Albert to Jennie, camp near Fort Hays, Kan., April 27, 1867:

I yesterday borrowed from the Commandant of the Post a nice new Sibley tent—a regular pavilion-palace (such a one as I intend to have for you, when you come out to cross the great plains!)—capable of accommodating 20 persons very comfortably,—and had it put up for my own especial habitation,—and occupy it all alone!—intending (while we stay here) to dwell in state, on an equal footing with Genl. Custer or any other General!—The centre pole is supported on an iron tripod, beneath which sits a conical (Sibley) tent stove, with a nice little pipe extending through the capped hole in the dome or cupola—for you see I borrowed the whole outfit;—and it was not an unnecessary proceeding either, I assure you, even at this season of the year, for the Adjutant [1st Lt. Myles Moylan*] assured me that ice formed to a considerable thickness on a bucket of water standing in his tent last night, and yet yesterday was quite agreeably warm. . . .

. . . We received [a letter] from Genl. Gibbs. He says the Band is progressing finely—and that it is rumored that General Sherman is to meet us, on our return, at Fort Harker, with half a dozen ladies:—But the General had not then heard of the Cheyennes. Our troops (a squadron of the 7th Cavalry and some Infantry) have had a fight with them near Fort Lyon, and killed seven. I dare not tell you how many desertions we are having! They are of nightly occurrence! As many as 10 non-commissioned officers and privates have left in one night, with horses and arms! With approval of Genl. Custer I sent out a detail of 1 sergeant and 3 privates the other day, to shoot buffalo, and they all forgot to return! Query, were they all gobbled by the Indians? We think not.

During April 1867 eighty-five men deserted from the 7th Cavalry, of whom sixty-five were from the eight troops camped on Big Creek. Barnitz's troop lost twelve. The action near Fort Lyon was a skirmish on April 15 by a detachment from Troop C under 1st Lt. Matthew Berry. One soldier was wounded. No indians were reported killed.

Albert to Jennie, camp near Fort Hays, Kan., April 30, 1867:

It is still believed that we *are* eventually to go west, and Fort Garling [Garland, Colorado] is spoken of in this connection quite as frequently as Puebla. It is not unlikely that we will go to both places—nor yet unlikely that we shall go to some half a dozen other places in addition! That, in fact, we will be "deployed as skirmishers"—one company or a squadron here, and another there, and every one do whatsoever seemeth right in his own eyes! But *when* we will go, that is the question! . . . I think it will not do to go off and leave the Indians to their innocent pass times. They must be looked after—even if it be from afar. We must keep them from laying up any great supply of buffalo meat this summer, and cause them to feel uneasy in their dreams, even if we can accomplish nothing more.

Albert's journal, May 3, 1867:

Genl. Hancock & Staff, Genl. Smith and Detacht. 37th Inf. arrived this afternoon from Fort Dodge, where Genl. Hancock was made a favorable treaty with the Kiowas and Arapahoes. Lieut. Jackson of my company also arrived today with the wagons and led horses of the regiment. Only 2 wagons, however, for each company were brought, whereas we left three. Some disease has broken out among the horses which he has brought up, supposed by some to be glandis, but Genl. Smith pronounces it lung fever, and says the horses only require physic and bran mashes, or something of the kind to insure a recovery! Very probable, but where can one obtain the "bran"? 28 horses have died out of those left behind, from the disease.

Albert to Jennie, camp near Fort Hays, Kan., May 4, 1867:

Have been remodeling the camp, and having a grand review, and inspection, mounted—Genl. Hancock & Staff being the "Reviewers"—and then this evening, as hitherto announced, in orders, we had a grand foot race, and a horse race! Genls. Hancock, Smith, Davidson, Custer and every body being present! I was one of the judges!—Each company selected its best running man, the winner to be excused from all duty for 30 days, and the company he belonged to to be excused from guard duty for one week! Company "A" (Capt. [Louis M.] Hamilton's*) came out ahead—and Company "G" not far behind. A Cavalry horse—of Capt. [Frederick W.] Benteen's* Company ran against their fastest horse from the Post, and won! Cavalry *far* ahead! . . .

Well Jennie, we are to remain here until the grass grows—three weeks at least.—and what do you think? General Custer is going to send for his wife to come on here!—and he tells me that if I wish you to come out, now is the time to send for you!!!! But I cannot "read my title clear" to do any such thing, as yet, and so I won't do it.

Albert to Jennie, camp near Fort Hays, Kan., May 6, 1867:

[Postscript] Our horses are beginning to look very well again. We are now getting hay, which has been brought on of late in addition to the grain and grazing. The grass is coming up finely—also the flowers. Discipline is very rigidly enforced. Swearing has been done away with, almost entirely. Both men and officers being prohibited by general orders! That's good. I had previously put a stop to it in my company. We have dress parade every evening, and present a fine appearance. Most of the officers have succeeded in borrowing Sibley tents—and nearly all have in addition wall-tents. I have a Sibley tent, a wall tent, two wall-tent flies, and in addition several spare "A" tents—as the tents have all come up. Capt. West furnished the officers a repast of ice cream last evening!—a great surprise!—made of condensed milk, I believe, and ice from the Post. I purchased a barrel of apples the other day—green apples—from a man who had hauled them all the way from Missouri (for the use of my company)—and a bushel for myself! Green apples mind, and very fine flavored, at $5 per bushel. The Suttler has got on a new stock of goods.

The Infantry is here, and the Artillery, under Brevt. Lt. Col. Parsons, has gone back to Fort Riley. Our camp is very clean. It is thoroughly policed every day—not a bit of dirt, or whisp of hay, or particle of manure left any where in camp, all hauled away. General Custer has become "billious" notwithstanding! He appears to be mad about something, and is very much on his dignity! *and* all the officers stand equally on theirs, so he does not make much by the operation! He has evidently incurred the censure of Genl. Hancock, or some one, in some way, or else Nasby's bitters [a reference to editorialist Petroleum V. Nasby's unflattering newspaper remarks about Custer's support of President Andrew Johnson], which are now received here often, do not set well on his stomach!—all of which, however, is confidential! He is really quite "obstreperous."

Albert to Jennie, camp near Fort Hays, Kan., May 9, 1867:

[Postscript] 6 a.m. May 10, 1867. I am officer of the Day, (as usual!). Every time that a new Officer of the Day has been detailed of late, he has found it very convenient to become sick, and get relieved, during his tour! I think I will have to take the hint, if this thing continues much longer, and do likewise!—for it isn't pleasant, of late, to carry out all Genl. Custer's caprices, in the matter of arrests. If I hear that Jennie is on the way here, and that the command is about to move, I shall be almost certain to become sick in consequence!! . . .

These are views of the 7th Cavalry camp on Big Creek, near Fort Hays. Although photographed during the 1869 encampment, they suggest similar scenes of the 1867 encampment in which the Barnitzes participated.

General Custer leans against a tent pole, while seated at left are brother Tom and wife Elizabeth. Photograph taken during 1869 encampment at Big Creek.

Custer plucked stolid, dependable Myles Moylan from the ranks and made him regimental adjutant, then had to force other officers to drop their snobbish refusal to socialize with a former enlisted man. He served in the 7th Cavalry for twenty-six years, fought at the Little Bighorn and Wounded Knee, and was severely wounded at Bear Paw Mountain.

Capt. Benteen, Wallingford, Nolan [Nowlan], Jackson, and I don't know how many others report sick! (in consequence of the general *"cussedness"* of things, I suppose!!)

Albert's journal:

May 13, 1867. . . . A report received that 3000 Indians are in the vicinity of Lookout Station. The whole cavalry command, with the exception of sick and necessary guard, ordered to march at once, to go out and look after said Injuns! We will not see one, of course. The tents are to be left standing. One company of the 37th Inf. to accompany us. We are ordered to take 3 days rations in haversacks of the men, and one feed of forage with us, and be prepared to be separated from our wagons from 3 to 5 days. Weather hot.

May 14, 1867. We marched the whole distance to Lookout Station, 18 miles, without a solitary halt! Thus does General Custer expend his cavalry. There are great inducements, certainly, for officers to take care of their horses. On reaching Lookout, (at 1 o'clock this morning,) I was told to let the men lie down in line, and hold their horses and get what sleep they could, and towards morning to let them build a fire near the creek, in a low place, and make coffee, and be in readiness to march at half an hour before daylight. We marched about daylight toward the cliffs west of Lookout, where we turned south, marched a mile or two, halted our horses, gathered buffalo-chips, and made great smokes, and then started back to the station, whence, after a few minutes halt we continued the march back to the camp near Fort Hayes where we now are—without halting again on our way, except a few minutes—not more than *two* minutes, in my Squadron—at Big Creek Station. The day was extremely hot. Immediately upon my arrival in camp I was met by the Adjutant [Moylan], who informed me that he was directed by the "Brevet Major General Commanding," (Custer,) to place me in close arrest in my tent! Well, I went to my tent, laid aside my sabre, and tried for an hour or so to think what offense I had unwittingly committed, but all to no purpose, until finally I received an official copy of Special Orders No. 58, d. Hd. Qrs. 7th U.S. Cavalry, May 14, 1867, and my suppositions were at an end! The mystery was solved! I hadn't fed my horses, on the morning of the 14th instant, at camp near Lookout Station, and had then and there abandoned government forage intended for the horses of my command!—which allegations were false in every particular, as the Brevet Major General commanding might readily have satisfied himself had he been pleased in the plenitude of his power and his very high mightiness to have ordered an investigation. The fact was that the horses of my squadron were fed *before those of any other squadron in the command,* and that *no* forage was abandoned, but that, on the contrary, every ounce that could be obtained (an issue having been made there by the A.R.Q.M. [acting regimental quartermaster]) was carefully loaded into the wagons! Well, I will not humor the redoubtable "Brevet Major General commanding" by applying for an extension of my limits, but will patiently abide my time, and wait for the upshot of this affair!

Albert to Jennie, camp near Fort Hays, Kan., May 15, 1867:

Things are becoming very unpleasant here. General Custer is very injudicious in his administration, and spares no effort to render himself generally obnoxious. I have utterly lost all the little confidence I ever had in his ability as an officer—and all admiration for his character, as a man, and to speak the plain truth I am thoroughly *disgusted* with him! He is the most complete example of a petty tyrant that I have ever seen. You would be filled with utter amazement, if I were to give you a few instances of his cruelty to the men, and discourtesy to the officers, as an illustration of "what manner of man" he is!—but I forebear, for the present, any further allusion to him. Of course, what I write in regard to him is for yourself. I do not care, for the present, to have it attain any publicity—but Jennie, it is *very* discouraging to an officer who is disposed, upon all occasions, to do his duty faithfully, and I might almost say with "religious zeal!" If General Custer is to remain long in command of the regiment, as now appears probable, I don't know how matters will result. I fear that it will prove an additional inducement for me to resign. I will not do so rashly however, nor without a careful comparison of all the relative advantages and disadvantages of being in or out of the service. But, indeed, I fear that the arbitrary method pursued by Genl Custer will be a source of such constant and *unmitigated* annoyance, that an officer cannot long serve under him with any degree of credit, or with proper feelings of self-respect. I know that what I say will worry you a little—and perhaps I should not have written it, but I feel that it will be an additional inducement for you to remain quietly "in the States" and await the result! . . . I try to be contented, and abide in hope, and if I could only feel some of your happiness—present and prospective—I would be measurably contented, for the time. I am well—and not entirely *despondent!*—nor without plenty of sympathy!—We are "all in the same box!"—as Genl. Custer is—well I will not resort to a simile! but simply observe that he is "no respecter of persons!"

Albert's journal, May 17, 1867:

Today Genl. Custer required Capt. West, Officer of the Day, to have the heads of six men (of Cos. "E" & "H", 7th Cav.) shaved close to the scalp on one side of a line drawn over the head from the base of the nose to the occipital bone, (while that on the other side of the head was left untouched!) and in this condition the men were then transported through all the streets of the camp, to their own great humiliation, and the exceeding mortification, disgrace, and disgust of all right-minded officers and men in camp. The men were afterwards returned to close confinement. Now all this shocking spectacle (no new thing in camp either) was occasioned simply by the fact that these men, impelled by hunger, had gone to the Post, half a mile distant, without a pass, in order to purchase some canned fruit, with which they immediately returned, not having been absent quite three quarters of an hour, and not absent from roll call, or any duty! The scurvey is very bad in camp now, not less than 75 (seventy-five) cases being reported, and all for want of a proper diet, and the men are perfectly crazy for canned fruits or fresh vegetables, a fact which makes the infliction of such a punishment for an offense of this nature, if offense it may be called, additionally atrocious. No man but an incarnate fiend could take pleasure in such an abuse of authority, and I have greatly missed my guess if the "Brevet Major General commanding" is not fast losing whatever little influence for good he may have once possessed in the Regiment, and if he does not moreover eventually come to grief, as a consequence of his tyrannical conduct. Charles Clarke, a Bugler, of my company, was

ordered by the officer of the day, to perform the office of Barber
in the foregoing cases, an additional outrage. Thus does one bad
example lead to others.

Albert's journal, May 18, 1867:

I was released from arrest, and returned to duty today per S.O.
[Special Order] No. 62, d. Hd. Qrs. 7th Cav. How very consider-
ate in the "Brevet Major General commanding!" I suppose he
thinks I ought to feel under great obligations to him for his
kindness in the matter! Well I do!

Albert to Jennie, camp near Fort Hays, Kan., May 18, 1867:

I don't want you to come, although Mrs. Genl. Custer, and Miss
Darrough are here now,—arrived yesterday, with Genl. Smith—
and although Mrs. Genl. Gibbs and the Band &c will be here in a
few days—and it is mainly because I have become so thoroughly
disgusted with Genl. Custer, that I will not ask even the *slightest*
favor of him, and if you were here, I should be in a measure
dependent on him for many little indulgences! As it is, I am
perfectly independent. I never approach him except in an official
capacity, and then I make my business as brief as possible. Were
we to be together for years, I should never associate with him on
terms of any intimacy and why? simply because by his recent
unfeeling treatment of enlisted men of this command and shameful discourtesy to officers, he has proved himself unworthy of the
respect of all right-minded men. I do not particularize, because it
would be tiresome, and you (being a little civilian!) would scarcely
be any the wizer if I should enter into details! No, Jennie, if you
are still at home, abide in patience for a time. . . .

. . . I have not called on Mrs. Custer, or Miss Darrow (how *is* it
spelled?) yet,—and I believe only a few of the officers have done
so—but I will be officer of the day tomorrow, and then, after
guard mounting I must necessarily report, in person, to the General for orders, and may possibly meet the ladies. If so, very well.
If not, why then they may consider me unsociable if they like, for I
will not visit the General in a thousand years, except officially!—
And you would like to know how they are situated? Very pleasantly, I can assure you. The General has removed his tent—or

tents rather, for he has I don't know how many now, to a pleasant place on the stream two or three hundred yards in rear of camp, and has had bowers and screens of evergreens erected, and triumphal arches, and I know not what all else. He has a large square Hospital tent, among other things—nearly as large as the little chapel at Fort Riley—and so the ladies will be very comfortable, I have no doubt. If you *should* come, Jennie . . . then I am going to have things nice too! I will have a rival bower of my own!—for I will not mix up with the Darrow outfit at all! I am going to be independent entirely! . . .

. . . Genl. Gibbs will probably remain here, or with the ladies, at least, if we take the field again—(as we will, of course,)—he is too old to stand hard service. He is an excellent man,—in the Army—and is very much respected by all. He is always genial, and reliable—and not a martinet, like Custer—although a perfect disciplinarian. We will *not* have a general Indian war, this Summer—only the Cheyennes and part of the Sioux to fight, it appears.

Jennie, just as I had finished the foregoing, I heard 30 or 40 shots fired on the picket line, and hastily put on my arms, and ordered a horse saddled, and turned out the troop, under arms, had the roll called, and reported to the Adjutant, and learned cause of the alarm—14 men of H, E, & M Troops had just deserted—gone off armed and mounted!—broke through the guards and departed. So they go! If Genl. Custer remains long in command, I fear that recruiting will have to go on rapidly to keep the regiment replenished!

Albert's journal, May 23, 1867:

The great supper of "Buffalo Hunters" (officers of the 7th Cavalry who had engaged in competition to see who of two parties could kill the most buffalo in one day) came off in camp the other night, the 21st. The festivities were suddenly interrupted about midnight, or near that time, by a shower of balls through camp, occasioned by the firing of guards upon a party of deserters—4 men who were going off with their horses and arms, and who returned the fire quite briskly! The companies were hastily turned out under arms, the rolls called, and absentees reported. The next night another similar alarm occurred, more men having deserted.

One sergeant, ([Charles] Fillmore,) the Farrier (Welch [Thomas Walsh]) and 5 Privates of my company deserted while out grazing horses the other day, taking with their their (selected) horses, saddle blankets, halters, bridles and Lariats. Sent Blouse to Post Tailor for alteration today.

For a month, in his letters, Barnitz had conducted a lengthy debate with himself over whether Jennie should join him. Primitive living conditions, uncertainty over the regiment's future operations, and tensions created by Custer's behavior argued against it. At last, perhaps losing patience with Albert's continuing indecision, Jennie made the decision herself. She left East Cleveland on May 21 and reached the Big Creek camp a week later.

Jennie to her mother, camp near Fort Hays, Kan., June 1, 1867 (misdated, should be May 31):

I arrived here all safe, Tuesday noon, precisely a week from the day I started. Another expedition against the Indians will leave here tomorrow, but one company is to remain here at the Post—& as *I* am here Albert's is that company. Aren't we fortunate? We are really delightfully situated. How I wish you could look in upon us. We have a hospital tent, large enough to accommodate a hundred persons. The only one here but Gen. Custer's. In one corner of it is a stove, in the opposite one is our bed—the bedstead being made of poles nailed together. We have no floor to our tent—but have it carpeted with empty coffee sacks put down with wooden pins. The cedar tree grows here in abundance. We have had those planted all around our tent. We have another wall tent for dining room. Have two very good servants, who cook just what they please, & just as they please. Have some strange dishes & some very nice ones. We have the nicest fruits (canned) & jellies & jams here that I ever tasted—also portable lemonade, put up in a concentrated form—it is delicious. Mrs. Gen. Custer, Mrs Gen Gibbs, Miss Darraugh, Mrs Wallingford & myself are all the ladies here. The officers are very pleasant it seems as if they could not do enough for me. I wrote you from Fort Riley—giving you an account of my journey there. The Quartermaster, Mr [1st Lt. and Bvt. Capt. Charles] Brewster* of this Reg. was my company here. We came in an ambulance, & I shall never forget the journey I assure you. You see, Gen Hancock has issued an order to this effect—"that no one or company shall cross the plains without an escort of fifteen men"—but as this escort is infantry, & delays were very much, & as Mr Brewster was very anxious to come through quickly, he refused to take the escort . . . & we came, Mr Brewster his servant—driver & myself. He had three revolvers on the seat before him, & those were our only protection. . . . Oh! you can have no idea how I felt coming across those plains—expecting every moment to see any number of Indians. Once we thought we saw some—& Mr B. was terrified enough . . . but we got through all safe & I can hardly tell or describe to you the relief I felt, when this fort came in view. Albert was of course overjoyed to see me & it was so fortunate that I came just as I did for otherwise he would have gone out on this expedition. Now we are to stay.

By the end of May, Custer felt himself strong enough to take the field. His mission, as defined in orders of May 21 from Colonel Smith, was "to hunt out and chastise the Cheyennes and that portion of the Sioux who are their allies between the Smoky Hill and the Platte." With six troops of the 7th Cavalry and a long wagon train, Custer marched on June 1. Troop F was sent to Monument Station to patrol the Smoky Hill route, while Barnitz's Troop G remained with the infantry at the camp on Big Creek. Colonel Smith established district headquarters here, and Major Gibbs exercised immediate command.

Jennie's journal:

June 2, 1867. . . . Have had a delightful day. It has been quiet & Albert has been with me nearly all the time. We have talked & read & slept. It has been intensely warm. It seems so strange at night to listen to the guard outside as he gives the command to halt & give countersign. It seems strange to see two pistols & ammunition in the chair by our bed, & another under our pillow, to have instructions given me what to do in case of an attack, & yet I dont feel in the least afraid.

June 3, 1867. We moved our tent to day, beside Gens. Custer & Gibbs. It is a pleasant spot, & we will have it fitted up nicely. I have spent the afternoon with Mrs. Gibbs.

June 4, 1867. Mrs. Gibbs brought me potatoes for dinner. Mrs. Custer & Gen Smith called this morning. To night the General took tea with us after which I walked with him to his quarters, to hear the band, & two old officers, friends of his. He is a very gallant old gentleman. The officers who are here call often. Albert & I take a nice little walk every evening. I enjoy it so much. Oh! I know we shall not be so happily situated any length of time. What could I do if Albert is ordered away. . . .

June 5, 1867. . . . Mr Stouch [1st Lt. George W. H. Stouch, 3d Infantry], Mr Brewster & Gen Gibbs were here, when the alarm was given about 10 O C that Mrs Custer Miss Darrough, & Col Weir [Bvt. Lt. Col. & 1st Lt. Thomas B. Weir,* 7th Cavalry, who was serving on Colonel Smith's staff as Acting Assistant Adjutant General of the district] had gone out walking & had not returned. The camp was aroused, guns were fired, bugles sounded, & after a great deal of excitement they were found all safe. Gen Gibbs was so intoxicated he could not give an order, scarcely walk. Oh! it is dreadful! If Albert should ever do so, what would I do. The guns were fired so at random & in every direction that we were really in great danger of being shot. Some fell down in the grass, or went into ravines to escape the balls, but at last everything was quiet. . . .

June 6, 1867. . . . To night we were invited to Gen Gibbs. The Gen. was drunk, as usual! It is lightning to night & looks like a storm. Oh I am afraid of storms here, but we will hope for the best.

June 7, 1867. Oh! what a night I passed. Such a storm I had hardly conceived of. Gen Smith who has always lived on the plains says he never saw anything equal to it. The lightning was chain & burst like rockets, & some said fairly hissed & fell like stars. The whole air was filled with electricity. The thunder I cannot describe. Much heavier than cannonading, & so very near us. It was terrific. I was calm & perfectly overcome. The rain fell in torrents, the wind blew fearfully, but we did not think of high water. At about 3 O'C a m Gen Smith came to our tent & screamed, "For God's sake Barnitz get up, we are under water." I was obliged to look for my things got dressed soon. With one shoe & one of Alberts boots, & took my watch jewelry & money & went out never expecting to see my things again. The sight was fearful. The creek upon which we were encamped & which had been very shallow the previous day, now was a mighty rushing river, & I think I never saw so strong a current. A few feet back of us, where before had been dry land, was another river madly rushing along, so we were entirely surrounded on a little spot of land, & the water constantly rising. What reason had we to hope. Nearly all felt for a time that there was no escape. The ladies were out half dressed, with hair over their shoulders, & to add to the terror of the scene, drowning men went floating past us shrieking for help, & we could not save them. Oh I can never forget those cries for help, never never. Nine were drowned. Some were saved. The water was rising as rapidly as a man could step back to keep from it. At last daylight came, & were people ever more thankful for light? After while the water commenced falling, & we began to hope. During the day the water was so low we could *possibly* have crossed, & how strange we did not, but *drunken* Generals thought it would rain no more & we stayed.

June 8, 1867. Mr & Mrs Capt [Arthur B.] Carpenter [37th Infantry] dined with me. About midnight Col Weir came & alarmed us again. It was raining harder than I ever heard it, it seems to me. Almost a water spout & the wind blew even harder than the night before. I dressed myself again & went with Albert to Mrs Gen Custers in that fearful storm. They sent men out who came back and reported that the stream could not be crossed, that we had better risk our lives where we were. Once more we gave up. Mrs Custer says, "Well, we will all go down together. I am glad the Gen doesn't know of it." We went home to our tent. I packed my trunk with all the calmness imaginable, & have wondered since how I did it. A number of officers came in & stayed the remainder of the night. After waiting & waiting,

June 9, daylight came again, & the water again commenced falling, & this time we moved & are now on the crest of a hill where we feel safe, comparatively. What an experience! May I never have to pass through such another!

By the spring of 1867, the Union Pacific Railroad—Eastern Division, soon to be renamed the Kansas Pacific, had reached Salina, 185 miles west of the Missouri River. Company directors thought to reach the Pacific through the southwestern territories, and in the summer of 1867 they launched a surveying expedition to explore possible routes. In the absence

*of the chief of the party, company treasurer William Jackson Palmer, the
first stage of the survey proceeded under the leadership of W. W. Wright,
who as a Union general had managed General Sherman's railroad operations in Georgia and was now superintendent of the Kansas Pacific.
Because of Indian hostilities, the Wright party needed an escort, at least as
far as Fort Lyon, Colorado. The assignment fell to Barnitz's troop. At the
same time, Colonel Smith decreed that the ladies must abandon the camp
on Big Creek. Once more the Barnitzes parted as Jennie sadly returned to
her Ohio home.*

June 15, 1867. Albert received orders to day to be ready to
march Monday morning at daylight as escort for Gen Wright.
What am I to do. I cannot stay here without him.

June 16, 1867. Alberts company was out for inspection. How I
hate to see it. . . . Gen Smith came down at 8 O'C and told me to
be ready to go in three hours, as all the ladies were going through
to Harker with him in ambulances. I had intended to go 8 miles
farther west with the engineering party & take the stage there, so
as to be with Albert till the last minute, but I must give it up, & say
good bye to night. It seems to me I cannot go home, but know it is
best. Will I ever be more reconciled to these separations? Will I
ever be able to part from Albert more easily, or must I all my life
endure this agony? I must go, there is no other way. A number
have called to say good bye, but I could not bear to devote one
moment to them. I wanted to be alone with my darling Albert.

June 17, 1867. We left last night at 12 O'C. Mrs Gen Custer,
Mrs Gen Gibbs, Mrs Wallingford, Miss Darrough, & myself & Gen
Smith & Col Weir with our escort of 20 mounted men. And now I
feel that it was better, that it was easier for *me* to leave Albert than
it would have been for me to have waited & seen him go. I am glad
the parting is over. Oh! how sad they are! We have driven very
fast. Reached Fort Harker, 65 miles, before dark having stopped
six hours. Dined at Wilsons Creek. Have written to Albert. I went
to Mrs Willards having been previously invited. [Bvt.] Col. [and
Maj. Henry C.] Merriam [38th Infantry] & wife were there. The
rest of the ladies had no particular acquaintances & slept in their
ambulances, taking their meals with [Bvt.] Col [and Capt. Verling
K.] Hart [37th Infantry]. I am sick & tired & sad. Where is my
darling to night?

Jennie to Albert, Fort Harker, Kan., June 19, 1867:

We reached here Monday evening at dark—& found that the high water has carried off the bridges and that it will be impossible for us to leave here for a week. I stayed with Mrs Willard the first night, but Mrs. Dr. Sternberg [wife of Assistant Surgeon George M. Sternberg*] heard I was here, indeed had heard I was coming & came over at once, & insisted on my staying with her every moment that I am here. She is delightfully situated in new quarters—has five spacious rooms—very handsomely furnished, china & silver for her table, excellent servants—then the Doctor has a farm near here, which he has cultivated—& his table is furnished from it—onions, radishes, green peas, etc. etc. Of course he is more certain of remaining here than others & can surround himself with all those things. The other ladies are taking meals in Officers Mess, & sleeping in ambulances, having no particular acquaintances here. I spend a good deal of time with them every day. Have become better acquainted than I ever should under other circumstances & like them all very much. Have had any amount of sympathy on account of being compelled to ride with poor Mrs. W[allingford] & that baby oh that baby! I did try to be kind to her Albert—& "took up my cross"—& held it once while it was sleeping, but the other ladies have all the responsibility of her now. The very stage I thought of coming through in—was attacked & obliged to go back. Think of it! A man was killed by Indians a few miles from here night before last & two wounded, one of whom was brought in last night. Our party is really delightful & very congenial (one exception, Mrs W-) The very kindest feelings exist between us—& we all talk very freely about other people.

The party left Fort Harker on June 21 by railroad and, after a pause at Fort Riley, Jennie continued to Cleveland, arriving on June 27.

5. Action at Fort Wallace, June 1867

Fort Wallace under construction in June 1867, as depicted for *Harper's Weekly,* July 27, 1867. Barnitz and his cavalry troop are in foreground.

Harper's Weekly issue of July 27 portrayed Barnitz's fight with Cheyennes at Fort Wallace on June 26, 1867.

Albert to Jennie, Fort Wallace, Kan., June 29, 1867:

Our route to this place was without incident worthy of note, except that the moccasin tracks of Indians were found about our camps in the mornings, and on going into camp on the north fork of the Smoky, 14 miles east of here on the afternoon of the 23d inst. numerous pony tracks, the remains of camp fires, bark gnawed & pealed from the small cottonwood trees, and other "signs" indicated that a large body of Indians had been there but a few hours previous, and caused us to exercise redoubled vigilance. In a short time Indians were reported advancing, and my command was quickly under arms, the mules and horses driven in from grazing &c, but the objects seen proved to be scouts in advance of two Denver coaches, which soon came up, filled with soldiers, as escort, and accompanied by a small force of cavalry—one of my own men among their number. From them I learned that a few days previous [June 21] the Indians had appeared in force, about Fort Wallace, and attempted to drive off the stock and had also made attacks upon the various stage stations in the vicinity and had attempted to burn them with a kind of torpedo arrows—made by placing a percussion cap on the point of the arrow blade, and encasing the same in a little cotton sack, containing about a thimble full of gun-powder! I was shown several of the arrows, thus prepared, the caps of which had split, but failed to explode—the arrows being probably too short. I learned further that Sergeant Dunnell [William H. Dummell] of my company, who had gone in command of the escort which I sent to accompany Genl. Hancock (one morning while you were asleep you remember!) had been killed on the same occasion, while gallantly charging an overwhelming force of the Indians, and attempting to drive them from the vicinity of the fort. We placed a handsome head-stone at his grave on our arrival here, one of my men carving the letters very nicely. The gallantry of Sergeant Dunnell was very highly spoken of by those who witnessed the charge from the Fort. He had but 3 soldiers and a citizen with him. The soldiers were all killed, and the citizen, being finely mounted barely escaped. It is generally believed that Sergeant Dunnell

63

would not have been killed had he been properly sustained by
Sergeant [William] Hamlin, of Company "I" 7th Cav. who was
ordered to charge at the same time, with about 8 men of that
company, but who shamefully retreated, just at a critical moment,
with all his men, leaving Sergeant Dunnell and his comrades to be
surrounded and slaughtered by the Indians! But more of him
hereafter. In consequence of his shameful misconduct on a subsequent occasion, of which I will presently give you an account, it
is a wonder that my own scalp-lock has not been danced about by
some smoky camp fire, beyond the hills ere this!

But to my narrative: We arrived here on the afternoon of the
24th inst. The same evening Lieuts. [Samuel M.] Robbins* &
[William W.] Cook[e]*, 7th Cavalry, arrived from Genl. Custer's
command, with Company "D" escorting a train of 20 wagons, to
obtain supplies. They started back the next day. They report
Genl. Custer somewhere on the head waters of the Republican,
and its tributaries, some where about 180 miles North-East of
here, his command somewhat scattered—Captain West with his
company being on Beaver Creek, upon which stream the Indians
are supposed to have some of their villages. Genl. Hancock [en
route to Denver] had taken all the cavalry from this post [Troop I
of the 7th, Capt. Myles W. Keogh*] a few days before my arrival
here. He is expected back in about a week. I found but a handful
of Infantry at the post and a few citizens.

The post is handsomely situated on high ground about a quarter of a mile distant from the south fork of the Smoky, a small
stream of pure and never failing water, beyond which the prairie
gradually rises for a distance of five miles, where the view is
bounded by a range of magnificent bluffs, quite mountainous in
appearance, and the summits of which are so clearly defined in
the pure atmosphere of this climate that the head of an Indian
could be readily seen if one should appear above the hills. . . .
Beyond the Smoky, at the distance of 3 miles, in a South-Easternly
direction is a bold cliff of rocks standing alone on the prairie. It is
the stone quarry from which the material for the new buildings
which are now in process of construction here is brought. The
stone is of a yellowish hue—somewhat variegated, sprinkled with
red and brown though some of the blocks are nearly white. It is
very soft when first quarried, and is dressed with carpenter's tools!

A dashing romantic with a fondness for the bottle, Myles W. Keogh was an Irish soldier of fortune with a distinguished Civil War record. He commanded Troop I in 1866–76 and died at the Little Bighorn. His horse, Comanche, was the only living being found on the Custer Battlefield.

Fort Wallace, Kansas, June 26, 1867. "Dr. Bell (W.A.) of Phila. an amateur photographic artist with the engineering party, took a photograph of myself and the other officers at the post, sitting in front of the commandant's quarters, with cavalry horses, and the boundless prairie in the back ground, on the day of the battle. . . . He also photographed the body of Serg't Wylliams, after it was brought to the post, just to show our friends at Washington, the Indian Agents, what fiends we have to deal with!" Albert to Jennie, June 29, 1867. Actually, the building is the temporary adjutant's office, as the sign indicates. None of the officers' quarters had yet been completed. Note also canvas roof and antelope skull above door. Barnitz is seated in the center. Seated to his right is Lt. James M. Bell, who commanded the 7th Cavalry detachment at Fort Wallace. Officer standing with rifle is probably Lt. Frederick H. Beecher, killed a year later in the Battle of Beecher's Island.

They actually saw it up into blocks of the proper size, and then plane it with an ordinary jack plane!—but it soon hardens, and resists the weather admirably. Five large buildings (of stone) have been completed here, and others are under way. Those finished are the Suttler's Store, commissary building, one company's quarters, a citizens and officer's mess house. The officers all live in tents, or board buildings at present. One large stone stable for cavalry, a temporary structure however, has been finished.

The officers of the post are at present, 1st Lieut. Joseph Hale, 3d Inf, commandant, 1st Lieut. D. Mortimer Lee, 37th Inf. Post Adjutant, 1st Lieut. F.H. Beecher* 3d Inf. (a nephew of Henry Ward Beecher) Post Quartermaster & Commissary, Dr. T.S. Turner, Assist. Surgeon U.S.A., Post Surgeon—in charge of the Post Hospital. Joseph M. Badger, a son of Revd. Norman Badger, Professor of Languages &c at Kenyon College, and my esteemed "patron" while there, is Post Sutler. Lieut. [James M.] Bell,* 7th Cav. is here, in command of the detachment of cavalry of Co. "I". All the officers here are very good, worthy men, and not a *drinking* set! Lieut. Hale is a man of fine abilities, and a very good man. You would like him exceedingly. He resembles Ralph Waldo Emerson somewhat in appearance, but is younger.

Having now given you some preliminary ideas, I will proceed to give you some account of quite a desperate little fight which I have had with the Indians, and which our citizen friends persist in dignifying by the name of a "battle." Indeed the soldiers of the garrison are very much impressed with its magnitude, and it was doubtless the most extensive engagement that has occurred for some time, on these plains, if I except the [Fetterman] massacre near Fort Phil. Kearney [Wyoming, December 21, 1866], which was more an ambuscade than a fight.

You must know then that upon my arrival here I found the small garrison under some apprehension of a renewed attack from the Indians, and it was not deemed prudent to be even a few hundred yards from the fort or our own encampment, which was only a short distance from here, without arms, lest the Indians should suddenly make a dash, and we be found like the foolish virgins! Well, not having any grain for my horses, I was accustomed to send them all to graze, at a point about two miles down the stream, in the valley, posting videttes on the high ground, at a

mile distant on either hand, trusting that in the event of a dash by
the Indians, and an attempted stampede, the mounted men about
20 in number, whom I kept among them, armed with their carbines, might be able to move them in to the Post before the
Indians could get among them. I was accustomed to send them
out after breakfast, keeping them fastened to a picket-rope, or
lariatted near at night, with a strong guard among them. Well, on
the morning of Wednesday, June 26, just as I was about starting to
breakfast, I saw a commotion at the Post, men running to and fro,
and emerging from their quarters and tents with arms, and at
once mistrusting the presence of Indians, I ordered the men to
seize their arms, and run out and bring in the horses (which were
lariatted near where they could get a little grass), and in the
meantime I learned that the Indians were approaching in considerable force, and that a large party were already running off the
mules and stage horses from the Ponds-creek Stage Station. In
less than a minute my horses were coming in, and I at once
ordered them to be saddled, and the command formed for action,
and mounting my own horse, which had been quickly saddled (the
sorrel—the vicious one you remember!) and accompanied by
[Edward] Botzer, one of my Trumpeters, I rode out to the North
West, to the high ground to reconnoitre, directing Serg't [Francis
S.] Gordon to form the command, mount, and follow. I had not
ridden more than half a mile, and completed some hasty observations (discovering small parties of Indians on the ridges, all round
the horizon to the west, and north, and a cloud of dust arising
from the direction of the Stage Station), when I saw my company
approaching, at a gallop, and also a small party of cavalry coming
out from the Post to join me. As my troop came up, I deployed the
1st Platoon, under Serg't Gordon, my 1st Sergeant, as Skirmishers, ordering him to proceed at a steady gallop, keeping the
horses well in hand, towards the North-West, the apparent centre
of the enemy's line, and to direct his movements towards a group
of Indians among whom was one mounted on a white horse, and
upon approaching sufficiently near, to charge as foragers, cau-
tioning the men to swing to the left in the charge, and endeavor to
head off a force which I now saw attempting to escape from the
station. I directed the detachment from Company I to cooperate
with the skirmishers, and the 2nd Platoon (under Serg't [Josiah]

Haines, my Quartermaster Sergeant) to follow in reserve, at 200 paces in rear of the Skirmishers; just as I had completed my formation, and was moving forward in fine style—(the whole formation being done while going forward at a gallop,) Serg't Gordon was thrown from his horse, and considerably bruised, the horse having stepped into a prairie-dog hole, and he was left behind, attempting to follow on foot, until the horse could be caught,—the horse however (a superb animal, one of the finest on the plains) made directly for the Indians, and fearing that he would fall into the hands of the enemy, I started in pursuit, and after repeated efforts, succeeded in catching the bridle, and bringing him to a stand, and sending him back to the Sergeant. In the meantime, seeing that the Indians from the Station were likely to get past my Skirmish line, before it could reach them, I sent Botzer to Sergeant Haines, with directions for the 2nd Platoon to bear more to the right, and with a few men who were somewhat dispersed, I struck myself toward the center—midway between the skirmish line and the reserve, which had now come up abreast of it. It was just at this juncture, and as the skirmish line were becoming engaged with the Indians, that I sorely missed the absence of Sergeant Gordon, who had not yet come up—(he being far in the rear by the time his horse was caught,) for most unfortunately Serg't Hamlin, of Co. "I", was the senior non-commissioned officer with the line—the skirmishers—and no sooner had the Indians found themselves too closely pressed, than being reinforced by another party from behind a ridge, and as their only remaining course, they turned suddenly upon my line, and came literally *sailing* in, uttering their peculiar *Hi!—Hi!—Hi!* and terminating it with the war-whoop—their ponies, gaily decked with feathers and scalp-locks, tossing their proud little heads high in the air, and looking wildly from side to side, as their riders poured in a rapid fire from their repeating arms, or sending their keen arrows with fearful accuracy and force. I had no sooner seen the turn that affairs were taking, than dreading lest the skirmish line should turn in flight, and thus be at the mercy of their savage pursuers, than I shouted to the men who were with me to hasten to the support of the skirmish line, and signalling to Sergeant Haines, who (through his constitutional stupidity!) was bearing too much to the right—(though warmly engaged, and fighting

with great gallantry) to do the same, I dashed with all speed towards the skirmish line, but before I could reach it, the men began
to waver, and urged by Sergeant Hamlin to retreat, (who himself
made off at all speed followed by a few of his men,) the men began
to turn about, and fall back in confusion, nor could I reach them
in time to prevent so direful a result, although by signalling them
to turn about and face the enemy, I succeeded in inducing some
of the most intrepid ones to again confront the enemy, and afford
another moments precious time for the reserve platoon (now in
entire confusion however) to move towards a concentration with
us,—but it was only by singling out individuals, one or two men
here and there from among the confused mass of retreating men,
and inducing each to turn and fire one or two shots, or beat back
the diabolical fiends with the sabre, that I was at length enabled to
check the pursuit long enough to measurably concentrate my
men. Sergeant Gordon now fortunately reached us, and with his
assistance, though not until after a good deal of desultory
fighting, I was enabled to effectively check our pursuers, and
drive them back beyond the hills. I now placed Serg't Hamlin in
arrest, and ordered him to the post, hastily reformed my command, and dismounting a portion of the men, determined to hold
the ground at all hazards, until an ambulance, for which I at once
sent, could come from the post, and remove the dead and
wounded. Going meanwhile to the summit of a ridge, I took a
deliberate look at the fiends, who were drawn up in fine order,
upon the summit of another ridge beyond, busily engaged in
reloading their arms, and preparing, as I supposed, to renew the
fight. With my glass I was able to distinguish their hideous
countenances, and the barbaric magnificence of their array, as
they sat with their plumed lances, their bows, and shields, and
their gleaming weapons, only awaiting apparently for the signal of
their chief to make another descent! But their leading chief,
"Roman Nose" had already (as we believe) been killed in the fight,
and the "Dog Soldiers" (as the Cheyennes style themselves) had
paid dearly in the encounter, and so they were not eager to renew
the onset. I now returned to my command, advanced a dismounted skirmish line to the north and west, to cover and protect
the horses, and waited patiently for the arrival of an ambulance,
and removal of the wounded, and all the dead whose bodies could

then be found, when I again moved forward, with a part of my
men dismounted to the point where I had last seen the enemy,
and a mile beyond, but not the head of even a solitary Indian was
anywhere visible above the ridges, and not a pony track was visible
on the hard dry ground of the hot prairie, and so I at length
returned to the Post, and made arrangements for the burial of the
dead, visited the wounded in the hospital, and put things in
proper shape for a repulse of the Indians, should they return in
force, and make an attempt to capture the post. The dead were
buried with martial honors, all my own company, Genl. Wright
and others of the surveying party, the troops of the garrison,
myself and all the officers being in the procession. Parties of
laborers, and occasional details of soldiers have been working at
intervals ever since, digging rifle pits, and we now have things in a
very fair shape for defense, should the Indians make their appearance. I cannot say that I deem such an event probable, and
yet it is well for one always to be on the safe side. [Pvt. John G.]
Hummell was wounded severely—a bullet wound through the
thigh, and a lance thrust in the side. But the Surgeon thinks he
will recover. Sergeant [Frederick] Wyllyams—the one who fixed
the tin protection to our stove pipe,—and who was such a gentle-
manly soldier, was killed. The Indians stripped, scalped, and
horribly mutilated his body. I dare not tell you how fearfully! He
had fought bravely, but had incautiously become separated from
the command, and was surrounded by overwhelming numbers.
The Indians stripped, or partially stripped all the dead whose
bodies fell within their reach. They did this almost instantly.
When [Charles] Clarke, the chief Bugler was killed and fell from
his horse (while following me from the centre across to the skirmish line—a very hot ride, by the way, for us all!) a powerful
Indian was seen to reach down, as he rode at full speed, seize the
body with one hand, and jerk it across his pony, strip off the
clothes in an instant, dash out the brains with a tomahawk, and
hasten on for another victim!—But I would only sicken you with
additional details of the fight. My own scalp seems to have been in
considerable request—although not by any means ornamental as a
trophy. Corporal [Prentice G.] Harris says that he saw an Indian,
who appeared to be a chief, swing a pole which he carried, with a
bunch of feathers tied to a string, on the end, rapidly around his

head five or six times, and then point it at me, when instantly half
a dozen Indians started for me, each firing a number of shots, but
I was not touched. One Indian dashed towards me, as I rode from
the centre to the left, and fired several shots at me over his pony's
head, and then when opposite me turned, and rode parallel with
me, on my right side, lying lengthwise on his pony, and firing
from under his pony's neck, his left arm being thrown over the
pony's neck, and grasping his rifle! The shots came *very* close! But
I was just then too much concerned for the fate of my command
to pay much heed to his firing. I only pointed my revolver at him,
a few times, as if I was about to fire, and thus disconcerted him a
little, I suppose; but I was reserving my shots for a more favorable
opportunity, and *Oh! Darling!* had I not been successful in check-
ing the tide of adversity, and driving back our pursuers, your eyes
would have been tearful when tidings from this far land had
reached you, apprising you of the dread result!—for it would
have been scarcely possible for any one to have reached the
Post—the distance being so great, and the Indian ponies so fleet!
The men would have fallen one by one, and possibly no one
would have escaped to tell the tale! But *dear* Jennie, do not be
fearful on my account hereafter, more than formerly, will you? I
will always do my duty, of course, faithfully, and fearlessly, and
leave the result with the All-Wise Giver of Life; and should it be
my fortune to fall in some future engagement, console yourself
with the reflection that I am not dead, but only transferred to a
higher and nobler sphere of existence, where I will await your
coming, with tender and fond solicitude, as the one dear being
without whom I would not choose to live!

I do not forget out tender parting, Jennie,—nor that your eyes
were *so* tearful, and that you would not be consoled! You will not
doubt that your going away was like the going away of all happiness from my life—and yet I could not wish you to remain, Jennie!
No, it would have been cruel to desire you to remain, even for a
day after an opportunity, however wretched, presented itself for
your safe return to the serener, and more salubrious atmosphere
of the Lake—and *Home!* I fear that you will think me sad—
unusually sad perhaps,—and yet I am not. I have passed through
such trying vicissitudes of life that I am not now rendered quite
despondent by adversity, and scarcely elated in seasons of joy. I

dream of you very often—almost nightly I may say, and so long to be with you *always!*—but this *cannot* be, and so I must ever be reconciled to wait!

Dr. Bell (W.A.) of Phila. an amateur photographic artist with the engineering party, took a photograph of myself and the other officers of the post, sitting in front of the commandant's quarters, with cavalry horses, and the boundless prairie in the back ground, on the afternoon of the day of the battle. He will print some copies for us when the days are less light. He also photographed the body of Serg't Wyllyams, after it was brought to the post, just to show our friends at Washington, the Indian Agents, what fiends we have to deal with!—He also photographed the buildings of the Post, and Fort Harker, and Castle Rock &c. &c. He promises to finish me copies of all in due time. . . . It is not now certain that I will go to Fort Lyon! Genl. Wright declines to go further without a larger escort. He wants 200 men! This being the case, it may be difficult for him to obtain the required force, and in that case he may return to St. Louis!—Genl. Smith is at Harker I suppose? We have no news from any where. . . .

By the way, Major Cooper (7th Cav.) shot himself—purposely—through the head—committed suicide a week or two ago! Reason, "he had got out of whiskey!"—so say Lieuts. Robbins & Cook[e]. He was with Genl. Custer, but of course you see the papers, and I don't.

> Head Quarters Company "G", 7th U.S. Cav.
> Camp near Fort Wallace, Kansas
> June 28, 1867

Lieut. T.B. Weir, 7th U.S. Cav.
A.A.A.G. Dist. Uppr. Ark's.
      Sir—

      I have the honor to report my arrival at this Post, with my command, en route for Fort Lyon, Colorado, as escort to the engineering party under the direction of Genl. Wright, pursuant to Special Field Orders No. 43, d. Hd Qrs. Dist. Uppr. Ark's, June 16, 1867.

I have further to inform you that at about 6 o'clock on the morning of the 26th inst., Indians being reported in the vicinity, attempting to drive off the stock from Ponds-Creek Stage Station, 3 miles west of here, I hastily mounted my command, and uniting with the same a few men of Company "I" 7th Cavalry, who were at the Post, moved out, and after a rapid ride of three miles succeeded in heading off a party of the Indians (about 75 in number,) who were endeavoring to escape Northward with stock from the Station, and engaged them, at close quarters, with carbine and sabre. They fought with great courage, and being strongly reenforced by another and larger band, which came suddenly around a point, from the North-West, they returned the charge, with the utmost vigor and determination, and for a time my little force was in serious peril, but was at length successful in repulsing the Indians, and driving them from the field, of which I retained possession until the arrival of an ambulance for which I had sent, and the removal of the dead and wounded, when I renewed the pursuit, with a view, mainly, to ascertain if possible and beyond a doubt the direction in which the Indians were ultimately retreating; but having followed them to a point at which they were last seen in force (about 5 miles N.W. from the Post,) I found that they had dispersed in various directions, and entirely disappeared, leaving no trail.

My loss in the engagement was: 1 sergeant, 1 corporal, 1 Trumpeter and 3 Privates killed. 2 Corporals and 4 Privates wounded. Corporal [James K.] Ludlow it is believed can not recover; he having been shot entirely through the body (the abdomen) with a "revenge arrow." None of the other wounds are believed to be necessarily fatal.

I inclose herewith a list of the names of the killed and wounded.

My command behaved well, indeed I may say admirably, in view of all the circumstances, with the exception of Sergeant Hamlin, Company "I" 7th Cavalry, whom I placed in arrest, and sent from the field for cowardice. He is said to have behaved very badly on a former occasion. His place can readily be filled by selection from the gallant men of his company who participated in the engagement. [Sergeant Hamlin deserted on August 11, 1867.]

The Indian force present during the engagement is variously estimated. I should place it at not less than 200 warriors, and think that it may have greatly exceeded that number, as, in addition to the main force, which acted in concert, (and after the engagement withdrew to a safe distance, and confronted us in admirable order—much resembling two squadrons of cavalry, formed by platoons, and closed in mass, with an interval of about 30 paces between the columns,) there were also single scouts or small groups of Indians upon all the commanding ridges, extending through an arc of 90° from west to north. The Indians were doubtless Cheyennes & Sioux, with probably a few Arapahoes. All were most admirably mounted and armed; many had repeating rifles or carbines, and every Indian appeared to have at least one revolver, in addition to his powerful bow and arrows; some of the latter were shot with such force as to pierce through the hard beech wood of our saddle trees, and the two thicknesses of rawhide covering! Several of the killed were shot through with numerous arrows, besides being literally riddled with balls. Many of the Indians carried lances, in addition to their other weapons. They were usually mounted on ponies, though a few had large horses. The ponies, however, were of remarkable size, very fleet and powerful. Our own horses were generally no match for them, either in speed or endurance.

The Indians appeared to have a system of signalling, with mirrors, by means of which the bands were guided in their movements.

The loss of the enemy is of course not satisfactorily known, as they succeeded in carrying off their dead, and wounded; it is believed, however, to have been quite as severe as our own, and the probabilities are that it was much greater, as several of the men whose horses had fallen (having stepped into prairie dog holes, which were numerous,) and who were thrown in consequence, used their carbines at very close quarters (the Indians crowding eagerly around them) and with manifest effect. There appears to be little room for doubt that "Roman Nose" (a leading chief of the Cheyennes) was killed. A chief mounted on a white horse, and fully answering the description of him as given by Mr. Kimbell, an employee at Pond's Creek stage station (who had seen him at the station in the morning, while attempting to run off the stock, and who had known him previously,) was killed by Corporal Harris, who first engaged him with a sabre, as he was attempting to plunge a lance through Private [Patrick] Hardiman [Hardy-

List of killed and wounded in an engagement with Indians, near Fort Wallace, June 26th, 1867

Name	Rank	Company	Killed	Wounded Badly	Slightly	
Frederick Wyllyams	Sergeant	"G" 7th Cav	1			Scalped & horribly mutilated
Charles Clarke	Bugler	"	1			Lived until following day
James Douglass	Corporal	"	1			
Frank Reahme	Private	"	1			
Nathan Trial	"	"E"	1			Scalped
[John] Welsh [Welch]	"	"G"	1			Body not recovered although repeated efforts have been made to find it. Probably carried off by the Indians, as the bodies of several of the others were carried by the Indians, on their ponies to some distance from where they fell.
James K. Ludlow	Corporal	"I"		1		
Johns Rivers	"	"G"			1	
John G. Humell	Private	"G"		1		
Peter Britton	"	"		1		
Hugh Riley	"	"I"		1		
Thomas Townley	"	"			1	
			6	4	2	

Albert Barnitz
Captain 7th U.S. Cavalry.

man], (whose carbine was empty, and whose sabre had unfortunately become disengaged from the scabbard in the pursuit and
been lost,) and indeed by placing his carbine against the stomach
of the "Big Chief," and shooting him through. As the Indian fell
forward on the neck of his horse, two others who were rapidly
approaching were observed to ride up on either side and seizing
his arms conduct horse and rider to the rear. My force in the
engagement was 49 men. The manner in which the Indians mutilated such of our dead as they were able to snatch up on their
ponies, and carry to a safe distance, was truly diabolical. I lost 5
horses in the engagement, 2 were killed and 3 fell into the hands
of the enemy, their riders having been killed. 4 others were
wounded. The latter, it is believed, will all eventually recover. The
Indians were only successful in escaping with 2 horses and one
mule from the stage station.

Very respectfully,

your obedient servant

Albert Barnitz,

Capt. 7th U.S. Cav.

*Barnitz's action at Fort Wallace, the first of any magnitude fought by
the 7th Cavalry, attracted considerable press attention and earned the
captain well-merited acclaim from his superiors as well as from correspondents.*

*After breaking off with Barnitz, the warriors rode north and that same
afternoon, June 26, fell on the wagon train under Lieutenants Robbins
and Cooke that Custer had sent to Fort Wallace for supplies. Placing the
wagons in two parallel columns surrounded by dismounted skirmishers, the
officers conducted an able defense. For three hours the Indians circled and
thrust unsuccessfully at the train and its defenders, then withdrew upon the
approach of Captain West with two troops of the 7th Cavalry dispatched by
Custer to strengthen the train's escort.*

*From the Big Creek camp, Custer had led the six troops under his
immediate command north to Fort McPherson, on the Platte River, where
he arrived on June 10. Here he parleyed with Pawnee Killer, who
professed peace, and with General Sherman, who cautioned his subordi-
nate against being so trustful of Indians and ordered him to scour the
headwaters of the Republican River. From the forks of the Republican on
the twenty-second, Custer sent the supply train under Lieutenant Cooke*

toward Fort Wallace. Lieutenant Robbins's Troop D went as escort, while
Captain West's Troop K went along, too, with orders to scout Beaver Creek
while Robbins and Cooke proceeded to Fort Wallace. On the twenty-
fourth elements of Custer's command skirmished with Pawnee Killer's
Sioux warriors. This gave rise to concern for the safety of the supply train,
and the next day Custer ordered Capt. Edward Myers* with Troop E to
reinforce West. It was West's and Myers's troops that lifted the siege of the
wagon train on the twenty-sixth.

William A. Bell, the Wright Expedition's photographer mentioned by
Barnitz, authored one of the classic travel narratives of the frontier, New
Tracks in North America *(London, 1869; reprint, Albuquerque,*
1965). It contains a description of Barnitz's fight and an engraving based
on the photograph he took of Sergeant Wyllyams's corpse.

The soldiers erred in thinking Roman Nose had been killed. He did not
participate in this engagement. The Indian slain by Corporal Harris was
in fact a Sioux. Roman Nose died instead in the celebrated Battle of
Beecher's Island, September 17–25, 1868.

Jennie to Albert, East Cleveland, Ohio, July 15, 1867:

Thank you a thousand times, darling, for your long, long letter
giving me so full an account of that fearful, *fearful* battle. Oh! how
gladly would I fly to you, and stay with you forever, and share
your fate, whatever it may be. I try to be cheerful here, so they will
think I am happy, but how often I am entertaining company in
the parlor, when my heart is aching, and I long to be alone, in my
own quiet room. I think of the coming winter, and it comforts me,
and I wish that *then*—we would be separated from the whole
world—and live only for each other. Oh! when we are together
the time is too precious to be given to society—to strangers. We
will stay at home next winter, won't we dearest? I should not
complain in the least, if we are sent to some remote one company
Post—*then* I could give all my time to *you*. Poor Sergeant Wylliams!
How well I remember him! You have not forgotten the boquet of
wild flowers he left on our table, when we were out walking, have
you? Someone, I think Dr [William H.] Forwood, has sent me two
copies of the Philadelphia Press, containing a lengthy account of
the fight, in which Capt Barnitz—"a tried soldier and an unflinch-
ing patriot"—participated. I spend a great deal of time in the
Reading Room, and read everything that pertains to the Indians.

. . . Oh, my heart is filled with gratitude to Him, who preserved and protected you, in those moments of danger. What a comfort it is, to feel that I can leave you in His hands in the future, trusting, *believing*, that He will take care of you.

. . . I was shocked to hear of Maj. Coopers death—but I do not think it is any loss to the Regiment. A sad end to a useless life! What an affliction for his wife, who is said to be a lovely woman. I am glad to learn that Gen Custer is moving down to the Smoky Hill route.

Albert to Jennie, camp near Fort Wallace, Kan., July 1, 1867:

Things continue about *statu in quo* here. The Indians take great pleasure in raising a fellow being's hair, as formerly,—at a little distance from this post—although since the date of my fight with them they have not been seen about here—and yet we keep ourselves mightily on the alert for them—especially at night. We do not intend to be caught napping, at all events. Every night the command is turned out at least three or four times—the sentinels firing on wolves, or other objects which they mistake for Indians creeping up in the darkness—for we have no moon now, and the sentinels have to be doubly vigilant. It must seem very amusing to people in Ohio to be told that certain of their acquaintances are really engaged in war, in these, to them, peaceful times! I suppose they can't realize it at all!—and yet away out here, it is the serious business of our lives! Well, I sometimes laugh myself, to think of it!—and yet it is not a very laughable matter, I am sure, to see a poor fellow every now and then with his scalp gone, and his body full of bullet holes, and revenge arrows, and his clothes taken off, and limbs gashed in every conceivable manner—but that is what we are compelled to witness daily here! Yesterday a train coming in with supplies for the Stage Company, was ambuscaded by a few Indians, about 15 or 20 miles east of here, and a citizen who was riding a few hundred yards ahead, on the alert for "Lo" lost his Henry rifle (16 shooter,) revolver, and scalp,—and his clothes too, which were jerked off in a jiffy—for the Indians are really becoming civilized to the extent of wearing white men's clothes occasionally, out here! Today, an ox-train, guarded by citizens, which passed here yesterday, going west, returned for safety—having had to fight Indians all the time after they had got a few miles west of this post! The Indians captured two of their wagons, at one time, but they succeeded in retaking them, losing, as I learn one man killed (and "sculped") and another slightly wounded. A Denver coach which came in this afternoon, with a small, worn-out, cavalry and Infantry escort, reports having fought Indians all the way from "Big Timbers" 50 miles west of here to this place. One of the soldiers was wounded. They killed an Indian, and, as they believe, wounded others. The weather is intensely hot. Thermometer indicated 102° today in the shade, but there are fortunately 40 tons of ice here! . . .

We caught a large grey wolf—Timber wolf—*alive* yesterday! Ran him down on horseback, and surrounded him!—I send my horses 2 miles to graze daily;—dangerous business!—but it *must* be done.

Albert to Jennie, camp near Fort Wallace, Kan., July 4, 1867:

Well, yesterday afternoon Genl. Hancock & party arrived, on return from Denver City, and having encamped near the Post, the General sent for me, and we had quite a social little talk in regard to the Indians &c &c. The General expressed himself as quite highly pleased with my management of "Lo, the poor Indian!" (and I learn this evening that he is about to issue a complimentary order in regard to the affair, but whether from press of business, &c, the matter will be forgotten, or not, I have no means of knowing. He is really very busy.)

The General's arrival resulted in my being sent, with 30 men, a little before dark last evening, to Goose Creek, 11 miles west of here, to meet a lumber train which was expected to encamp there last night (the Genl. having passed it on his way here,) and escort it to this post. Just after I had got started a most *terrific* thunder storm set in, and it became *very* dark! *pitch dark*—except when the whole country was illuminated by the fearful flashes of lightning! Wasn't I glad that Jennie wasn't along—or any where in this country! Well, I found the train about 9 o'clock, and escorted it safely to this post this morning. It consisted of 40 wagons, each drawn by about 20 oxen; the lumber, pine, is from Denver, and intended for completing the buildings of this post.

6. Cholera, Court-Martial, and A Long, Hot Summer
July–September 1867

George Armstrong Custer. The portraits of George, wife Elizabeth, and brother Tom in this chapter and those of 7th Cavalry officers were contained in an album Albert presented to Jennie for Christmas 1877 and now in the possession of a great granddaughter, Mrs. F. Michael Trevitt.

For Barnitz and his troop, the rest of the summer of 1867 brought heat, dust, long, tiring, and seemingly pointless marches, the boredom of camp life, and the dreaded scourge of cholera. By doubling up with another division of the surveying expedition and its escort (twenty-five black soldiers of the 38th Infantry), General Wright felt strong enough to venture forth to Fort Lyon. The parties left Fort Wallace on July 8 and reached Fort Lyon on July 15. Here Barnitz first encountered the cholera.

Albert to Jennie, camp near Fort Lyon, Colo., July 18, 1867:

Mr. [William E.] Chandler, Assist Treasurer U.S.A. or assist. *Secretary* of the Treasury, or something [First Assistant Secretary of the Treasury], arrived here yesterday, with "excursion party"—They were escorted to within a few miles of this Post by a couple companies of the colored troops, but the "moaks" [blacks] are now quarantined below here, as the cholera has been carrying off some of them on the way, and Genl. Penrose, who is in command here, is fearful about having them come on.

Albert to Jennie, camp near Fort Lyon, Colo., July 20, 1867:

I found Col. Merriam here with his colored troops, in *quarantine!* He has had 20 cases of cholera among his soldiers, and 6 of them have died. Besides this the Surgeon's wife has died and the Surgeon is very low—in relapse—and not expected to recover. The Surgeon ([Henry R.] Tilton) from the Post came down with me to day, to attend the patients. At present there are five mild cases among the colored troops—all convalescing.

At Fort Lyon a troop of the 3rd Cavalry replaced Barnitz's troop as escort to the Wright party. Barnitz and his men turned back toward Fort Wallace on July 20, reaching their destination on July 25.

Albert to Jennie, camp near Fort Wallace, Kan., July 28, 1867:

We are becoming very fashionable out here! We are having the cholera just like other people, and are beginning to feel quite as important as city folks! Only think, seven dead men in an evening (all of the 7th Cavalry) isn't a small beginning at all, considering that this is reputed to be a remarkably healthful climate! Yes, seven dead men in an evening, and more the following day; and would you believe it, I turned Chaplain, and read the burial service over them, and the firing was done in right good style—for you know it wouldn't do to go and act "skeery" about it, or every body would "up and die," right off! But I confess to being a little skeery notwithstanding—(on your account, darling!) I would really much rather see two Indians than one man with the cholera, and I am not remarkably fond of Indians either! . . .

. . . Found . Genl. Custer's command encamped near the Post—the General himself having gone post haste, with an escort of 75 picked men, to Harker, to see "Libby!"—They do say that he just squandered that cavalry along the road!—that whenever a horse gave out or a man took sick, or became faint from sunstroke, that man or horse or both remained by the road side until the arrival of Lo, the poor Cheyenne, who acts as public scavenger on these highways, and there was an end of the matter!—I do not credit the rumor however—though the occasional arrival in camp of a broken down and riderless horse, with blood upon the saddle, gives some credence countenance to the story.

On June 27 the Robbins–Cooke supply train reached Custer. He then pushed his command hard in searching the headstreams of the Republican for the Sioux and Cheyennes. On July 6 he descended into the Platte Valley and, telegraphing to Fort Sedgwick, learned that General Sherman had sent orders for the 7th to hasten to the protection of the Smoky Hill route. The orders had been dispatched to Custer in charge of 2d Lt. Lyman H. Kidder and a ten-man detail of the 2d Cavalry on June 27, more than a week earlier, but had not reached him. The troops marched at once for Fort Wallace. En route they found the mutilated remains of Kidder and his men, cut down by pursuing warriors.

En route, too, desertion threatened to destroy the command as weary, hungry troopers, lured by the relative safety of the nearby Platte road, slipped away. On July 6–8 a total of thirty-four men deserted, and there was evidence of a plot that would have taken a third of the command. When thirteen men broke away in broad daylight on July 7, Custer ordered Maj. Joel H. Elliott* and other officers in pursuit with instructions to bring none back alive. Seven made good their escape, but Elliott brought back six,

Elizabeth Custer.

Tom Custer.

three wounded in an exchange of gunfire, one fatally. Custer ostentatiously refused medical aid but later quietly instructed the surgeon to care for them. As the column marched deeper into Indian country, away from the Platte road, the danger of desertion diminished.

Custer's troops limped into Fort Wallace on July 13, low on provisions, exhausted by long, punishing marches in broiling heat, and generally unfit for field duty without a period of rest and refitting. Sherman had expected Custer to receive further orders from General Hancock, but he had already passed through Fort Wallace. With a picked detachment of seventy-five officers and enlisted men, therefore, Custer headed east on July 15. The ostensible purpose of the journey was to obtain fresh orders from Hancock and to hasten badly needed supplies to his command at Fort Wallace. But as Barnitz's letter to Jennie makes clear, the officers remaining at Wallace perceived another reason: their commander had not seen his wife for six weeks.

The forced march was as hard as Barnitz intimates. With few pauses, the troops pushed through to Fort Hays, 150 miles in about 55 hours, arriving on the morning of July 18. Wornout horses were left along the way, and a party sent back for a straggler had a brush with Indians in which two fallen men were abandoned. An infantry detail later found one dead and one wounded.

Leaving the detachment at Fort Hays, Custer and three companions went on in ambulances to Fort Harker, where they arrived at about two o'clock on the morning of July 19. Here Custer talked briefly with a sleep-befuddled Colonel Smith and, apparently with his blessing, boarded the three o'clock train for Fort Riley. A few hours' journey by rail united him with Libbie that same day.

Barnitz's letter of July 28 continues:

Well, I not only found Genl. Custer's command here, (under Major Elliott) but I found the cholera too, and the grave-diggers, and coffin-makers appeared to think that these were troublous times! It was the very night after my arrival that so many deaths occurred. Since then, the epidemic has been abating—there have been numerous cases of cholera—or cholerac symptoms, but only an occasional death since. I did not go into camp with the regiment, but put my command nearly a mile away from the affected camp, and as yet have had no symptoms of cholera among us, and Jennie, dear, you must not be fearful, for don't you mind?—the

"Good Man" knows what's best for us, and if he desires that a human being should take sick, and vomit, and all that, why I suppose we ought to be reconciled, and not go and cry about it! Isn't that the true theory?—I enforce the strictest sanatary regulations in my camp, and if taking a nice bath every evening, and having nice clean sheets, and white pillow cases, and everything, will do any good, why then you need not feel at all concerned about your Albert, and all will be well. . . . But Jennie, I have not told you *all* about the cholera. I have some very sad news to communicate. Your friend Mrs. Dr. Sternberg, of Fort Harker, is dead! She died with the cholera only 6 hours after she was attacked. Lieut. [Charles G.] Cox,* of the 7th Cavalry (a new appointee—who held the position of Attorney General [Adjutant General] of Colorado at the time he received his appointment as 2nd Lietenant!) has just returned here from Fort Harker, with Capt. Keogh's troop. He says that he was at Mrs. Sternberg's funeral,—that there were 15 deaths at Harker on the day before his departure, and 13 the day previous, and that the day he left the mortality was so great that it was not deemed prudent to let people know how many were dying. He says it was perfectly fearful! The women and "citizens" were leaving as rapidly as possible—over 300 hands on the R.R. had quit work and were fleeing from the "wrath to come" in perfect panic! Lieut. Weir was taken down with the cholera just before we left! Two died out of Lieut. Coxes command. Mrs. Willard and Baldwin had left. How glad I am darling, that you did not remain at Harker one moment longer than was absolutely necessary! . . .

As Genl. Custers command was crossing from the Platte to this point, they accidentally discovered the remains of 12 men, who had recently been killed, scalped and mangled by the Indians. At the time, it was not known who the men were, but subsequent disclosures show that they were a Lieutenant of the 2nd U.S. Cavalry [Kidder], 10 men of that regiment, and a guide, who had been sent to communicate with Genl. Custer, and had missed the way, and fallen among thieves—or Indians rather—and had all been killed within the space of a few rods! So they go! We will fool away the Summer here, without adequate force to accomplish anything, and next Summer we will repeat the experiences of this! It needs *not less* than 40,000 men to make a speedy end of this

Indian business, and we haven't a fourth of this number, and our troops are scattered in parties too small to accomplish anything, through an area of about 10,000 square miles! By actual statistics 9,700 Indians, of various tribes, are *known* to be on the war path, and others are wavering, or supposed to be leagued with our enemies. Well, a different policy will have to be instituted in the management of Indian affairs, or I fear that by next summer there will be few officers or men left of the regular forces now here. The officers, many of them, will resign, and the men will avail themselves of the only opportunity that will be afforded them for getting home, as soon as they arrive once more in the vicinity of the settlements! This is truly a bad state of things, and quite unnecessary I think. It is a "penny wise and pounds foolish" policy, which will produce such results.

P.S. to letter of July 28, Aug. 1, 1867:

The cholera appears to have lost its epidemic form. One man buried last evening, and another this morning, but most of the patients appear to be convalescing. I have some hopes that my company will escape entirely—although I sent one man to the hospital—a *tent* at the Post!—this morning who was quite ill—and with strong premonitory symptoms of cholera. His sickness may have been caused, however, by the oppressive heat, as he was taken sick while out on the herd—herding horses. By the way, we had quite a little alarm today. Some mules had wandered off from the Post, it appears, and half a dozen teamsters went in search of them, and luckily found them a few miles away. As they came in sight of the Post, the impression some how got started that they were Indians, and was strengthened by the fact that the teamsters commenced firing at prairie-dogs, or something, and thereupon there was a general commotion in this vicinity! A signal gun was fired at the post, the pickets commenced circling at a gallop, on the distant hills, the herds of mules and horses were started in, at the gallop, from all directions, the Artillery run out, and placed in position, and the troops double-quicked out to meet and protect the animals, and every thing really had very much the appearance of an approaching fight, when at length the origin of the alarm was discovered, the teamsters arrested, and placed in limbo, in very uneasy positions!—and the herds were again started out, and everything returned to a peace footing. I was just engaged, with tracing cloth, and a set of mathematical instruments in making a map of the country between here and Fort Lyon, for Genl. Hancock, when the alarm was started, and I hastily rolled up my papers &c, and put things in shape, and then, having ordered the company under arms, I took my telescope, mounted an army wagon, and proceeded to take a survey of the situation, which resulted in a conviction that the supposed Indians were "mulewhackers," and the whole thing a scare, and so I didn't do much unnecessary mustering around.

Jennie had already learned from other sources of the death of Mrs. Sternberg, as recorded in her journal on July 20, 1867:

Have heard this week of the death of Mrs Dr Sternberg. I cannot feel reconciled to it. For her to die away off there of that dreadful disease Cholera! When we met we were friends at once & my longer acquaintance made me love her more. Members of the same church & meeting as we did we were very naturally drawn together, but she possessed a high moral principle which I have seldom seen among the ladies of the Army, & this alone would have made me admire her. She said to Mrs Custer at Harker, "I should have had Mrs Barnitz stay with me, while at Harker, if she had had to brought here by force." Poor Dr Sternberg. He loved her so much they were so devoted & happy. It seems to me he will be inconsolable. There are very few who can fill her place.

Albert to Jennie, camp near Fort Wallace, Kan., Aug. 5, 1867:

Col. Weir has recovered from the cholera, it appears, as I see his autograph affixed to orders and various documents dated July 24. Capt. Hamilton is expected here to day, escorting a train. He will bring the latest news from Harker and Hayes, and our future movements will depend on the word he will bring. Mr. [Theodore R.] Davis, the Artist [for *Harper's Weekly*, who had been with the regiment since April], writes from Harker that Genl. Custer has the "measels"—that is the mild way of phrasing it, when an officer is in arrest. I think it quite likely that he has been placed in arrest, for going to Harker without permission, and especially for the way he went there—making Fort Hayes, 165 miles, in 56 hours, with a detachment of 75 picked men, from a broken down command, which had just arrived from the Platte, after a terrible forced march, and without taking any time to rest! (If he *has* the measels, I hope he has them powerful bad!!) Genl. Custer is not popular here! The officers of the regiment do not speak of him in amiable terms!—But of course, Jennie, I only tell *you* this. It would do no good to promulgate it! I will not take time to tell you of his barbarous conduct on the way here from the Platte—how he ordered certain men shot, for attempted desertion, and then hauled them through the hot sun for days, without allowing them medical attendance—positively forbidding the surgeons to attend them (one has since died of his wounds)—Capt. West does not love him, and threatens to make certain developments!

Rising on the morning of July 19, Colonel Smith saw Custer's hasty nighttime passage in clearer perspective, especially when he learned that the 7th's commander had not come by stagecoach, as assumed, but with an escort. Smith ordered Custer to return at once to Fort Harker, then placed him under arrest, with confinement at Fort Riley in view of the cholera then rampant at Harker. The next day a message arrived from General Hancock urging the action that Smith had just taken.

The charges Smith preferred against Custer were twofold: absence without leave in coming to Hays, Harker, and Riley; and conduct to the prejudice of good order and military discipline in the manner in which he conducted the march. Three specifications supported the second charge: that he overtaxed an already unfit detachment in the interest of private affairs, that he used government ambulances and mules for a private journey from Hays to Harker, and that he failed to take proper measures to relieve the detail sent back for the straggler and to recover the two soldiers of this detail supposed to have been killed by Indians.

An additional charge of conduct to the prejudice of good order and military discipline was preferred by Captain West, commander of Troop K. Specifications supporting this charge alleged that Custer had ordered deserters shot without trial and had denied them medical attention when brought in wounded. Two of the wounded deserters, including the one who died, belonged to West's troop. Moreover, West himself was under charges preferred by Custer at Fort Wallace for repeated instances of drunkenness on duty.

The letter of August 5 continues:

Genl. Hancock has redeemed his promise to send supplies here—hard bread and forage, at least. Train after train continues to arrive daily, "Bull-Trains," "Mexican Trains" and every thing, bringing corn and "crackers" mainly! Genl. Smith continues to partake of commissary stores under a different name! It is called *lemonade!*—He has written a *wonderful* letter to Major Elliott, censuring him very much for not killing very many Indians, and telling him to "kill *innumerable* Indians!—spare none but women and children" &c. &c. Oh, its funny Jennie, dear! it is really *very* funny! To people who are not behind the scenes war presents a very brilliant aspect, I have no doubt!—but to us, who are initiated it is just *ridiculous!* I pledge you sincerely, I would not give one hour with "my darling" for all the military glory in the world! . . .

. . . 50 copies of Harpers Magazine (of July 27) (Giving views of Fort Wallace, and the desperate battle with the Cheyennes) have been received here—and the officers are all indignant at the statement which it contains that my company was "driven back to the Fort!" &c.—It is well known here that I started out at 5.30 a.m. and did not return within 2 miles of the Post—*not within sight*—until about 2 p.m.!—and had received no reinforcements in the mean time! Many other papers have been received here, giving accounts of the fight—from all of which it appears that I have gained quite a notoriety, and yet I would not give one hour with "my *darling*" for all the notoriety or *fame* even, in the world. I know the value of it very well, Jennie! I know that I shall be utterly forgotten within a month, by all who may have glanced over the reports. I only say this as showing that I do not care for fame, or glory—unless, indeed it brings with it such advancement as will enable me to make Jennie very happy,—and this I do not at all expect. Why Capt's (Michael V.) Sheridan* and Benteen 7th Cav. have been brevetted Lieutenant Colonels in the Regular Army, to date from March 2, 1867, for *nothing!* Capt. Benteen only arrived here about a week ago, from Fort Hayes, direct, where he has been doing nothing, ever since I left. And Capt. West brevetted Colonel from same date!—and *I* who have done *far* more than either of them, hundreds of times over, in the volunteer service even—(and *they* have done *nothing* in the *regular army*) am not noticed! Well, I don't "knuckle down tight" and make application I suppose, and I will die several times before I do it, and this is probably the reason. Genl. Hancock was going to issue a furious complimentary order in regard to the engagement of the 26th, so he assured many officers here! As soon as he got out of the Indian country he forgot it I suppose,—and poor old Genl. Smith was too much engaged in pouring down "toddies" to even give the matter serious attention!—But why do I go on about things? . . .

. . . And so it appears that Genl. Custer really has the "measels"—got 'em by order of Genl. Hancock, through Genl. Smith!—and has been allowed to go to Fort Riley and remain there with his wife pending his recovery! I would like to be slightly afflicted myself, on similar terms! The cholera appears to be subsiding here. We have about one death per day now on the average. Serg't King of Co. "A" [Sgt. John Farrer], a good non-commissioned officer was buried this morning. I buried one of my men, Private [James] Brown, on the 3rd. He died with dysentery, the surgeon said—had only been sick about 36 hours.

Jennie's journal, Aug. 15, 1867:

Found in a letter to Phila. Press that Genl. Custer is under arrest by order of Genl. Hancock for going to Fort Riley to see Libbie without orders. *I am glad.* He had Albert put under arrest so wrongfully once. I dont think it is wrong for me to feel so, then Albert will not have to be controlled by him for a little longer. Yes I am glad.

Jennie to Albert, East Cleveland, Ohio, Aug. 25, 1867:

Are you pleased with Genl. Hancock's removal? [Orders of August 19, 1867, replaced Hancock with Maj. Gen. Philip H. Sheridan, who enjoyed an extended leave before assuming command of the Department of the Missouri.] I think he was not very popular but I will not talk any more about wars or Generals, for you hear nothing else where you are—will only say that I seriously hope if Gen. Custer's attack is not fatal, it will be *protracted*—so you will be relieved of his presence. How fortunate *you* have been in this during the summer.

Rested and refitted, eight troops of the 7th Cavalry under Major Elliott broke camp at Fort Wallace on August 12, 1867, and embarked on a series of scouting expeditions to search out the hostile Indians. The operations were characterized mainly by long, exhausting marches, heat, dust, bad water, and an absence of Indians. The first scout took the command from Fort Wallace to the upper reaches of the Saline River and ended at Fort Hays on August 17.

Albert to Jennie, camp near Monument Station, Kan., Aug. 13, 1867:

I am out again with the "ride-abouts"—going to look up some Cheyennes! Have had a hard and tiresome march to day—over the hot plains—the torrid plains!—prairie fires surging every where in the distance, and clouds of dust rising along the column—for it has only rained twice since you left, and the heat has been fearful at times, and the grass looks as though it had been dried in an oven, and the streams are all dry—even the Smoky is dry—not a drop of water to be found except by digging in the dry sand of the channel, and *it* (the water which we obtain thus) isn't very delicious—tastes as though it had been filtered through several mud holes!—(which is the fact). . . .

. . . We are to have peace soon it seems!—Genl. Sherman, and the Peace Commissioners have met, and decided upon it, it appears, and the big councils are to be held up on the Platte in the full moon of September and at Larned in the full moon of October, and the presents will be distributed, and the new guns, and everything, and then we will go into winter quarters before Christmas, and in the Spring we will repeat the pleasant little farce of a Big Indian War, and a hand-full of men to carry it on.

Of course the peace won't amount to any thing, except that it will enable the Commisioners to distribute presents!—But may be some more extensive preparations will be made for the next war. The Indians must be thoroughly whipped before they will respect us, or keep any peace, and they haven't been whipped yet very much to speak of.

An act of Congress of July 20, 1867, had authorized the formation of a peace commission to confer with the hostile Plains tribes and try to per-

suade them to give up the territory traversed by the major travel routes in exchange for reservations north of the Platte and south of the Arkansas. As the commission organized, the 7th continued to scout the plains of Kansas.

Albert to Jennie, sutler's store, Fort Hays, Kan., Aug. 18, 1867:

We have marched 160 miles, through a beautiful country, the finest that I have yet seen in Kansas. A country covered with rich buffalo grass—(perfectly thick, like a nice carpet, or rug) abounding with streams of good water, and all kinds of game which frequents the Great Plains. There were *millions* of buffalo! and they were very tame. When we would encamp, they would remain about us for hours, upon the slopes within easy range, and we had such an abundance of tongues, and haunches, and hearts and livers that we had no wish for any more! We didn't see an Indian on the march! Only saw a few pony tracks, and some distant smokes. The days have been cool and delightful, with a splendid moon. We usually had reveille at 1.30 or 2 a.m. and marched at 3 or 4 a.m., and encamped about 1 or 2 p.m. On arriving here we find that there is a battalion of Kansas militia (cavalry) scouting on the Saline directly North of here, and in search of a large Indian force said to be in that neighborhood.

After two more brief scouts of the Saline, six troops under Major Elliott marched on August 24 for the headwaters of the Republican, where Indians had been reported.

Albert's journal, Aug. 24, 1867:

Command marched with pack train, and *without* forage, expecting to subsist their horses on the dry buffalo grass of the plains, and march probably 40 miles per day, with thermometer at 110° in the shade, on an *average*, between sunrise and sunset! It is simply ridiculous, and can't be done! Besides many of the horses are already in poor condition as regards shoes—some are altogether bare-footed, and their feet will inevitably wear down to the quick, and they will become lame, and have to be abandoned, and how their riders will be able to manage on foot, is more than I know, as Major Elliott, like his illustrious predecessor, is averse to having the men dismount and walk occasionally on a march, as they should, and thereby rest both themselves and horses, and a consequence of his bad management in this respect, when the men become actually dismounted from any cause, they will be unable to walk more than two or three miles before their feet become blistered, or they sink down from exhaustion.

I cannot but regard our present expedition, conducted as I well know it will be, as a supremely ridiculous piece of business; besides, it is quite uncalled for under existing orders—it is in fact in positive violation of orders that have been officially received at this Post, and are notorious—(viz: that all hostilities are to be suspended until after the councils) and it will be utterly barren of all good results. We will not see an Indian, in all probability, as they will be on the alert, and leave "for parts unknown," and undiscoverable, as soon as they hear of our approach, unless indeed, after counting us carefully, by peering through a bunch of tall grass, or a "Soap Plant" from the top of some distant ridge, they discover that we are greatly inferior in numbers, and conclude that they can "wipe us out" without much difficulty, and in that case we may find the expedition even more unprofitable! Our men are in the main a set of uninstructed recruits, who cant hit a barn door at 300 yards, with a carbine, and much less an Indian, whereas the Indians are experienced hunters, and don't fire without a fair prospect of hitting something.

The march turned out about as Barnitz predicted. On September 2 Elliott's weary column dragged into Fort Wallace once more.

Albert to Jennie, camp near Fort Wallace, Kan., Sept. 3, 1867:

We—the detachment which Major Elliott and myself found here awaiting us, (consisting of the sick and convalescent mainly, with Lieuts Jackson, Brewster & Wallingford,—the Adjutant, Lieut. Moylan having gone off to Harker during our absence, with the Regimental Records) have been moving camp to day, to a site about a mile further from the Post, beyond the Smoky, and this afternoon the command, including the remainder of my own company, arrived, with the regimental remains!—all that was left after the raid, and that worn out "well-nigh unto death!" Lieut. Robbins suggests as an appropriate epitaph for the 7th Cavalry "The Marched-to-death!" Very pathetic, isn't it,—and very appropriate! Certainly, the regiment has marched more miles than ever any cavalry regiment has done in the same length of time "since the world was made!"—and has accomplished just as little as was possible! You should have seen us up there on the Republican—or on Beaver Creek, and Prairie-Dog Creek, and Bow-Creek, and Throw-away-Creek, and the rest of them, making moccasins for our horses of fresh buffalo hide,—many of their shoes being worn out or lost, and their feet worn out and bleeding,—and you should have seen us eating our very hasty breakfasts shortly after midnight, and setting forward over the ravine-abounding prairies, as though we were in search of all *lost humanity*! and we all felt and knew that it was a very foolish and tiresome business! When you go after Indians in any force they of course run away from you if they can, and they always can unless you are able to move very rapidly, and know just where they are, or unless you are very cautious, marching in the ravines, and having the scouts and flankers go very stealthily up the sides of adjoining ridges from time to time, and peep through a bunch of tall grass, over the surrounding country, in such a manner as to see, but not be seen by even the most inquisitive eye, aided even by a field glass. If this course were followed, and the horses kept in good condition, it might be possible once in a while to get sight [of] an Indian, but Regimental Commanders in these latter days are not much wiser than Braddock of the older times, and refuse to fight Indians or even follow Indians in Indian fashion. General Custer could not have existed without hearing the sweet sound of fifteen or twenty bugles at least a dozen times during the day, and repeatedly at night, and he liked to march upon the "divides"— the high ridges, and to encamp where we could have a magnificent prospect, and where camp-fires would look *gorgeous* from afar!—all of which would have been quite unobjectionable in time of peace, but when it is considered that we were always in hot pursuit ("imaginably") of numerous Indians, making fearful marches,—pushing on, and on until the horses were nearly ready to drop from exhaustion,—until, in fact many of them *did* drop, and had to be abandoned, (and shot)—it was simply stupidity, and that of the grossest, and most unpardonable kind,—and quite unfortunately as I have thought, and very much to the surprise of all (who are not stupid, even at this late hour), Major Elliott, however excellent an officer in other respects, has pursued a nearly similar course! He loves the sound of the bugle very much, and a hill-top is, as he conceives, a very charming place to be! Well, we didn't find any Indians, as a result—which was probably well enough,—for we knew before we started, and officially too, that hostilities had been suspended by order, on our side, until after the forthcoming pow-wows—but if we didn't mean to find any Indians, why then march so hard; why use up so many horses, and have to abandon upwards of 40 of them, besides certain mules, well-knowing that one cavalry horse which has stood a summer's campaign on the Plains will be worth next year any two—or for that matter *five* "American Horses" freshly brought from the *States*?—and why march so hard, if we meant nothing by it, when we might have gone up to the wild-plumb patches, and luxuriated in the shady groves, and feasted our horses in the deep grass of tranquil meadows, surrounded by the towering bluffs— affording the most charming and delightful scenery, and springs of pure, never-failing water? If any body can tell me, I would like to hear the individual speak up! . . .

By the way, we visited Capt Arms' Battle-Field up there toward the Republican, and found one dead horse and the remains of one dead negro! It appears that he didn't find the Indians after all, so much as they found *him*! He reported 40 horses killed— there or thereabouts—on his returns! It appears that the Indians attacked his camp unexpectedly and stampeded about 70 of his horses!—and gave him a general waking up, wounding I believe about 35 of his men, and with the aid of two companies of the Kansas Cavalry which were near, and came to his assistance, (and were speedily demoralized, and losing two men killed, a few wounded, and many horses) he managed to get out of the scrape after a fashion, and the whole force drifted back to Fort Hayes without any unnecessary procrastination, and gave out that they had fought with the utmost desperation, and for a period which exceeded in duration anything hitherto conceived of, by fighting humanity,—but I guess they didn't think the 7th Cavalry would go over that ground, and carefully examine the indications! The Kansas troops are a set to contemplate with curiosity,—and the "Moaks" are in the same category! None of them have any particular business with Indians! The Kansas men only went with us about 70 miles on our late ramble, and then we parted company, and left them to find their way back to Hayes, while we "took off" to the North-West. But Jennie, I never get through gossiping!

On August 21–22, 1867, a command consisting of a troop of the 10th Cavalry, one of the two black mounted regiments, and two companies of the 18th Kansas Volunteers, all under Capt. George A. Armes of the 10th Cavalry, clashed with a large force of Sioux and Cheyenne warriors on Prairie Dog Creek. The troops suffered losses of three men killed and thirty-five wounded.

Elliott's command remained in camp near Fort Wallace until September 19.

Albert to Jennie, camp near Fort Wallace, Kan., Sept. 7, 1867:

You have several times asked about the particulars of Maj. Cooper's death. Well, it appears that he had been drinking pretty freely, until the command arrived upon Medicine-Lake—away up in Nebraska many days march from any where, and there the whiskey was all exhausted, and no more could be got, and as a consequence of the sudden withdrawal of his supplies the Major took *delirium tremens*, as is supposed—though his symptoms were not closely observed—and shot himself through the head with a revolver—expiring immediately. He leaves a lovely wife it is said who has very recently given birth to a son. She resides at Lexington, Ky. Major Cooper had some soldierly qualities, and was a man of warm sympathies, and generous impulses, but he had so far injured himself mentally and physically, by constant and inordinate indulgence in his favorite Bourbon whiskey—or whiskey of any kind or quality in fact,—that he had utterly disqualified himself for being of any great service to his country in the profession of arms, and so his loss was not felt severely.

Albert to Jennie, camp near Fort Wallace, Kan., Sept. 13, 1867:

It is very warm this afternoon. I have just been playing *chess* with Lieut. Brewster. He is a very good chess player, but I do succeed in beating him now and then, which always astonishes him very much! The Major and Capt Benteen, and a few others play cribbage nearly all the time, but I never take any interest in games of cards. Have only played 3 or 4 games of . . . *cards*—since you left. I have plenty of time now, very little to do, in fact, except sign my name, receive the reports at roll-calls, return the salute, and say "Dismiss the Troop." O, yes, have a dress parade every evening, upon which occasion we put on all our good clothes, white gloves and sashes, and make a very creditable display—for our own gratification, solely!—we have no visitors—no spectators, except our own dear selves! And yet notwithstanding this we *are* quite dressy—or as Lieut. [Frank Y.] Commagere* says "Knobby"—I don't know where he picked up that word! I have my boots blacked I don't know how many times every day—when they become dusty,—have an extra pair in process of blacking nearly all the time! . . . You should see my new wall-tent. Everything looks so clean and neat. My floor is carpeted deeply with new gunnysacks—not those *thin* grain sacks which *we* used to have, but great, thick, bright-looking sacks, which make a carpet like hemp-matting, and I have a nice mattress, filled with new-mown prairie hay—and every thing very neat, and inviting. O, *wouldn't* you like to be here darling? I would really like to have you here now. . . . We have such a nice mess too—Major Elliott, Dr. [I. T.] Coates, Lieuts. Jackson & Brewster and myself. We have a nice large roast of excellent beef every day, for dinner, broiled steak, and fish for breakfast, with toast, coffee, tea, canned fruits and vegetables &c. &c. You see I am just giving you a view of our domestic arrangements—for I haven't any thing else to write about at present, and I know you feel an interest in every thing that concerns us. We have a spring of *excellent* water now. I selected the spot, and engineered the digging in a place where few supposed that I would find water. The supply is quite inexhaustable. . . .

You inquire about Lieut. Commagere. He is much the same individual as formerly, very social, but decidedly lazy, and careless about military matters; he was left in command of Company "K" when Capt. West went away—a very nice position—but the Major has recently relieved him, and assigned him to duty with Company "H"—under Capt. Benteen, directing in the order that the Captain should "require him to be present at every roll call, and try to teach him some of the duties of a soldier!" I am aware that Colonel Merriam wasn't popular. I don't know the reason—

except it be, perhaps, that he commands the "Moaks." I agree with
you about Mrs. M. She is quite "common place." There! I only
intended to write a few lines.

*With a scent of peace in the air, Major Elliott's command broke camp at
Fort Wallace on September 19 and marched to Fort Hays, arriving on
September 24. A new post was under construction, and a new town had
taken root.*

Albert to Jennie, camp near Fort Hays, Kan., Sept. 25, 1867:

Now *New* Fort Hayes is on the right bank of *Big Creek*, about 12
or 15 miles S.W. of *Old* Ft. Hayes. A nice stone Fort or Block
House has been built, or completed rather, since we marched
toward Fort Wallace. The Garrison—certain Companies of the
38th Inf. (colored) live in tents. About 100 cords of wood are piled
around so as to make an admirable "Fort" or protection against
the Indians, and the blockhouse will enable four (or 6) mountain
howitzers to rake the whole country from the upper story. We are
encamped within half a mile of, and below the Post. The stream in
this vicinity is bordered with a fine growth of cottonwoods &c. &c.
We are encamped right in the bend of the creek.

By the way, "Hayes City" has been built since we marched west
(to Wallace,) a month ago! It now contains 20 frame houses, (and
more going up,) besides many wall tents. I rode over there in an
ambulance, this morning, to purchase supplies for our mess, and
we bought eggs at 50 cts per doz, potatoes at $4.00 per bushel (too
high), onions @ 12 cts per lb. &c. &c. &c.—The cars (construction)
trains are now running within 12 miles of here, and the cars
(passenger) will be here within 15 days at *furthest!* "*Rome*"—a rival
of Hayes City contains 4 or 5 stores, and a number of dwellings,
and is just across the creek from Hayes City. It was built before the
latter city. It really sounds like civilization to hear the sound of
planes, saws and hammers in Hayes City! "Hayes City" is now
nearly as large as *Salina* was when I came through there in the
Spring. A great many of the officers have been summoned to Fort
Leavenworth, as witnesses on Genl. Custer's trial—among others,
Capt. Hamilton, Lt. Cook, Lt. Moylan, (with Regl. Records,) Capt.
West, Lt. [Thomas W.] Custer* [brother of the General], &c.

&c.—and to day Maj. Elliott and Lt. Jackson. I may be ordered presently, but I was not at Ft. Wallace when Genl. Custer left (without leave,) nor with him on his march to the Platte.

As Major Elliott had been summoned to Fort Leavenworth for the Custer court-martial, command of four troops of the 7th Cavalry fell to Barnitz along with orders to march them to Fort Harker. The column left on September 27 and arrived at Fort Harker two days later.

Albert to Jennie, sutler's store, Fort Harker, Kan., Sept. 29, 1867:

I have just arrived here this afternoon, in command of the Detachment 7th Cavalry, (Co's A, D, G & M) as I wrote you a few days since. . . .

My march to this point was very pleasant, and without incident worthy of note. I find that quite a change has taken place here since I left, 6 months ago! The R.R. has come, or probably I should say the *cars* have come and Ellsworth City has grown up, even since the flood, and innumerable stone buildings are going up at the Post, and broad stone pavement going down, and flashy-looking Artillerymen are standing around in their gay uniforms, their caps surmounted with scarlet plumes &c.

Genl. Gibbs is in command, and of course, the first thing that he thought of, when I rode in, a mile or so ahead of the command, and reported, was his *band*! Nothing would do but he must send out the band, to escort us to our camp! The band looked very gay, indeed, all the members mounted on grey horses. The band preceded the command to, and through the Post,—through the sacred parade ground even!—to the great wonder, and probably great edification of all lookers on!—and Genl. Gibbs sent his ambulance and his compliments to me (I having returned to the command, after reporting, and selecting a camping ground) and requested me to come to his residence &c. &c. The General looks remarkably well, in a complete suit of Navy flannel, with heavy gold watch guard, majors shoulder straps, of his own unique pattern, with the two silver stars of a (Brevet) Major General between the leaves.

Well, Jennie, I have received orders upon my arrival here, to hold myself in readiness to march to Fort Larned, to escort the Indian Commissioners (Genl. Sherman &c &c.) Am to receive the recruits who are here awaiting me, mounted, armed and equipped, and am to make immediate requisition for every thing that I want, clothing, tents, arms, horses &c &c. &c, for the *Squadron*, Companies "G" & "M",—the other two companies also remaining under my command for the present, and are encamped with me, but they are to become part of the garrison of this Post for the winter, while my squadron, it is said, will, after the council, go to Fort Leavenworth, to winter quarters! I do not believe any thing until it occurs, but I do *hope* we will go there for Jennie's sake.

7. Council at Medicine Lodge, October 1867

Scenes at the Medicine Lodge treaty council as sketched for the *Harpers Weekly* issue of November 16, 1867.

By the summer of 1867, a military solution to the Plains Indian problem seemed increasingly remote. On the northern plains, Red Cloud's Sioux continued to block the Bozeman Trail to the Montana goldfields despite a heavy commitment of soldiers to its defense. On the southern plains, Hancock's brave martial display had served only to stir up the native inhabitants and send them on a bloody rampage across the Kansas prairies. In Washington, peace advocates gained control of Indian policy. Under the act of July 20, 1867, a peace commission was organized to negotiate a settlement of the issues underlying the continuing conflict. The commission consisted of Commissioner of Indian Affairs Nathaniel G. Taylor, Senator John B. Henderson, Samuel F. Tappan, John B. Sanborn, and Gen. William T. Sherman, Gen. Alfred H. Terry, and Gen. William S. Harney (retired). An effort to arrange a conference with Red Cloud at Fort Laramie failed, and the commissioners turned south for a meeting with the tribes of the southern plains, set for mid-October at a popular sun dance ground on Medicine Lodge Creek, seventy miles south of Fort Larned.

The commission was to pick up part of its escort, Troops G and M of the 7th Cavalry, at Fort Harker and then proceed to Larned for two companies of infantry. With Major Elliott detained at Fort Leavenworth as a witness in the Custer court-martial, Barnitz expected to command the escort. The post hummed with preparations.

Albert to Jennie, camp near Fort Harker, Kan., Oct. 5, 1867:

I am getting everything in perfect readiness for the reception of the commissioners, and for the march to the big "Medicine-Lodge!" Have had all the horses shod, and new shoes made, and nails pointed, to be carried along on the march—have drawn a number of new horses—some fine ones too—have had 35 Recruits assigned to my company, and about 25 to the other company of my squadron—have drawn new tents, and clothing, and plenty of ammunition. Have 44,000 rounds for the carbines, and 10,000 rounds for the Gatling Guns, and a quantity for the revolvers, and I have new spades, and pick-axes, and hatchets, and axes, and curry combs, and horse brushes and every thing (. . . but you want to hear about the ladies who are going with Genl. Sherman! and about the preparations that Mrs. Genl. Gibbs is making for the grand reception, and every thing, don't you darling?) Yes, and

I have had the Gatling Guns (the revolving, and flying artillery)
put in the nicest order—the grounds policed, the recruits drilled
in the riding school and the manual of arms. . . .

. . . Mrs. Genl. Gibbs appears to be having all her silver ware
put in the very best possible order, and Genl. Sherman is expected
to occupy the biggest room in the house! 20 large hospital tents
have been erected for the lesser personages of the party, and a big
tall "liberty pole" with a golden globe on top, is to be erected on
the parade, on Monday, and an immense new garrison flag will be
flung out, amid the volleys of artillery, as the man who "marched
down to the sea" approaches! [Bvt.] Col. [and Capt. George W.]
Bradley [A.Q.M.] is not here now. He has been relieved by [Bvt.]
Maj. [and Capt. Henry] Inman* [A.Q.M.], lately Q.M. at Fort
Union, New Mexico. He is an excellent officer, and his workshops,
for repairs of govt. wagons, harness &c. &c. make this look like
some great manufacturing metropolis. He is putting down a stone
pavement 18-1/2 feet wide all around the parade ground, and
lengthways and across through the center.

Seven new Lieutenants are here—Lieutenants of the 7th
Cavalry—all are so anxious to go along! I have had to prevail
upon the Genl. [Gibbs] to assign one or two temporarily to my
command. [One was Edward S. Godfrey,* soon to be permanently
assigned to Barnitz's troop.] Two are graduates of West Point.
About 5 of them are first class men, and will make good officers,
and fine social companions—of the other two I have not formed
so favorable an opinion. They are too much of the Lieut Commagere style!—very nice young men however.

*To the disappointment of all, General Sherman was not with the
commission when it arrived at Fort Harker on October 7. He had been
summoned to Washington and his place on the commission taken by Brig.
Gen. Christopher C. Augur. To Barnitz's even keener disappointment,
Major Elliott accompanied the commission bearing orders to command the
escort. Piqued, Barnitz obtained Major Gibbs's consent to remain at
Harker but reconsidered upon learning that he would retain command of
the cavalry squadron under Elliott as overall escort commander. The
procession left Harker on October 8 and, bypassing Larned, reached
Medicine Lodge Creek on the fourteenth. En route a company of the 3d*

Three of Barnitz's close associates were (left to right) Lieutenants Edward S. Godfrey, Francis M. Gibson, and Edward Law. Godfrey grew a huge mustache and became a general. Both he and Gibson served in the 7th Cavalry for more than two decades and fought at the Little Bighorn. Law, scion of a prominent Philadelphia family, dropped out of the army in 1870, became a lawyer and politician, and drowned in a boating accident in the Schuylkill River in 1881.

A close friend of Barnitz and descended from patriot Nathan Hale, "Holy Owen" Hale died in the charge on the Nez Percé village at Bear Paw Mountain in 1877.

Infantry and one of the 5th from Larned joined the escort, together with Jesse H. Leavenworth,* the Kiowa–Comanche agent, and Edward W. Wynkoop, the Cheyenne–Arapaho agent. Also accompanying the commission were Kansas governor Samuel J. Crawford and Senator Edmund G. Ross.

Albert to Jennie, camp 70 miles south of Fort Larned, Kan., Oct. 14, 1867:

We arrived here this morning. The Kiowas, Arapahoes, [Plains] Apaches, and a few other tribes are here, or represented, and the Cheyennes are coming. We will be here several days. A courier is just going post haste to Larned for supplies, and I send this. The prospects for peace (for this winter, at least!) are very favorable, and then we will be at Leavenworth without doubt I suppose! I wish you could see all the Indians here! I won't fall in love with any of their dirty little squaws!

Albert to Jennie, camp on Medicine Lodge Creek, Kan., Oct. 16, 1867:

Well, there are a great many Indians here now—probably 7000 in all [closer to 5,000], big and little, and there are daily accessions to the number. A large band of Comanches came in yesterday, and a band of Cheyennes last night. The big Council will come off on Saturday, and a general peace will doubtless be concluded,—which will last till Spring, I suppose!—though the Commissioners seem to believe that it will be *permanent*! Possibly it may hold for a longer period than I imagine, and I do hope it will.

Albert's journal:

Oct. 17, 1867. Visited Indian (Arrapahoe) camp at night, went to "White Mans" Lodge, and to dance, in company with Maj. Elliott, Maj. [Henry] Douglass 3d Inf, Lieuts [George W. H.] Stouch [Thomas S.] Wallace & Godfrey, Gov. Crawford of Kansas &c &c. Bardley, the scout, was along, as interpreter. The Indians have had 150 ponies stolen last night. They suppose the thieves were Pawnees. We believe it more than probable that they were whites. This evening an Arrapahoe, whom I have never noticed before brought and presented me a pair of moccasins. . . .

Oct. 19, 1867. The Indian council commenced to day. Senator Ross addressed them and a number of the leading chiefs replied. The proceedings are to be continued tomorrow. The council is held in a grove near here.

Oct. 20, 1867. Was present to day again at the Council. The Indians had little to say. A band of Osages arrived. Senator Henderson explained the terms of proposed treaty and requested the Indians to come up and sign it tomorrow. . . .

Oct. 21, 1867. . . . Indians signed treaty. Presents distributed—among other things 65 new revolvers!—and hundreds of new butcher knives! The distribution of presents was quite amusing! The Indians have recovered about 50 of their stolen ponies. The revolvers were made by the Union Arms Company.

Oct. 22, 1867. The weather has been very fine ever since our arrival here. We are drilling daily, and the camp is daily thronged with Indian spectators, of all ages, sexes, and tribes. Last night "White Man" an Arrapahoe Indian brought me a young squaw, which he assured me was "heap good" and which he desired to present to me as a companion for the evening! I showed him Jennies picture, and explained to him that *she* was my squaw, and that one squaw was amply sufficient and two squaws "*no wano!*" whereupon he begged a candle, and disappeared, taking Mrs. "White Man" along. (She was very elegantly ornamented with vermillion, and seemed to have been especially gotten up for the occasion!) The distribution of Indian goods still continues, and daily "talks" are held by the commissioners with certain of the chiefs.

Oct. 23, 1867. In the evening I furnished horses for a party to visit Indian Medicine Lodge (Kiowa) 5 or 6 miles below here, but the trip was deferred until it was too late to proceed, and it was decided to visit certain Indian camps in this vicinity instead. I accordingly rode around with the party, consisting of Senator Henderson, of Missouri, various newspaper Reporters, Mr. Karney and [Philip] McCusker, the Interpreter. We first visited the Comanche camp, and after riding through it, inspecting tents, ponies, saddles, &c we stopped at the tent or lodge of "Ten Bears"* the old head chief. A young and handsome squaw held our horses, while we went in and had a long talk with the old man, whom we found sitting quite *en-dishabille*, on his couch, his favorite squaw by his side, and several of his children around him. His saddle, an elegant Spanish tree, with silver mountings, plated bridle bits & buccles &c hung on a frame in his lodge and a nice bugle, of an antique pattern hung on the pommel of the saddle. The old man said he could not blow the bugle very well, but was practicing! He said the name by which Comanches were known among themselves was "Nim," which McCusker explained to mean "a people," and added that a Comanche usually calls himself "Nim-nim" (which he says literally signifies a people of people.) While we were in the lodge the old man, three or four sons, grown men, and some of the children came in. The old man conversed awhile with each of us, and especially with Senator Henderson, informing him that he (Ten Bears) had been in Washington, in the winter of 1862 or 3. . . . We afterwards went and witnessed the process of dressing buffaloe robes, and Senator Henderson tried his hand at it, the squaws standing by and laughing aheap. We then went to the Kiowa camp, and called at Satantas* tent and at Kicking Bird's* but neither were in. Talked with the Indians, squaws and papooses, and then came back to camp.

Oct. 24, 1867. Am officer of the day. Several men of the cavalry were arrested yesterday for stealing blankets, and to day General Harney made an investigation into the matter, threatening summary punishment. Weather very fine, a little foggy at night. Satank* made speech.

Oct. 25, 1867. The troops continue to drill daily, the cavalry rather, the Infantry appear to consider themselves very proficient in drill already. The Indians throng the camp as usual, and sometimes are really annoying when one wishes to write—favoring us with their company at all hours, and whether agreeable the same or not, and very frequently taking "supper" with us, by "special request." Weather fine—morning foggy.

To day I saw an Indian with a little bunch of feathers, buffaloes hair &c, made up into something resembling a doll baby, and learned from him that it was a charm, and that he considered himself impervious to bullets while he wore that, and he would not be persuaded otherwise, but insisted that bullets would glance from him, and that he could remain unharmed, and invulnerable!

I dare say that if he should be shot through the body his opinion would still remain unshaken! Such is faith—or credulity.

Albert to Jennie, camp on Medicine Lodge Creek, Kan., Oct. 25, 1867:

You would really be surprised were I to tell you how much I attend to in any given 24 hours. First in the morning there is reveille—*now* at sun-rise—or a little before—when I attend roll call—immediately afterwards follows stable call, when I walk about in the vicinity of the horses for one hour, when I inspect them, and order them to be fed, and then go to my tent and prepare for breakfast. (All the officers mess together, 7 of us [Major Elliott, Captain Barnitz, Lieutenants Jackson, Godfrey, Bradford L. Bassett*, and Owen Hale*; the seventh has escaped identification], and a surgeon, in a large hospital tent.) After breakfast I am usually busy with official matters until 10.30 a.m. when drill call sounds, and I superintend drill until 11.30 a.m. when recall sounds, and I come in and prepare for dinner—from 1.30 till 2.30 I am again present at drill, in the manual of arms, and school of the squadron, and then I am occupied in various ways until 4 p.m. when I am again present at the stables for an hour, and then prepare for supper,—at which half a dozen big chiefs usually invite themselves to be present!—(sometimes with their squaws; and papooses!) and follows retreat roll call, and later tattoo, and you would really be surprised to see how many papers I sign, and how many official letters I write in the interim! I occasionally take rides of an hour or so to the Indian camps—but our own camp is daily *filled* with Indians and it is scarcely necessary to visit *them*!

Albert's journal:

Oct. 26, 1867. The Cheyennes have not yet come in. It is now 8 p.m.—and night cold. The Arrapahoe Indians continue to dance and sing, and fire off pistols and carbines as usual! They generally keep up their dances, and nocturnal noises of all kinds, especially the firing of pistols in our vicinity until near daybreak—but to night they are more than commonly noisy. . . .

Oct. 27, 1867. Shortly after I had retired last night the Indians became very demonstrative in our vicinity, firing perhaps 200 shots, and yelling "aheap," about our camp, and "Stumbling-bear"* came in, and lay down in front of one of our fires, and as the Indians had been observed repeatedly counting all our saddles during the day, it began to be suspected that the Indians might be going to seize the occasion of the arrival of the Cheyennes for a general attack. Accordingly the officer of the day was instructed to have company commanders require their men to load the magazines of their carbines and sleep on their arms, ready for immediate action if occasion required. The night, however, passed off without any descent of the savages! This morning I found the first ice in my water bucket. Took a dose of quinine and 10 drops tincture of the muriate of iron this morning, as I felt a little agueish. Indians have been pilfering little things from me of late. I attribute the thefts to squaws and Indian children, who require close watching.

About noon to day the Cheyennes arrived, they crossed the creek on our front and emerged from the woods, in line of battle, firing their guns into the air, singing and yelling! One portion of the tribe—about a squadron formed in line in front of my camp, on a little rise of ground about 150 yards distant, and behind them and on their left flank about 200 Arapahos sat on their ponies, with bows strung, and on the other side of camp the Comanches, and Kioways, and Apaches were out in force—and for half an hour or so the intentions of the Indians were at least questionable. I had taken the precaution to have all the horses brought in and tied to the picket line before the arrival of the Cheyennes, and on their approach, I buckled on my pistols, and had all the men quietly retire to their tents, and put on their belts and cartridge boxes, and be ready in an instant in case the Indians should make a charge, but finally the head chief, Black Kettle,* held a talk with the commissioners, and afterward withdrew his warriors to their camp, which is located across the stream at the distance of 3/4 of a mile from our own camp. The day has been very pleasant. The council will come off tomorrow, and we will probably be able to start for Fort Harker tomorrow evening, or Tuesday morning. The moon changed last night. It is now said that the Cheyennes were only waiting for the new moon to come in. They were gaily dressed and painted to day, and presented a truly grand and formidable appearance as they came in sight! I wish *Jennie* could have seen them!

Oct. 28, 1867. The big council with the Cheyennes and Arapahos came off to day, in front of the commissioners tents. I was present and took down the speeches. After the council the Cheyennes were with great difficulty persuaded to sign the treaty. They were superstitious in regard to touching the pen, or perhaps they supposed that by doing so they would be "signing away their rights"—which is doubtless the true state of affairs, *as they have no idea that* they are giving up, or that they have ever given up the country which they claim as their own, the country north of the Arkansas. The treaty all amounts to nothing, and we will certainly have another war sooner or later with the Cheyennes, at least, and probably with the other Indians, in consequence of misunderstanding of the terms of present and previous treaties.

In the evening I rode over with Crankcerzada, an Apache Indian, to the Apache and Cheyenne camps, to find a buffalo robe which a squaw had taken to dress. Failed to find it, and Crankcerzada professing to feel sorry about the matter *presented* me with one, which I think is the identical robe! At night a great bondfire was kindled in front of the commissioners tents and the Arapahos seranaded us in Indian fashion. Dancing, singing, firing pistols &c in fine style. Yellow Bear, their big war chief and some lesser chiefs were present, mounted on their Ponies, with grand head dresses, and ridges down their backs, composed of eagle feathers, and carrying their lances, with a single eagle feather dangling therefrom. The pow-wow has just concluded, and we have had tattoo roll call. A high wind, (from the north) such as we have not had for perhaps two months has just sprung up, and tents are with difficulty kept up. We are to start at day light tomorrow morning for Fort Harker and winter quarters.

Oct. 29, 1867. Heavy storm last night, and violent wind from the North. Scene at breaking up of camp, and distribution of remnants quite amusing. I succeeded in procuring 20 pairs of cavalry trowsers, and five Cavalry overcoats, gratuitously, from Genl. Sanborn, and sent them to Sergeant Gordon, for distribution among the men of Company "G". Broke camp, and started for Fort Larned, and civilization at 8 a.m. Wind cold and in our faces severe and dust troublesome. Reached the stream known by us as "Little Medicine" (8 miles from Indian villages, or encampments) about 11 a.m., and encamped near the stream in a nook sheltered by trees and surrounding hills. Water excellent, grass good, and fuel plentiful. Lieut. Stouch encamped near us, across the stream, with his company of the 3d Inf. but the commissioners went on, with [Bvt.] Major [and Capt. David H.] Brotherton's company, 5th Inf. as escort, toward Ft. Larned. . . . Henry C. Olney, sometime of Osh-kosh Wis., and correspondent of New York Tribune &c joined us this evening, and bespoke quarters in my tent during the march to Larned, having been forgotten by the commissioners, as it appears, perhaps purposely. I am not fascinated with the young man. He had an unpleasant altercation with a demoralized teamster at Medicine Lodge Creek, and received a stab, which came near proving fatal. We have a large fire in front of our quarters to night, a big log-heap. The night is cold, quiet, and starry.

After a two-day rest at Fort Larned, the command resumed the march and arrived at Fort Harker on November 4.

The Medicine Lodge treaties provided for concentrating the southern plains tribes on two large reservations in western Indian Territory (later Oklahoma), the Kiowas, Comanches, and Plains Apaches on one and the Cheyennes and Arapahos on the other. The treaties promised clothing and other presents for thirty years, schools for the young, and help in beginning to farm for the adults. In return, the tribes relinquished claim to all territory outside the reservations. As Barnitz suggests, however, the Indians only vaguely understood the contents of the treaties, and less than a year was to pass before another war broke out on the southern plains.

Among the prominent chiefs who signed were the Kiowas Satank, Satanta, Kicking Bird, Woman's Heart, and Stumbling Bear; Comanches Ten Bears, Silver Brooch, Horse Back, and Iron Mountain; Cheyennes Bull Bear, Black Kettle, Tall Bull, and White Horse; and the Arapaho Little Raven.

In the Fort Laramie Treaty of 1868, the peace commission at length concluded similar arrangements with the Sioux, ending hostilities on the Bozeman Trail and establishing the Great Sioux Reservation in Dakota Territory. This treaty, too, laid the groundwork for future conflict, one in which the 7th Cavalry would play a prominent role and its colorful lieutenant colonel achieve an enduring place in history and legend.

8.   Fort Leavenworth, November 1867–April 1868

Fort Leavenworth in 1867.

Albert to Jennie, camp near Fort Harker, Kan., Nov. 7, 1867:

This morning Capt. Parsons' Light Battery "B", 4th Artillery left this Post for Fort Leavenworth, where it is to be stationed this winter. It presented a fine appearance, as it moved out,—6 pieces of Artillery, each drawn by 6 horses, 6 caissons and limber-boxes, and two forges, each drawn by 6 horses, and cannoneers all mounted, and 22 wagons; besides some from the Post, loaded with hay. The Battery will march all the way. The Artillery drill is quite imposing—the Battery has been drilling here daily.

To day a dispatch from Hd. Qrs. Dept. of the Mo. was received here stating that orders for six companies 7th Cavalry to report at Fort Leavenworth, have just been forwarded by mail. We will probably receive the orders to night. We will doubtless march. I say *we* because I presume that there is now no doubt that I shall go there.

Companies "H" (Capt. Benteen,) & "M" (Lieut. Hale) have been designated to remain at this post during the winter [with Major Elliott as post commander]. I feel a little sorry for Lieut. Hale, as he has been very anxious to go to Leavenworth, mainly because he thought that, if stationed there, the opportunities would be more favorable for him to secure a leave of absence, during the winter, to go home, (to Troy N.Y.) and induce some young lady, of whom, as it appears, he has been long enamored, to say "yes!"— . . . . Really, this is not a very unpleasant place to be stationed now, and if it had fallen to my lot to be left here I should doubtless have acquiesced without serious murmers of complaint. The Post has changed very much since you were here. The large building at end of the Parade, formerly occupied by Genl. Gibbs, and now by [Bvt.] Col. [and Maj. Thomas C.] English [5th Infantry], who at present commands the District, has been very greatly modified. It has a large portico extending along the entire front—it is quite wide, and very ornamental—and the house has many other additions, and a nice garden behind, inclosed with a neat, painted fence. All the dwellings are elegantly painted, and grained now. Doors rose-wood color, or something. In the centre of the Parade stands a tall white flag staff, which has cost several hundred

dollars, and from its top floats the broad garrison flag, about 20 ×
30 feet in size. Around the base of the flag staff is an octagonal, and
very handsome fence; the inclosure is entered by an ornamental
gate, and ascending a couple of broad steps you find yourself on a
platform, or balcony, about 15 or 20 feet in diameter. The boards
of the floor radiate from the centre—the flag staff—and are
painted brown, or drab. The fence is painted white. At the R.R.
track stands a very large new Depot, or ware-house building for
storing the quartermasters supplies. Another large stable has been
built, and all are painted white. Two large frame buildings, Captains quarters, containing *numerous* rooms, are going up on the
opposite side of the Parade from what were Dr. Sternberg's quarters while you were here—(and which are now occupied by Genl.
Gibbs, who is at present in command of the Post.) The Captain's
quarters which I have mentioned are two story buildings. There
are many other new buildings and out-buildings, which were not
here in June. Among others, a very large brown frame building
for the Depot Quartermaster's office, and for the occupation of
his clerks. The Depot Quartermaster, Brevet Major Inman, . . .
is an energetic and accomplished officer. . . .

Fort Larned, too, is improving. I hardly knew the place any
more. Many fine, large, stone buildings have gone up, ware
houses, officers quarters, Barracks, &c., all far superior to those at
Fort Riley, and others are in process of construction, and an
elegant large stone building is going up at Zarah, and others are in
contemplation, and the work will be pressed forward rapidly, and
buildings are going up at Monument Station, and elsewhere; so
that it really appears that this whole frontier will eventually become inhabitable—for troops—and possibly the experiment of
bringing ladies out here to reside for a *very* brief time would not
be so hazardous in future as in the past! No other young wife will
ever be enabled to have such "pleasant" experiences as you have
had, *beloved one*! While I write the band—the 7th Cavalry band—
the idolized of General Gibbs is discoursing sweet music in front
of my tent. The band has really improved wonderfully, and is now
elegantly uniformed.

Since I commenced writing I have learned that the companies
which are to go to Leavenworth have been designated by tele-
graph, this afternoon, and that Company "G" is among the

number. So you can get ready to put on your bonnet, Jennie dear! . . .

I told you that many new officers have reported. The regiment is now full, I believe, though some have been granted permission to delay, and will not arrive for a month or so yet. You may therefore expect to see many new faces in "our Regiment"—some are handsome, and some are not so much so. I have now two Lieutenants. Lieut. [James T.] Leavy,* who came part of the way with you, and Lieut. Godfrey, a recent graduate from the Academy, and a "splendid" young man—quite handsome, and a good officer. He was temporarily assigned before I started for the Indian encampment, and immediately placed in charge of the Gatling Guns, which we took along—and which, together with others—are to go with us to Leavenworth,—and then Lieut. Godfrey will doubtless be returned to duty with the company. He has now been permanetly assigned to the company—Lieut. Jackson has been promoted 1st Lieutenant, and assigned to Company "F"—which is to go to Leavenworth, too, it appears.

Under Major Gibbs, Troops A, D, G, and K marched from Fort Harker on November 13 and arrived at Fort Leavenworth five days later.

Albert to Jennie, Fort Leavenworth, Kan., Nov. 19, 1867:

I write you a hasty line for the mail, which is about to close. The command arrived here yesterday, and Capt. (Brevet Colonel) West's company was placed in quarters at the *Post*, and all the other companies were sent to the *Attache's* Barracks, four or five hundred yards from the Post. These barracks are simply long, frame, barn-like buildings, white-washed within and without. They are provided with bunks, and large heating stoves, and are not uncomfortable, but are far, very far from what we expected, and ought to have. The Infantry and Artillery occupy all the barracks at the Post—the very troops that ought to be shown the least favor, in view of the recent rough experiences of the Cavalry, and their *prospective* experiences but you may not be able to see just how all this affects us; I will tell you. All the officers are to be quartered with their commands. At the Post, the quarters are superb, and the grounds, and everything quite lovely—perfectly *charming*—but here the officers quarters are very unpleasantly situated—scarcely 100 yards from the barracks of the men, and not a tree, or green plat of grass in view from the front, and from the back windows nothing can be seen except the dingy little kitchens! Oh, it is too bad entirely! The rooms are comfortable enough, large enough, and nicely plastered, but oh, how unpleasantly situated! I could have sat down and taken a hearty cry, when I was told to select my quarters from those that are available here!—but I didn't however—I did the next best thing—I went and saw Mrs. Gibbs and Custer, and represented the case to them, and they declared that it was really too bad, and that General Smith had all along intended to have the Infantry vacate the buildings at the Post, and put the Cavalry in there, but unfortunately Genl. Smith (who still commands the Department [in Sheridan's absence on leave],) is still absent at St. Louis. He is expected back to day. There are barracks and quarters for one other company, still unoccupied at the Post, but the company for whom they are intended (Co. "F" 7th Cav. [Capt. George W. Yates*]) has not yet arrived. Genl. Gibbs says that he is anxious to have all the married officers stationed at the Post, and that if the other officers concerned are willing to waive their rank, he will so order it. I am not *very* sanguine that all will consent to do so, but possibly they may—in that case, we will be at the Post, and will be nicely situated—we will have carpet, chairs, tables, pictures, &c. &c. to buy—and larger curtains, of course—but we need not keep house, unless you wish, for the officers' mess is *elegant*—as good as any first class hotel—and terms only $1. per day for each person, and it is *not* a bachelor's mess, as I had been previously informed, although no ladies are boarding there at *present*. [Bvt. Brig.] Genl. [and Maj. Chauncey] McKeever [departmental Adjutant General] & wife, Col. ——— and wife, and many others have been boarding there for several months, but have now gone to house keeping—so as to be able to give parties &c. I suppose. Mrs. Custer and Gibbs and Mrs. [Algernon E.] Smith,* I suppose will keep house—We will not have to buy any *stoves* as the Quartermaster's Department furnishes them. Two very elegant ones were yesterday put up in my present quarters.

The old dragoon barracks and duplex officers quarters at Fort Leavenworth such as the Barnitzes occupied in 1867–68 and 1869–70.

Commander of the "Band Box Troop" of the 7th Cavalry, Captain George Yates roused Barnitz's antipathy by securing a choice assignment that he thought rightfully his. Yates died with Custer at the Little Bighorn.

Algernon E. Smith. One of Barnitz's closest associates, "Fresh" Smith was plagued by a Civil War wound that limited the use of one of his arms. A Custer loyalist, he died at the Little Bighorn.

Albert to Jennie, Leavenworth City, Kan., Nov. 20, 1867:

Captains Hamilton and Myers have very kindly and considerately waived their rank in my favor, and accordingly Company "G" will move into the vacant barracks at the Post to day, and myself and Lieutenants will be quartered there, and we will be *so* nicely situated.

Albert's journal, Nov. 20, 1867:

Just as I was about to retire I was notified by the Post Adjutant that it was found to be necessary to detail me as officer of the day, to relieve Col. West who "could not be found!" He has been very much under the influence of liquor for several days, and at last accounts,—or "when last heard from" was entirely unable to perform his duties properly, as officer of the day, a sad state of affairs truly! Col. West or Capt. Hamilton should have gone on before me, but the Adjutant says he has been in search of them, and finds that they are both "sick!" This is a mild way of stating it! Lieut. Leavy of my company is in the city, absent without leave—drunk, more or less. Lieut. Robbins do. [ditto] Lieut. [H. Walworth] Smith*, "Salty" [Algernon E. Smith was known as "Fresh" Smith, in contrast] do—&c &c to the end of the chapter.

Albert to Jennie, Fort Leavenworth, Kan., Nov. 21, 1867:

I wrote you the other day that I had selected quarters. I have to day selected others, those at present occupied by Genl. Custer, but which he is to vacate forthwith, as he and Genl. Gibbs will be quartered together. I have applied to have his house assigned to me as quarters for myself and one of my Lieutenants, who will only occupy one room. We will have a kitchen & dining room and two servants rooms &c in basement &c. &c., also a cellar. A large balcony, hall, sitting room, sleeping room and dressing room on first floor, and two rooms on second floor and two on 3d floor and many clothes presses and closets, and the wood work grained, windows large, *fine prospect*. Elegant well in rear with revolving chain pump, wood house and stable for private horses also at end of back yard. The rooms are not large—only about 15 or 16 feet square but they are very cozy—a fire place in each room, and stoves—ornamented—will be furnished by the Q.M. without cost if we prefer. The quarters are double—but entirely separate if we wish—another similar set such as I have described on other half of same building, even the balconies, which are broad and spacious are separate. . . .

How will you like to hear "morning gun"—the big cannon go "boom!" every morning, at daylight? You must become accustomed to it! Guard Mountings and Dress Parades, just in front of our balcony, will be very fine indeed. There is a *Post Band* of 22 instruments besides the regimental band, and everything is excessively military—and nothing else! There is a hack stand at the Post, where carriages are always in readiness. I will be *considerably busy* this winter, though, Jennie, so please do not imagine that I will have nothing to do but wear dressing gowns and sit around "idle like"—or you will be sadly mistaken! I shall have to kiss you in haste and be off to stables very early in the morning sometimes. I think that we will have a mess of our own after a little time, without doubt! [Bvt. Maj.] General [and Col. William] Hoffman [3d Infantry] commands the Post here.

Albert's journal:

Nov. 21, 1867. We had dress parade this ev'g, and our appearance was very creditable as I hear. The "Battery" looked well in their scarlet plumes &c. I purchased 7 doz. white gloves for my company this ev'g, in order to enable the men to appear to advantage. The cost $3.00 per doz = $21.

Lieuts. Robbins, [H. W.] Smith and Leavy are in arrest I learn, for drunkenness, and absence without leave. They do not deserve one particle of sympathy. Drunken soldiers or officers are very uncertain and unserviceable beings.

Nov. 22, 1867. . . . Lieut. Leavy returned at 3-1/2 o'clock this morning, not excessively sober, and informed me that he intended to resign. He was notified of his arrest this morning, and Lieuts. Robbins & Smith, who got back last night, were also notified this morning that they are in arrest. Genl. Gibbs present on Dress Parade this ev'g—and very "military!"

Nov. 23, 1867. I am detailed again for officer of the day tomorrow! Details are heavy now, in consequence of so many officers being in arrest. The following is the list of

"Unfortunates!"

1. Brevt. Maj. Genl. Custer, in arrest awaiting sentence
2. " Lieut Col. Myers, Captain, in arrest awaiting trial
3. Brevet Col. West, Captain, in arrest awaiting trial
4. Lieut Robbins,
5.   Smith
6.   Leavy
7.   Brewster
8.   Commagere

All except the first and last named were on big and apparently interminable "sprees" as the prime reason of their being placed in arrest, though superadded thereto, they were usually absent without leave, and neglecting duty generally, and a reformation is very essential for the good of the service!

Albert to Jennie, Fort Leavenworth, Kan., Nov. 25, 1867:

Oh, we will be *very* nicely fixed Jennie!—but *remember*, there will be no *permanence* in our housekeeping arrangements!—When spring comes the Indians will break out again, *of course*, and then I will have to be off, for the Field, and all furniture and everything will be consigned to an auctioneer, and sold for half its cost or less—*provided*, always, that I remain in the Army, as is probable. I *like* the Army very well, under a purely ideal state of affairs, but *practically* it is very pretty indeed, but hard work, and *incessant*. I actually can not find time in the 24 to glance over the daily paper, as affairs are now (7 officers of the regiment being in arrest, and all the duty devolving on the others!)—and *additional* duty, besides, rendered necessary, or at least *imposed* upon the other officers in consequence the neglects of the "poor unfortunates"— (the inebriates &c!)—all of which is for your own information!— But we look very pretty here Jennie! very handsome indeed, and I suppose outsiders think "Oh, those officers have *such* easy times! nothing on earth to do but to wear good clothes, and white gloves, and crimson sashes, and elicit admiration!" I sometimes laugh to

myself, when I think of all those nice books which you are going to
bring! I fear I will only have time to glance at the titles!

Albert's journal. Nov. 25, 1867:

The order publishing proceedings, findings and sentence in
case of Genl. Custer published to the command at Dress Parade
this ev'g. He is sentenced "to be suspended from rank and pay
proper for one year." Oh, that I too could be similarly suspended!
The fact is I am *sick and tired* of this *tread-mill life*. I am weary,
weary, weary, with never a moment to rest! Not the veriest convict
in a prison is more unfortunately and unhappily situated than an
officer of cavalry at this lovely Post. I have little time for reflection,
no time for relaxation, and to tell the truth, *very unhappy*—not
even the prospect of Jennie's arrival is sufficient to make me feel
elated,—for with imcompetent, unreasonable, and drunken
superiors, what can I expect! Will it ever be otherwise? Will I ever
be able to enjoy a moments rest in the society of the one to whom I
am so tenderly allied, and so devotedly attached, without having a
world of care and anxiety on my mind, without waiting and
watching for the ever recurring and hateful summons of the
bugle and the drum? Ah! me. In the Field it is tiresome and
arduous enough, but at a Post, such as this, when we should have
rest, and time and opportunity for enjoyment and improvement,
it is even worse. Even the men are *constantly* employed, and have
not a moment for relaxation or amusement. Is it any wonder that
they desert? Tomorrow they (of my company) will be paid, and I
will not be surprised if some of them disappear shortly afterward.
They have not been paid now for six months, and meanwhile they
have been sorely distressed for the want of many little necessaries,
even needles and thread, postage stamps and stationery have been
beyond their means of purchasing of late.

*The Custer court-martial, which convened at Fort Leavenworth on
September 15, 1867, and sat until October 11, brought together an array
of military notables and attracted wide public attention. The post commander, Colonel Hoffman, served as president of the court. Captain Parsons,
commander of the light battery of artillery at Leavenworth, served ably as*

defense counsel. Custer pleaded not guilty to all charges. After hearing extended testimony, however, the court found him, with some qualifications and exceptions, guilty as charged and sentenced him, as Barnitz records, to suspension from rank and command and forfeiture of pay for one year. On November 18 General Sherman announced General Grant's approval of the findings, at the same time remarking upon the lenience of the court in view of the gravity of the charges.

Custer's enemies, and they were many, agreed. But Custer and his friends saw the whole affair as a persecution gotten up by General Hancock to divert attention from the failure of his spring and summer operations. General Sheridan, Custer's wartime mentor and Hancock's successor as department commander, thought his friend too harshly treated and said so. He advertised his feelings by inviting the Custers to occupy his quarters at Fort Leavenworth during the winter. This offer they gratefully accepted.

Meantime, Captain Barnitz happily bought furniture and other household implements in Leavenworth City, moved into the quarters vacated by the Custers, and eagerly awaited the coming of Jennie.

Albert's journal, Nov. 26, 1867:

My company was paid off to day. The actual amount required greatly exceeded the estimates of the Paymaster, (Major Rodney Smith) and in consequence he was obliged to return to the City, for more money after he had paid off a portion of the troop. He returned just before Dress Parade, and I went to Genl. Gibbs and endeavored to have the company excused from Parade, in order that the Paymaster might proceed with the payment, but Genl. Gibbs would not consent! The silly old man! He made himself appear ridiculous subsequenty on parade, by his over-solicitude to have everything done exactly right (according to his variable notions of propriety!) which resulted in his having every thing done exactly wrong, to his own exceedingly great discomfiture and the no small exasperation of many of the officers, including the Adjutant! For my own part, the very ludicrous aspect of affairs (quite observable to all disinterested spectators,) made it very difficult for me to restrain an almost overpowering tendency to mirth!

Albert met Jennie in St. Louis on December 4, 1867, and together they traveled to Fort Leavenworth. On December 13 Jennie wrote to her mother:

I wish you could look in upon us to night, & see how cheerful our home is with our two large fires in fireplaces. . . . Two rooms we have furnished very beautifully. We received the boxes all safe yesterday. The Express charges were seventeen dollars & seventy five cents. Everything came safely. It must have been a very great trouble to pack them so carefully. Whose idea was it, putting in the hickory nuts. They were very acceptable, & Albert was so pleased with the cake. It would amuse you. For a little while he was going to cut it at once, then he decided to wait until we had company, & it is now put away for that purpose. . . . I have employed a colored girl to come to work for me next Wednesday. We have every convenience for housekeeping—even our stove is up, & I am quite sure Albert prefers it, though he is perfectly willing that I should take my choice. There are some very pleasant persons here. I had twelve calls after tea last evening, which will give you a little idea of our evenings. Three ladies and nine gentlemen. Every two weeks there is a Hop, at which they have elegant suppers, & every two weeks a promenade concert. We have a Theatre—Tableaux etc.

Gen. Custer has been tried & this is his sentence. He is deprived of his rank & pay proper for one year. That is he will not wear his uniform or have anything to do during that time, & will receive about sixty five dollars per month [in allowances]. They do not seem to care much.

My friend Mr Commagere has been very unfortunate. He had difficulty with a Col. Parsons who is here. Col. Parsons called him a liar. Mr Commagere said nothing, & because Mr Commagere did not *challenge* Col. Parsons—the officers held a meeting, & decided that Mr C. was not a fit associate, & hereafter no one would speak to him, & he has been obliged to resign. I am so sorry for him.

It is very cold, the wind is blowing hard. Albert's orderly has been standing out by our door all day, & I have just prevailed upon him to let him come in & warm as there is no one here this evening. He did seem so thankful. I do pity the enlisted men.

I had two negroes here one day cleaning house. Mrs. Custer did not leave the house as clean as she might. This Post is beautiful. The streets are macadamized—nice board sidewalks everywhere which are kept very clean swept off by the men. Some of the officers quarters may really be called elegant, & nearly all the luxuries of New York find their way out here, & it seems to me there is as much style here as on Fifth Avenue. We ride in Barouches always. There is a stand near here. We were indeed Very fortunate in being sent here. I wish you would all visit me.

Jennie's diary records a constant whirl of visits, dinners, parades, concerts, and hops. Every day the officers and their wives paid and received calls. Jennie also penned her impressions of some of their associates. "I never liked Mrs. Gibbs so well before." Of Mrs. M. R. Morgan, wife of the departmental commissary of subsistence: "I like her exceedingly. She is very simple and unaffected & friendly." Of Captain Parsons's wife: "She is very lovely. At one time a West Point Belle I am told." But of Mrs. Lt. A. E. Smith: "I think she is very common place. Dresses well, but cannot talk any, & is not therefore a very desirable member of our dinner table." Capt. George W. Yates and Lts. James M. Bell and Edward S. Godfrey attracted favorable comment.

Jennie's journal:

Dec. 21, 1867. The days seem very short. Perhaps because they pass so pleasantly. In the morning we return from breakfast [at the officers' mess], then I read the morning paper, & do the dusting & picking up. We drive about two, come home, dress, read or sew some, & it is time for tea. The evenings are altogether taken up with making or receiving calls, & reading. We read aloud all the time evenings that we are not otherwise engaged, and so the days go by like one happy dream. Not one thing occurs that is unpleasant. No two persons I am sure were ever happier. Truly we take comfort in "unknown marvellous quantities." I cannot bear to think there will ever be a change. That our happy happy home will ever be broken up, Albert to go in one direction & I in another, as heretofore. Oh! those bitter hours of parting I cannot think of them without a shudder, but I will not make myself unhappy about the future when the present is so bright. "Sufficient unto the day etc." . . .

Dec. 25, 1867. Christmas! Albert because he had no opportunity of getting me a Christmas present gave me a hundred dollar bill, which some day I will spend as I choose. It has been a quiet day. Even more quiet than Sunday. Albert did not want to go to church, & I did not insist.

Dec. 26, 1867. This evening Maj Bell came & recommended a servant to me, & I decided to take her, but we shall not commence taking our meals here at once.

Jan. 1, 1868. Invited Mrs. [A. E.] Smith to receive calls with me to day. Had cake (the large fruit cake from home) two kinds of choice wine, ale & figs. They commenced calling about 10 O C. Had fifty calls, forty eight were officers, some of them of high rank. Five were gentlemen from the city one a judge. The day has passed very pleasantly & still it has sometimes been very stiff. We received a number of cards. I was very much worried this morning. My cake would not cut well, finally Albert undertook it & did nicely, then I dont know, it seemed such a responsibility to entertain so many, & I was afraid Baker would make some blunders, but he did very well. We had a good dinner of oysters, Roast Chicken, Lemon Pie etc. Everything was well cooked. Had a letter from Ma but it came when I had so much on my mind that I could not read it.

Jan. 14, 1868. Pay day for the privates & a trying day it is to Officers. I wish it did not come so often as it does. Albert is so worried. The men are almost unmanageable as soon as they have a dollar. Mr. Godfrey has been in a number of times. He was determined that I should go to the Hop, where I most certainly should have gone, had I felt able, but as I look well & would not tell him just what the matter is, he thinks my sickness is merely figured as an excuse to remain at home.

Jan. 20, 1868. Capt Yates called this morning to invite us to a surprise party to be given to Gen Smith tomorrow evening. They are to meet at [Bvt. Brig.] Gen [and Lt. Col. Langdon C.] Eastons [departmental quartermaster], to march in masse to Gen Smiths hdqrs preceded by the band. The party is made for Gen Eastons friends. . . .

Jan. 23, 1868. A leap year party at Gen Custers to night. None but unmarried persons are invited. . . .

Jan. 25, 1868. Have been to call on Mrs. H. Walworth Smith, who has just arrived. She is not particularly prepossessing. Has a nice little boy. Capt Weir came in & told us all about the party at Gen Custers. While we were at dinner Mrs Gen Easton & her friend Miss Lee called, & Mr Godfrey.

Jan. 31, 1868. This morning we called at the Sherwoods. Met a number of persons there. This evening we spent at Gen Gibbs & [Bvt.] Maj [and Capt. Daingerfield] Parkers [3d Infantry]. Every body wonders why I dont go out more. It does seem as if in Garrison they are not willing for any one to stay at home a day. The principal business is to go, but I am quite independent.

Feb. 1, 1868. Col Weir was in some time. He insists that I shall go out more. Oh! if I could only stay at home a little while in peace! I am so happy here, & our home is so pleasant, but we must go. To night is a Theatre party & Mr. [A. E.] Smith & Mr Godfrey came for us but I did not want to go & see the play of the Drunkard. Had a charming walk to night.

Feb. 2, 1868. Mrs. Smith came in & invited us to go to the City to church. We accepted. Mr Godfrey invited us to drive with him but we are to wait till next Sunday. We started for the city at 6 O'C, Mr & Mrs Smith, Mr Godfrey, & us. We could not find Mr [Calvin] Reasoners [Christian] church, or there was no service, so we went to hear Dr [George W.] Skinner [Unitarian]. We were introduced to all the family after service. He is very talented. A universalist. Said he saw by my face that I did not like the sermon.

Feb. 7, 1868. Mr. Godfrey came in feeling very badly because Albert had reproved him quite harshly for so much noise in his room. I apologized saying that Albert seemed more offended than he is, & begged he would not be offended. . . .

Feb. 11, 1868. Anniversary of our marriage. One year ago (to night) I said Good bye to home & friends to come to the far West. It has been a happy *happy* beautiful year. How much I have to be thankful for, but I tremble almost when I realize that perfect happiness is not for this world. We have been so happy! Happy in each other! Albert has given me a handsome set of Poe's Prose & Poetical works, 4 volumes, to day & is writing a "poem" which I long to see. [Bvt.] Col. [and Maj. James W.] Forsyth* [departmental inspector general] & Mr Leavy called to invite us to a Hop, at

[Bvt. Maj.] Gen [and Lt. Col. John W.] Davidsons [10th Cavalry] quarters to night. We went & I enjoyed it very much, till Capt [Thomas W.] Custer very unfortunately stepped on my dress which was very long ripped it so I had to come home. I regretted it. Mrs. Gen Custer & Miss Richmond called to day. This is a precious anniversary to me. I gave Albert a plain heavy ring.

Albert's journal, Feb. 13, 1868:

Went with Jennie & Mrs. & Lieut. A. E. Smith to Leavenworth City in ambulance, to have photographs taken. Went to Henrys gallery, and found the artist too much engaged to give us a sitting; then went to Noble's Gallery and had large negative made, standing, and one sitting with epaulettes.

Jennie to her mother, Fort Leavenworth, Kan., Feb. 18, 1868:

We are still getting along delightfully. I have two of the best servants in the world! How fortunate I was to get them. I go into the kitchen once every day. We have breakfast at 9 O'C, dinner at 5 O'C. At dinner I give my orders for breakfast, and go down once during the day to order dinner, and everything is done just as I direct. It does not cost us as much to keep house as to board, and we have the best of everything at such low prices of the Commissary. I have got some excellent recipes since I have been here of Mrs. Gen. Gibbs. . . . We have everything as nice as if we had company every day. Did you think on the 11 that it was the first anniversary of our marriage? We kept it, & made it a gala day. Had an unusually nice dinner, a bottle of the choicest wine, (which last we only use on great days), & attended a Hop in the evening. Albert gave me on that day a set of Poe's prose & poetical works—four large volumes handsomely bound—he also wrote a very nice little poem on "the first anniversary," which I will send you when I write again. We are determined to always observe that day, & hereafter will always endeavor to give a party on that day. Our series of Hops closes Friday evening, with a grand military ball. Persons are invited far & near. Tickets are eighteen dollars *each*, so you can imagine how fine it will be. All gayeties cease here this month as Lent commences, and persons are expected to be serious for the space of forty days. Well, it will be pleasant to rest.

Albert's journal:

Feb. 21, 1868. . . . Am officer of the day. Am just waiting until after midnight to make the guard rounds. Went to Leavenworth City in ambulance last ev'g, with Jennie, Lieut. [James W.] Steele 38th Inf. and Brevet Capt. Leavy 7th Cavalry, to witness performance of play, entitled "*Still Water Runs Deep*" by Mr. & Mrs. Fannehill, and the Dramatic Company of Fort Leavenworth. Play good—attendance small, except from the Post—and not of the best class of society. The after piece was "Marrying a husband at Sight."

There is a large military Ball in progress here to night—it is quite a brilliant affair. Upwards of 40 officers stationed here having each subscribed $18. to defray the expense. Jennie and myself did not care to go partly by reason of the extravagant expense, and partly because our evenings at home are so pleasant that we have little desire to participate in the unintellectual and formal gatherings which are so common at the Post this winter. We only attended three of the semi-weekly "Hops" which have been in progress here, although subscribing to all. The weather has been delightful and quite spring like all this month. . . .

Feb. 24, 1868. . . . I went to Leavenworth City to day, with Jennie, in Lieut Smiths (or Brewster's rather) ambulance. Went to Noble's photograph gallery, and got large photographs of self and Jennie and myself in same picture. Met Mr. Reasner, Christian minister, and took dinner with him at Brevort House. Took pistol to J. F. Schmeltzer No. 31 Delaware St. for repairs, also spur. Went to foundry and made arrangements to have spur buckle cast next Saturday, to replace one lost. Came home in time to attend drill, mounted, in School of Trooper,—at 2 p.m.

Genl. Gibbs is quite ill—has been so since the ball of 22nd.

There is to be a 'hop' to night at the quarters recently vacated by Genl. Davidson—an informal affair. Jennie is going with Lieut. Godfrey. I prefer to stay at home and read proceedings of Congress in the matter of impeachment of the President for attempted displacement of Secretary [of War Edwin M.] Stanton, a matter of which I had not heard the slightest mention until to day.

Jennie's journal:

Feb. 25, 1868. We decided to go to town to day. Before we
started Mr Cooke & Col Weir called, also Capt Custer, to invite us
to a Hop at Gen. Davidson's quarters to night, Albert did not care
to go so I went with Mr Godfrey who invited me. It was delightful.
It seems to me the pleasantest Hop I have attended. We had a
delightful time in town. Met Mr. Reasoner who went around
shopping with me, & then took us to dine with him at the Hotel.
He introduced me to a great many.

Feb. 26, 1868. I danced so much last night I am really tired &
lame to night. Had a pleasant nap to day. Mr Godfrey came in &
told me of quite a little affair of honor Mr [2d Lt. Edward] Law*
[7th Cavalry] & Capt Yates had over Miss Lee. They will have a
settlement to day. I read the evening paper to Mr Barnitz now
every day & something solid after it. He in turn reads me something from Shakespeare.

Albert's journal:

Feb. 29, 1868. Genl. Sheridan and staff arrived to day, shortly
after review and muster of the troops, and while the officers were
going around in a body to inspect quarters and stables, and
visiting the prisoners in guard house—his arrival was quite unan-
nounced, and was unattended with any formal demonstration,
although we are all duly sensible of his merit.

March 2, 1868. Am officer of the day, and busy making out a list
of the various prisoners, confined in the Post Guard House, to
enable the Provost Sergeant to take the proper ones out to work. I
find that there are 20 sentenced to break stones (some for 2 or 3
years), 19 under charges of desertion, and awaiting trial; 6 awaiting trial for minor offenses, and 5 undergoing sentence of hard
labor &c—quite a formidable array of incorrigible scoundrels—
for such they are, as a general thing.

The officers of the regiment were assembled by circular, at the
Adjutant's office to day, at 10.30 a.m. and went in a body to pay
their respects to Genl. Sheridan. He received us very cordially,
and invited us all to call upon him at the "cottage," where he has
his quarters.

March 3, 1868. On being relieved from guard, was left in command of the regiment by Capt. Hamilton. I shortly turned over the command to Capt. Yates, and went in ambulance with Brevet Major Bell & Jennie to Leavenworth City; went to Noble's Gallery and sat for card pictures and large photographs, (with Jennie) with understanding that we would order pictures if they were considered good, when we should see the proofs. Afterwards went to E. E. Henry's Gallery, 42 Delaware St., and sat together for card pictures, or rather I sat, Jennie stood by me. Henry is considered by far the best artist in the city. Some pictures of us hitherto made by Noble were not altogether satisfactory. Previous to going to Nobles we called on Mrs. & Capt. [Samuel L.] Barr (5th Inf.) at the Planter's House, and on Mrs. Capt. [William] Thompson* (7th Cav.) at her rooms on Cherokee St. Returned home at 4 p.m. In the ev'g called on Mrs. & Lieut. [John G.] Butler (Ord. Dept.) at their quarters near the Arsenal; on our way there, passed the "cottage" Genl. Sheridan's quarters; saw the General walking in the yard; he approached us, and bowed cordially, meeting us at the gate. I introduced Jennie, we conversed a moment and passed on, much pleased with the frank pleasant manner of the General. Had an agreeable visit at Lieut. Butlers. Before starting to the Arsenal we called on Mrs. & [Bvt.] Capt. [and 1st Lt. Henry A.] Huntington [4th Artillery] & on Capt. [John] Livers [Military Storekeeper] and Daughter, and Mrs. & Genl. Easton—in the morning we called on Mrs. & Genl. Forsythe (she is Daughter of Ex Gov. [William] Dennison of Ohio.) The weather to day has been delightful.

March 6, 1868. Mrs. Genl. Hoffman, wife of the Post Commander, who has been quite ill for a long time, died last night. Her remains are to be taken to Pittsburgh. Genl. Hoffman and the Post Adjutant to start tomorrow at 2 o'clock with the remains. The Grass is quite green in yards & parade ground here. It has been raining incessantly all day. General Sheridan and Col. Forsythe called on us this ev'g. I had gone to "Officer's School" but Jennie entertained them very agreeably, I suppose. She appeared, when I came home, to have been much pleased with the General, and Colonel Forsythe as well.

Jennie to her mother, Fort Leavenworth, Kan., March 16, 1868:

You ask me why I do not write to you about Gen. Custer. Simply because I had forgotten it. I suppose you refer to his being taken up for murder. He was arrested on the charge of murder, that he did cause men to be shot last summer, who had attempted desertion but when overtaken had given up their arms & surrendered themselves prisoners. He had his trial in Leavenworth City [in January], but was acquitted. They have two young ladies with them this winter & seem to be enjoying the winter even better than when the Gen. is not in arrest, as *now*, he has nothing to do. They talk of going to Europe this summer. Gen. Gibbs has been quite sick. Albert has been in command of the Regiment a number of times. I was honored with a call from Gen. Sheridan a few evenings since. It was a very pleasant call. He is very communicative, & it is hard to realize when talking to him that he is invested with so much power, that he is the second man in our nation. He has two or three magnificent carriages & five horses & creates quite a sensation when he drives out. His staff officers are very gay so his arrival adds greatly to the interest & society of the Garrison. All things taken into consideration, I think there is no life in the world quite as pleasant as Garrison life. Every morning at 9 O'C is Guard Mounting on the Parade ground in front of our houses. The band is out, & the ladies usually sit out on their porticoes & see & talk with their friends. At sunset, of pleasant days, we have Dress Parade, which is very imposing. Then evenings everybody visits. It actually spoils me for any other life. I feel that any other life would seem very tame after spending such a delightful winter in Garrison.

Jennie's journal:

March 18, 1868. We have dress parades now every evening. All the ladies sit on their porches & The Officers distribute themselves around & it is certainly delightful. I fear I shall miss all these privileges badly, when I am away from them. There is no life quite like Garrison life. Every day dawns new, & we feel as much interested as if we had never seen the same before. I sit out a great portion of the time. Mrs McKeever & Mrs Gen. Forsyth (daughter of Gov. Dennison of Ohio) called. Mrs F is very agreeable. I think she will be very much liked here.

March 19, 1868. This thought comes to me always in the midst of our pleasure. In a few days all this will be over. Of course I am sad, though I say little about it. A great deal of company to night. We called at Capt Livers. Had an invitation to go out riding horseback but did not like to borrow a horse & saddle consequently declined.

March 23, 1868. Oh! how the thought comes constantly, in a few more days & our home will be broken up, & we shall be separated, but my last years experience ought to make me resigned. When I left Mrs Sternberg at Fort Harker, I thought how fortunate you are to be left here with your husband while I have to go home. It is unfair, but just after I left, the Cholera broke out, & in two weeks she was dead! These things ought to teach us to be contented with whatever is appointed to us, for our ways are ordered by One who sees not as we see, but who knoweth what for each is best, and who is perfect love. . . . Have called on Mrs Dr [John W.] Brewer & Mrs Gen Easton. Have Dress Parade every evening. We have a great deal of gayety on our porches. The Band plays a great deal now.

Albert's journal:

March 24, 1868. We are under marching orders, to leave for Fort Hays on the 10th of April, in light marching order. The weather is uncomfortably warm this evening—too warm to wear a coat or vest, with comfort.

My 1st Sergeant Francis S. Gordon was reduced to the ranks for absence without leave, and drunkenness, on the ev'g of 22d of March, and confined in the guard house. Since then the company has felt somewhat demoralized, as they sympathize with Gordon, who was quite a favorite. Some desertions have taken place, and more are anticipated.

March 25, 1868. Serg't Gordon was released from the Guard House this morning, and at once absconded.

Jennie's journal:

March 25, 1868. Went to see Mrs Custer & she & the Gen. advised me to get some heavy flannel for shirts for the field, & gave me her patterns & one of the Generals shirts to look at, & I sent for the ambulance & went at once to town, & got the heavy flannel.

March 26, 1868. Have been over to Mrs Smiths all the morning cutting out my shirt. Have the form cut out, & am going to make them at once. My first attempt. Mrs Brewer & Mrs Smith were here this evening.

March 27, 1868. Have been sewing busily. Col. West called. Mr. [Lt. Francis M.] Gibson* has been temporarily assigned to Alberts company & moved over here. I like him much. We have been using ice, it is so warm.

March 28, 1868. Have had a letter from Ma. Have finished Alberts flannel shirts and am quite proud of them.

April 4, 1868. Col West was here this morning. Maj. Elliott from Harker came about noon. He is very anxious for me to go out with the troops & offers me the use of his ambulance all summer. He will be in command of the Regiment. This evening we spent in calling at Gen McKeevers & Gen Forsyths. Very pleasantly. Oh but every time I come back to our pleasant home I think how soon I must go & leave Albert & everything. Oh there is nothing in this world so bad as to leave one's husband & particularly one so dear as my darling.

April 5, 1868. This morning Albert & I took our last walk in the woods. We gathered a lovely boquet of violets. Had a charming walk. A number must have been here to day. Had an invitation to go to church in the city, but we thought we would attend church in Garrison once more. Once more! this winter! What sad words!

April 6, 1868. Went to the city to get some photographs of Albert in his Navy shirts. Did not get home till 4 O C. Made a number of calls to night with Maj Elliott.

April 7, 1868. Have company almost constantly. Every body thinks he must come. Had a pass lent us over a portion of the Road to day. Company & excitement all the time, & all the time my heart is so heavy. Have made a number of calls.

April 8, 1868. Have commenced packing. How forlorn it is. Oh! how desolate. Have now called on all the families in Garrison. House full of company. Rev. Reasoner came up but I was too much torn up to invite him to dine with me. Nearly all the Officers have been here. My last night here. Oh that thought leaves me not for a moment. I dont want Albert away a moment. It seems as if my heart would break.

April 9, 1868. How my heart ached when I awoke & the thought flashed into my mind that I must leave here, leave Albert to day! What a day it has been. I have moved like a machine. Have been obliged time after time as I have been packing with Albert to leave the room till I could become composed. It has been almost impossible for me to talk to the multitude of people who have been here. Sometimes I have been obliged to stop as they have come to say good bye. Rev Mr Reasoner came up to say Good bye. Had a long visit with him. He complimented me very highly. Seems to think a great deal of me. We left Fort Leavenworth at 6 O C. A great many officers & ladies gathered around the ambulance as we were starting to say a last Good bye. Oh! how sad! We reached the cars in time. Albert & Mr Smith could not go to the cars with us, as the last ferry boat was going back. When Albert left the omnibus he left his gloves. For a moment I was sorry. Some gentlemen offered to go & carry them to him but upon taking a second thought I concluded to keep them. They look more like him than anything else possibly could! Took a sleeping car with Mrs Smith. We sat up & had a long talk, about our husbands of course. Went to bed about 10 O'C.

Albert's journal:

April 16, 1868. Since the date of my last entry in my diary until the date fixed for our departure for Fort Riley I was constantly *very busy* in getting my company and myself ready for the summers campaign on the Plains. Having boxes made for my surplus company property, which was to be left behind, and my own personal effects, and boxing and turning the same in for storage—fitting up a mess chest for the company, and one for myself—turning in surplus ordnance & ordnance stores, to the Leavenworth Arsenal, and drawing lariat ropes, picket pins & carbine sockets &c.—writing to Superintendents of Rail Roads &c for passes &c. &c., &c.—ad infinitum. I was indeed so very much

occupied as scarcely to have a moment's leisure for conversation
with Jennie, up till the date of her departure. She left for home on
the ev'g of the 9th inst.—going to the city in ambulance with Mrs.
A.E. Smith & Husband, in time to reach train (7.30 p.m.) on
North Mo. R.R. She went via St. Joe & Macon City to St. Louis,—
thence via Terre Haute, Indianapolis, Bellefountaine & Crestline.

She was not at all reconciled to the journey. For several days
previous to her departure it was rumored that one company of
cavalry was to be kept at Fort Leavenworth for a time, and, if the
Indians should remain quiet, all Summer, and all the officers of
the regiment who called on us, as well as others at the Post,
expressed themselves as highly solicitous that my company should
be the one selected to stay,—but it proved otherwise. Capt. Yates
(Co. "F") was patronizing to Genl. Gibbs and the Adjutant
[Lieutenant Moylan], and in consequence obtained the "post of
favor"—if not of honor. I was the only company commander who
was married, and should therefore, according to established us-
ages of the service have been selected to remain, if I desired to do
so, (and my wish in this matter was well known)—although I did
not go personally to Genl. Gibbs, as he perhaps expected, and
besides my company had the only engagement of any consequence with the Indians last summer, and marched further than
any company at the Post, and this should have entered somewhat
into the calculations of the inebriating old General—but it did
not, as the sequel has shown.

The 9th was a sad, busy cheerless day—nearly all the officers of
the Post, even Genl. Gibbs and Capt Yates among the number
called to bid Jennie good bye, having heard that she was going
home, and late in the ev'g we started for the Depot just in time to
procure tickets and get seats in the omnibus at the Planters house.
. . . Our wagon (the one containing the trunks) broke down just
as we reached the Planter's House, where fortunately the baggage
wagon was still in waiting. Went with Jennie across the Missouri
on the boat, had to get off the omnibus on the other side and
return at once to the boat without going to the Depot—the boat
was just making its last trip for the night—it had already left the
Missouri side before I (we—Capt Smith & self) reached it, after
leaving the omnibus, but it fortunately returned for us. I acciden-

tally dropped my gloves in the omnibus on leaving it and they were lost—unless Jennie happened to pick them up, which is scarcely probable.

On the 10th inst. at 9 a.m. the column consisting of Companies A D E G & K 7th Cav., preceded by the Regimental Band, marched around the parade ground, at Fort Leavenworth, receiving the parting salutations of the ladies and officers of the post & Department who were to remain; and then, as the Post Band struck up the tune of "The Girl I Left behind me" we marched off toward Fort Riley and the "Great Plains."

9. Camp Alfred Gibbs, April–July 1868

Major Alfred Gibbs, a scarred old veteran of Indian fighting, was the senior major of the 7th Cavalry. He won Barnitz's admiration, later his contempt. A rigid disciplinarian, Gibbs amused the regiment with his preoccupation with military trivia. The splendid 7th Cavalry Band, however, was largely his creation.

After the Medicine Lodge treaty council, the Indians moved south of the Arkansas River for the winter of 1867–68. From a temporary agency at Eureka Valley, near old Fort Cobb, Indian Territory, Agent Leavenworth pursued precarious relations with the Kiowas and Comanches. They threatened him, continued to raid in Texas, and in the spring began to drift northward toward Fort Larned in expectation of the annuity issues promised at Medicine Lodge. In May 1868 Leavenworth resigned as agent.

The Cheyennes and Arapahos spent the winter on the Cimarron River south of Fort Dodge. Agent Wynkoop, based at Fort Larned, issued occasional rations. In the spring these tribes moved north of the Arkansas and camped on the headwaters of Pawnee Fork and Walnut Creek. The chiefs seemed reconciled to the peace settlement, but there were indications that the young men were less ready to give up the buffalo country between the Platte and the Arkansas. Also, they harbored some grudges against the Kaw Indians, and early in June they launched a big raid against their old enemies. For this offense the Indian Bureau announced that the arms and ammunition promised at Medicine Lodge would be withheld. The news sparked fresh discontent among these tribes.

General Sheridan returned from his winter's leave in March 1868 and resumed command of the Department of the Missouri. Uncertain of the Indians' intentions, he had little choice but to dispose his forces along the travel routes and await developments. It was on this mission that Major Elliott led five troops of the 7th Cavalry out of Fort Leavenworth on April 10, 1868. Custer went home to Monroe, Michigan, to wait out the balance of his year's suspension. Major Gibbs with regimental headquarters and Troop F remained at Fort Leavenworth. The other troops of the 7th garrisoned Forts Harker, Dodge, Wallace, Lyon, and Reynolds.

Elliott's column marched by way of Fort Harker to Fort Hays, arriving on April 28. On May 25 he moved camp about twenty miles westward, to Ellis Station of the Kansas Pacific Railroad, and laid out on the north bank of Big Creek. He named the new site Camp Alfred Gibbs. Barnitz's letters to Jennie tell of camp life during the spring and early summer of 1868.

Albert's journal:

April 23, 1868. We marched at 7 o'clock this a.m. & reached Fort Harker about 2.30 or 3 p.m. My company in front required to follow Band at a jog trot—silence enjoined, as Maj. Elliott, who was moderately drunk on Dr. Lippincott's whiskey conceived that my men were making too much noise. Cold & rainy this afternoon. I have a good fire in my tent to night. Capt. Hamilton has a cask of beer.

April 24, 1868. We remained encamped near Fort Harker to day, the ladies of the Post visited us this afternoon came over in their elegant private ambulances. Mrs. English, Benteen, Inman & Steele, & Miss Dyer & others. Day cloudy, cold and dismal. All the officers of the regiment are invited to the Post to night to a ball given in our honor. We are to start at 8 p.m. in ambulances.

April 25, 1868. Camp on Wilson's Creek 22 miles from Ft. Harker. Col. West being Officer of the Day remained in camp last night, all the other officers went to the ball which was in Maj. Inman's office. Maj. Inman, like a sensible man always retires at tattoo, so he was not present. The fandango lasted till 3 o'clock this morning, and we only had time to get back to camp through the rain and darkness before reveillee sounded, (at 5 a.m.) and we broke camp and continued the march at 8 a.m. I was *excessively* sleepy, and (notwithstanding a good supper which was provided, and served at 2 o'clock a.m.) was thoroughly disappointed with the whole thing, and with myself for going in ambulance, so that I could not return to camp, (across the river) without waiting for the others. Have resolved to attend no more balls. Very tired and sleepy to day.

Albert to Jennie, camp near Fort Hays, Kan., April 30, 1868:

We are delightfully situated here, encamped on a lovely spot in a horse-shoe bend of Big Creek, just large enough for a spacious camp. A terrace between the plateau on which we are encamped, and the stream—all the way round the curve—and another similar one on the other side of the stream are overgrown with beautiful trees, elms, ash, and cottonwood mostly, with some wild plums, and grape vines—bluffs beyond the stream, and towards the East, through the opening by which you approach the camp, from the prairie, are seen the cars of the U.P.R.W. [Union Pacific Railway] passing and re-passing—and two miles away to our left, on going out on the prairie is Hayes City, with its R.R. depot, and ware houses, and no inconsiderable collection of houses—all *covered* with signs!—like the buildings of all western towns. Fort Hayes is, I think, by far the cleanest, and loveliest post that I have ever seen. It is about two miles off, just across the stream from Hayes City, on an elevated plateau, backed by swelling bluffs in the far distance. The stream on which we are encamped abounds with fish, and the officers who are not occupied have fine sport fishing. The 10th Cavalry (colored) are encamped about one mile from us, on the other side of the stream. The officers of that regiment are very attentive to those of the 7th—and have greatly feasted and treated to champaigne those who are "given" in that way! I have not been to the Post—nor in fact away from camp since we arrived here (on the 28th) as I prefer to get all my Muster Rolls, and returns complete before I ride about at all. We went out of our way slightly on arriving here and marched through the Post, with flying colors and the Band playing, and afterward came down here and encamped. The buffalo are numerous hereabouts, close to camp. We encountered a band of 28 Arrapahoes on our march from Harker, and held a short pow-wow. I recognized among them several whom I had seen at the council, and they also recognized me. They were all very friendly.

Jennie to Albert, East Cleveland, Ohio, April 26, 1868:

Gen. and Mrs Gibbs were in all my dreams last night, and as I dreamed that all the other ladies were sympathizing with me, because our pleasant home was broken up, and we were obliged to be separated, Mrs Gibbs was there with that same cold, unfeeling look and manner which is so characteristic of her, and which is chilling, even to think of. When I awoke my eyes were filled with tears, and my heart was desolate indeed.

Jennie to Albert, East Cleveland, Ohio, May 3, 1868:

With regard to Mr [A. E.] Smiths being transferred to your company, I hope you will consult your own interest and wishes, regardless of my little dislikes. I do not know that we would be compelled to be any more intimate if he is in your company than if he is in the same Reg. As an acquaintance, merely, Mrs. Smith is not disagreeable, and all familiarities can be easily avoided. If Mr. Smith is an efficient officer and it is for your interest to have him in your company, by all means endeavor to have the transfer made. Mr Godfrey you remember is to be married in the Fall. Should you retain him as your 1st Lieut and Mr Smith as your 2nd Lieut. your company would very likely be favored in many respects. I really hope that Capt. Leavy will not return. Please do what is best for yourself and company, and do not think of my little personal preferences. My greatest desire is for you to have an officer who will be able and willing to relieve you of some of the care and labor of the company, and I think Mr Smith might do this. . . .

Everybody asks me about Gen. Custer and are generally so prejudiced against him that they will not listen to any thing in his favor. You have no idea how generally unpopular he is, in civil life, since his last summer's campaign.

Albert to Jennie, camp near Fort Hays, Kan., May 8, 1868:

Our band discourses much sweet music these pleasant evenings—and in the mornings as well, and is improving,—and the silver instruments are kept excessively bright. We usually have music for three hours out of the 24. Buffalo hunting is the "rage" hereabouts now. Half a dozen of the officers usually start out every morning, in an ambulance, and have their horses led by orderlies, and come back in the evening with the humps and hind quarters and tongues of half a dozen buffaloes.

Albert to Jennie, camp near Fort Hays, Kan., May 17, 1868:

General Sheridan was here to visit us on the 15th, and he said that he would prefer to have us encamped for the summer about 15 miles west of here, and south of the R.R., if a suitable camping ground could be found,—otherwise at or near Downer's Station, but not, in any event north of the R.R. on the Saline, for the reason that the main body of Indians is believed to be south of

the Arkansas, and our being stationed on the Saline would leave
the R.R. and stage road, as well, more exposed to Indian aggres-
sions. . . .

[Bvt. Lt.] Colonels [J. Schuyler] Crosby [Acting Assistant Adjutant General] & [Thomas W. C.] Moore [aide-de-camp] accompanied General Sheridan on his visit. They were here all day, and
until 11 o'clock in the ev'g—Genl. S. inspecting the 7th & 10th
Cavalry in the mean time—and then left on the train for the end
of the track, which is now 25 miles this side of Fort Wallace,—
from there they intended to proceed to Fort Wallace on horseback, and then return. . . .

The weather has been delightful here since I last wrote, and our
camp is as lovely a place as you could wish to see. You ought to
witness a guard mounting here, or a Sunday morning inspection!
The men are incomparably neater in appearance than they were
at Leavenworth,—because they have more time probably—and
their arms are polished to perfection. There is a great rivalry
among the men of the various companies as to whom shall be
orderly—the man whose clothing arms and equipments are in the
best condition is selected by the Adjutant and new officer of the
day, as orderly for the commanding officer, and the one who is
deemed to be next in point of merit is chosen as orderly for the
Officer of the Day. The three next are selected for the post in
front of Head Quarters—the men on that post being relieved at 9
oclock to go on again at reveille. Sometimes it is next to impossible
to determine who should be selected—even the heads of the
screws in their carbines are closely scrutenized, and if they are not
polished even to the bottom of the little notch intended for the
point of the screw-driver, the man can not expect to be chosen as
orderly. There is a great rivalry between Companies A & K in this
matter, and I really believe that Col. West or Capt. Hamilton
would either one rather lose fifty dollars than that a man of the
other company should be selected instead of one from their own!
So this morning they were very much chagrined when [Pvt. Luke]
Mullen, of my company, whom you will remember, was selected as
orderly for the commanding officer! . . . The men were paraded
in blouses this morning, and it is not customary for them to wear
stocks, except when jackets are worn, but Mullen having failed to

"take orderly" the last time, when he appeared without a stock, and having observed that the wearer of a stock was his fortunate rival, took the precaution to have one on this morning! . . .

Well, I *did* think to put a dress coat in my chest, before leaving Leavenworth, and it was very fortunate, as all the officers dress to the full extent of their wardrobe,—and even then they can scarcely compare to advantage, with the men, when on duty. I have had no desertions since leaving Leavenworth—and there have only been two or three from the command. The men have fresh bread every day, as well as fresh beef, and potatoes—and plenty of buffalo meat. I have remembered the Sabbath day, as you require, to day!—that is I have not done any writing, except what I am now doing, nor any duty which I could avoid. Have not been to church, because there was none to attend—but in lieu of this all the officers, including half a dozen from Fort Dodge, who were here on a visit, participated in a social game of base ball! I have complied with the requirements of the "2nd Commandment"—that about "other Gods," I am sure—but I don't know whether you exactly remembered the proper number of the commandments yourself, did you? When you enjoined upon me the keeping of that one in particular, wasn't it the 11th? that one about *cussing*? instead, which you meant? (*vide* Deuteronomy, Chap V.)—Well I have kept the 11th, at all events—I suppose. I don't just remember that I have lost my temper about anything, of late! Have not drank any toddies, and havent chewed any since the Virginia-leaf disappeared. I don't think I will buy another pipe, as you recommend, for a pipe is a very inconvenient thing when one is on the march, and so I wont "bother with it."

. . . We have ice delivered every day, at 3 cts per lb. Our suttler has arrived, and opened part of his stores. He has one tent 34 feet long for a store room and another a hospital tent, which looks small in comparison with the first,—being not quite half as large,—as a place of resort for officers, who are supposed to be fond of beer! I don't expect to frequent it very much, if at all, so you needn't be alarmed for fear I will become addicted to beer! You see we are not entirely away from civilization, as we were last Summer, and I really think we will have a very pleasant Summer, if the Indians don't become hostile,—but I am not at all confident in their good intentions, even yet, and so I do not dare to hint that it may be possible for you to come out presently,—in a month or two—for fear something should occur to make me wish that I had not done so.

Jennie to Albert, East Cleveland, Ohio, May 24, 1868:

Mrs. A. E. Smith is now in Cleveland. . . . She gave me a good many little items—that you have probably not thought of—such as—your difficulty in getting the ferry boat—the evening we left—that Mr Ròbbins and Mr [H. W.] Smith will probably be dismissed from the service—that Capt. Brewster is in trouble also—that Tom Custer has reformed—owing to Miss Adams influence—that Capt. Hamilton is a very hard drinker, etc. etc. all of which of course interested me. She says she expects a letter from Mr Smith every day! Think of that, dear!

Albert to Jennie, camp 16 miles west of Fort Hays, Kan., May 27, 1868:

Will you be surprised to learn that we have changed camp? We left our old camp . . . on Monday morning, the 25th, and arrived here about 2 o'clock p.m. that day, during the prevalence of a violent hail storm. . . . Our present camp is not quite as pleasant as the former one on some accounts, but still, it is not unfavorably located. . . . About one mile west of us, on the rail road, and beyond a little bend in the creek is a R.R. water station [Ellis Station], and wood pile, with a cheap and altogether desolate looking frame house; a small low structure of poles, covered with shelter tents; and a kind of dug-out in the bank, the sides of which are carried up about four or five feet, above the level of the ground, with sods, and the whole is roofed with shingles or boards; this primitive establishment is occupied as a lodging house by the men employed about the station, about 20 in all, when they chance to be there. At present they are all absent on some labor up the road, except the man who attends to pumping the water, at the tank (with horse power,) a man who attends to sawing the wood, with horse power—one horse in an inclined box tread-mill—a small red-headed boy, with a very freckled face, short hair, and no hat, and who says his brother is 19 years old, and is a

brakeman "on the cars," and a slatternly woman, with unkempt
hair, who puts her head through a broken pane of glass in a
window of the desolate frame building, and inquires with some
trepedation what is the latest news about the Injuns! . . .

. . . Our camp is quite spacious, the officers tents being removed about 120 paces from those of the men—and the company
streets are 30 or 40 paces in width. The Suttler has put up his big
tent, braced, inside, with timbers & rafters. I suppose that he will
absorb most of the money paid to the men, and officers too for that
matter! I don't think he will absorb a great deal of *my* pay,—for we
have other use for our money, haven't we dear? . . .

On last Friday night we had quite a little episode, or tragedy, or
what not, in camp. The Quartermaster Maj. Bell had discharged
several teamsters upon reaching Fort Hayes, and they remained
loitering about Hayes City, without any visible occupation, and
finally several mules were stolen from our train, and it was suspected that they were concerned in the matter, and so a detective
was placed on the track of them and late on Friday night it was
ascertained that they were coming up that night to steal some
more; accordingly one relief of the reserve of the Guard was
stationed in the vicinity of the train, screened from observation,
and half a dozen officers volunteéred with a few picked men to
increase the force, stationing themselves where they could see
without being seen, and sure enough about midnight the suspected men arrived, and going to one of the wagons, got out a
couple of saddles, and carried them to the vicinity of some bushes,
near the stream, and then quietly unhitched half a dozen of the
best mules, and led them to where the saddles had been left, and
then, after a little consultation, concluded not to saddle them
there, but to lead them off, carrying the saddles with them; at this
juncture Lieut. Nowlan, the commissary, approached them, and
cried halt!—as they paid no heed to the challenge, after it was
several times repeated, but only made off all the faster, he took
deliberate aim at one of them, with his revolver, and fired, whereupon the man turned about and fired two shots at him, with his
revolver, and then made off again with the mules, but he had not
gone many steps when one of the shots fired at him took effect,
passing through his heart and he fell dead. The other men es-

caped, with some of the mules, but were pursued, and the mules recovered, and the men finally arrested at Hayes City.

I heard the firing at the time, and partially dressing myself and seizing my arms was about leaving my tent, to have the Troop "fall in," when listening a moment and not hearing any war whoops, or rather manifestations of the presence of Indians, I returned to bed, and was soon sound asleep, and did not know until the following morning what had occurred—thinking that the firing was upon prisoners attempting to escape from the Guard House.

You would be astonished at how little talk or concern such an occurrance creates in camp! I believe the subject was scarcely talked about at all, and I hardly think that half the men in the command had sufficient curiosity to walk up to where the man lay on a stretcher, in rear of the hospital tents, to look at him. A coroner's inquest was held over him the next day, by the U.S. Commissioner, and a few "good and lawful men" from Hayes City, and the verdict was "justifiable homocide," or something of that kind, and the body was very quietly put into the ground without any ceremony whatever. The man, whose name, or assumed name was Grant, was a character something like "Wild Bill," and dressed a good deal like him.

Albert to Jennie, Camp Alfred Gibbs, Kan., June 2, 1868:

Genl. Sheridan visited us again on Sunday last accompanied by Col. Forsyth, Col. Crosby, [Bvt. Brig.] Genl. [and Lt. Col. Alfred] Sully* [3d Infantry] (who has replaced Col. English in command of the District of the Upper Arkansas, Hd Qrs. at Fort Harker,) and Judge Grey, one of the Supreme Judges of Massachusetts. . . . General Sheridan never comes to see us without looking at every horse in the command! The party staid until after dinner—Col. Crosby and Capt. Cox dining with me—or at our mess rather, at my solicitation, and the others with Major Elliott. I will give you the bill of fare at "our mess" on that occasion,—as you may be curious to know. We had tomato soup, a roast haunch of Antelope, and a roast hind quarter of a nice fat buffalo calf, mashed potatoes, biscuits and butter, crackers, pickles, green peach pie, green peaches (canned) & cream (condensed), pound cake, tea & coffee &c. Our eating house & kitchen now consist of two wall tents facing each other, with a space between covered with a wall tent fly. . . .

Speaking of obscure posts reminds me that Col. West was ordered—not to a post exactly—but to an obscure camp, at the mouth of the Little Arkansas, about 70 miles south of Fort Harker, where he will have an independent command. He left with his company yesterday morning, with military honors, the whole command being formed, and presenting arms as he moved out. Capt. Barr of the 5th Infantry is there with his company, but Col. West will outrank him and take command. Col. Benteen or "Holy Owen" was going there, as was expected, but "Owen"—Hale—was not sent because Barr would outrank him, and I suppose Col. Benteen would quite as soon remain at Fort Harker—and has persuaded Genl. Sully to allow him to remain—and perhaps Col. West has used some influence in the matter, as I presume he is not anxious to be with the command when Genl. Custer returns, in the Fall, and he probably hopes to pave the way for some remote station during the winter. He has been conducting himself in a very exemplary manner of late, so far as attending to his duties is concerned, but there is something about him that I don't like,—I think he is very crafty, scheming, envious, selfish, malicious, and not to be trusted. Moral principle is what is lacking in the man. He is *exceedingly* selfish, and has no sense of right. Yet apart from this, he is a thorough soldier, when he desires to be so. But he "wobbles"—and is very uncertain! There, I guess you will think that there *is* something about him that I don't like! Well, I have not associated with him more than I could help, since his return to duty, notwithstanding that he has seemed very anxious to conciliate me, and cultivate my friendship. . . .

P.S., June 3, 1868. . . . Wouldn't you like to peep into my tent this morning, Jennie, and see how neatly everything is arranged? I have the floor all carpeted with nice grain sacks, and which overlap so that there is no trouble about sweeping. . . . I even have a heavy mat—a gunny sack—tacked down in front of my tent for a door mat—not so much to wipe feet on, as to prevent the grass from being worn, and so prevent dust. We are encamped with so much space between tents, and such a grassy lawn between—which like Betsy Trotwood's door yard is kept innocent of donkeys—and horses—that there is no reason for dust. And so we don't have any. On the right side, as you enter the door of my tent stands my iron bedstead, and at the head of it is a box containing my sheet iron stove (which I still keep for an emergency!) The box serving as a form on which to pile extra bed clothes—blankets—or clothing— Next to it—against the back pole of the tent, sits a box which you would scarcely recognize as the old wood box of our bedroom,—it has a shelter tent so neatly folded over it, and is otherwise somewhat altered in appearance. In it I keep spare boots—for I am so fortunate as to have four pairs—all neatly blackened, to be used upon occasion. On the back upright pole of my tent hangs my sabre, with the hilt and scabbard neatly burnished,—and also a camp hatchet, very sharp,—the blade in a neat leather case, or scabbard; above this are my spurs, and on the topmost peg hangs my hat—only to be worn when off duty, or on a buffalo hunt, or the march, or a scout [i.e., in garrison the kepi was required]. In the left hand far corner of my tent stands my table, the legs of which fit into sockets on two cross boards, which are nailed upon pegs driven into the ground, the boards being leveled (by driving down the pegs more or less) with a square and plumb-line. . . . The table is neatly covered with a clean, new shelter tent, the corners of which are buttoned about the corners of the table so that the sides hang very nicely. (You know each piece of shelter tent is provided with buttons & button holes.);— on the table sits my little desk, of course, and to the left of it a case for books. On the left hand side of the tent, as you enter sits my chest, and in the front corner, near it, the case for my desk, as a receptacle for "soiled linen"—i.e. gingham, Navy flannel &c. and upon it stands a new cedar water bucket, with brass hoops and bail, and a glass tumbler, and my wash basin, with a supply of clean towels are on a convenient arrangement near the door. . . . Of course you will remember that I have an arm chair, and two others of less pretensions, besides, and it may be well to inform you that my tent is closed at night, or in stormy weather with a row of straps and buckles, instead of the little tapes provided by the Quartermaster Department, and that the sides are rolled up in warm weather, and fastened up with straps and buckles, like the curtains of an ambulance. . . .

Perhaps you would like to know how we are going to occupy our time this summer, if the Indians don't require our attention, well, here is the roster, as published last evening.

Reveille, 1st call, 4.40 a.m.

Stable call immediately after.

Recall from stables, 6 a.m. when the horses will be sent to graze, under the supervision of the officer of the day, who will post the necessary videttes and guards, and select the grazing ground for the day.

Breakfast call 6.15 (I will breakfast at Guard Mount)

Fatigue call 6.45

Sick call 7.

Guard mount, 1st call 7.45

Guard mount, 2nd call 8.

Drill for instruction of non-com'd officers 8.50

Recall from drill 9.30

Water call 11

Dinner call 12

1st Sergeants call 1 p.m.

Recall from grazing 1.30

Drill call, (mounted) 4

Recall from drill 5.15

Water & stable call 6.

Recall from stables 7.

Retreat 7.15 p.m.

Tattoo 8.30

Taps 9

So you see we will be busy, Jennie!—Company commanders will drill their non-commissioned officers in the riding school at 8.50, and in the afternoon the non-commissioned officers will drill the men, the officers being present in superintendence. . . .

. . . Lieut. Godfrey . . . is still in Company "E"—but Lieut [John M.] Johnson has just arrived—together with Lieut. Gibson. I have not seen them yet, but my cooks are now preparing a supper for them—and probably Lieut. Godfrey will now be returned to duty with the company. I do not think that his assistance would be material! He is somewhat lazy, and a little slovenly, and not at all systematic, although he makes some pretentions in that way. I have now got my company into admirable trim, and every thing goes on swimmingly.

. . . Lieut. Robbins is still absent—at Harker. Lieut. Brewster will be here with Keogh [and I Troop, ordered from Lyon], I suppose. I have dropped Capt. Leavy as a deserter, and have so reported him, and the Adjutant General has ordered his arrest, wherever found. His conduct is perfectly unaccountable. He was about $3000 in debt here and at Leavenworth it appears!

Albert to Jennie, Camp Alfred Gibbs, Kan., June 20, 1868:

Capt. Custer was only on duty at Fort Leavenworth for a day or two, while on leave he is now here. Brevt. Lieut. Col. Keogh is ordered to Fort Harker, as Act'g Assist. Inspector General on Genl. Sully's staff—not a very high position by the way, as it is properly that of a 1st Lieut.—and takes $10 a month from his pay, (the allowance for commanding a company,)—but it is a very easy position, and I suppose even if not a very complimentary one, ought nevertheless to be accepted with gratitude! Lieut. Godfrey is at present stationed at Hayes City, to "captivate" deserters! Lieut. Johnson is in arrest, for some slight delinquency. Brevet Capt. [A. E.] Smith is slightly indisposed. Salty [H. W.] Smith is ordered to Fort Hayes for trial—Brevt. Lieut. Col. Keogh is to be a member of the court. Brewster is here, and looks very natural. I don't think he drinks much nowadays. Robbins is also here, and on duty. Genl. Sherman passed west over the R.R. last night. He did not stop. I am building a large Bakery,—in addition to being company commander, Officer of the Day, and President of three different boards of survey, at one time. I had to discontinue writing for a time, since commencing this letter, to go out to practice target firing, as all the officers fire daily now from 6.15 to 7.30 at 1,2,3,4 and 500 yards. I appear to be about the second best shot, on the average, Lieut. Nowlan being the best, I believe. I think I could make an Indian feel very unhappy at any moderate distance, if he would only stand quite still—which I suppose he wouldn't do ordinarily.

Albert to Jennie, Camp Alfred Gibbs, Kan., June 23, 1868:

I have just received a commission as Brevet Major U.S.A. "for gallant and meritorious services in action at Ashland Station, Va." I would like to send it to you, but I guess I will not do so at present. I hope that now, since they have begun to look up my record, they will continue to do so, and give me a couple of more brevets.

We hear to day from the Adjutant General that Brevet Capt.

Leavy is sick in Washington, and that he is to be taken up on the rolls again. [Pvt. William] Annard has received a letter from Sergeant Gordon, who sends regards to me, and says he has never drunk a drop of liquor since leaving, and that he is clerking in a store, and doing well, but would much rather be back in the army, in Company "G"—and that if he can be assured that he will not have to wear a ball and chain and have his head shaved, &c., he will gladly come back to the company. . . .

P.S. I open my letter to say that I have no majors straps and that if you happen to see a pair that will answer (yellow ground remember) you might send them—as I can get none here—just the gold *leaves*, without the straps, would answer well enough for a blouse—straps should not cost over $2—and leaves less. You see I think it probable that I will be still further brevetted, when these straps would not answer.

Jennie to Albert, East Cleveland, Ohio, June 28, 1868:

First of all, let me congratulate you on your Brevet. Of course I am delighted, and only hope your good luck will continue, until you have as many Brevets as you deserve. I searched the City over yesterday, for straps, but with poor success. I found a pair of Cav. straps—2nd Lieut's—and I have thought since I came home, that I might have taken those, and put the gold leaves on them. I can find some with the embroidered leaf here. I send you in this letter two leaves as a sample. They were fifty cents. I thought they would answer for the corners of your Navy flannel shirt collars—(Gen Custer told me he always wore his stars there) and possibly for a blouse. I can send to New York and get you a handsome pair or take those here. Tell me which you prefer to have me do, and speaking of those shirts, reminds me, that you have never told me how you like any of them. Do not forget it, when you write again.

Albert to Jennie, Camp Alfred Gibbs, Kan., June 26, 1868:

General Forsyth arrived very unexpectedly yesterday, and yesterday afternoon he inspected the whole command mounted, and to day dismounted, and the inspection was very thorough. I think my troop appeared to as good advantage as any, and all appeared well. I think Genl. Forsyth will find quite a contrast when he goes up to Wallace, to inspect his own regiment—the 10th (Cavalry) [in which he was a major, though detached as departmental inspector general]. He will wish he didn't belong to it! The General took dinner with me to day. What did we have? Why tomato soup, roast beef, new potatoes, butter and biscuits, fresh peach pie, cake with raisins in it, corn starch custard—excellent—coffee, and every thing good!

Albert to Jennie, Camp Alfred Gibbs, Kan., July 3, 1868:

General Forsyth made a very *thorough* inspection of this command. He had a tent assigned him, and a clerk from Department Hd. Qrs., and he "went through" all the retained Muster Rolls, Returns, books and papers of each company for this year in the most thorough and systematic manner. He told Major Elliott that he never saw Company Records in such perfect condition as those of my company, and he told other officers of the regiment the same thing, and will doubtless make a note of it in his report. He was acting under orders direct from the War Department, and one of his objects appears to have been to ascertain, if possible the cause of so many desertions having taken place from this regiment. We have lost upwards of 1200 men by desertion since the organization of the regiment! I guess the War Department people will have their eyes opened a little in regard to the cause of these desertions presently, when Genl. Forsyth's report is made. The General, in addition to his researches among the papers, sent for all the non-commissioned officers of each company in succession, and examined them separately in regard to the cause of desertions, condition of their rations &c. &c. &c.

Did I tell you in my last that I was building an oven, and bake house? It was completed day before yesterday, or rather the day before that, and we have since had two bakings of bread from it. It is quite a success. The bread is excellent—far superior to that furnished at Leavenworth—and partly for the reason that it is baked on the oven floor—which is of broad smooth stones—and not in pans.

Most of the officers prophesyed that it would be impossible, with our resources, to build a field oven, that would answer, but now they are all agreeably disappointed since it *has* been done. I had to originate and provide for every thing myself—except that Major Elliott advanced some money to purchase sheet iron for the arch, trusting to be reimbursed from the savings of the bakery—which will be large, and go to the Company Fund. The oven is capable of turning out 400 rations per day—or rather at one baking—and it might be heated several times a day, if more troops were here.

Albert to Jennie, Camp Alfred Gibbs, Kan., July 5, 1868:

The little leaves are very nice, and I am going to put them on one of the Navy shirts the next time I wear one. By the way I will tell you how I like the shirts. I find it impracticable to wear the blue flannel shirts at present, as they chafe my neck, in consequence of the extreme heat, and consequent perspiration—but when the days become a little cooler I expect to wear them often. They fit me nicely, and are much admired by all—but I can not wear flannel next to my skin at all, in hot weather (and these touch about my neck & wrists), I find, as it causes "prickly heat." The Gingham shirts are very cool and nice, but I am rather sorry that I did not have them made with bindings about the neck, instead of with permanent collars attached, as I find that the collars always become soiled in one day, so that I can not wear a shirt longer. My brown linen ones serve very well. I did not bring any white ones along. Perhaps I should have done so, if I had known how dressy we would be here. For a time nothing was allowed to be worn here unless in strict conformity with the regulations, but now officers are allowed to wear what they choose about their own tents—which results in their wearing white linen clothes throughout, and straw, or light felt hats, a great deal,—but they are not allowed to appear on any duty, even at stables, in anything not in accordance with the regulations. I am sorry that I did not have a nice blouse made while at Leavenworth. I find it quite difficult to keep pace with the men, in appearance, and I am quite sure that I would never "take orderly!" I had not time to tell you in my last letter that Genl. Gibbs had sent me a congratulatory letter enclosing two pairs of beautiful gilt leaves—the handsomest that I have ever seen—they are larger than those you sent. I have put them on my blouse. It was very thoughtful in the General, wasn't it, as well as very kind. I suppose he begins to feel rather sorry that he kept Capt. Yates there. On the 2nd Genl. Gibbs telegraphed that Col. Myers was cashiered, and sentence approved by the President. To day an order from Department Hd. Qrs. dated the 1st. inst., directs him to report without delay to Major Elliott for duty. Considerable uncertainty exists in consequence, as to whether he has been cashiered or not. If he has not been, I think that his trial will be a wholesome lesson to him. "Salty" [Smith] was tried last week, at Fort Hayes. His case is not serious, I think, and will amount to very little, in any event. Wallingford is to be tried, I believe. Capt. Thompson is here on a visit now,—as well as Lieut. Beecher and [William] Comstock, the scout. The latter is to go over to the head waters of the Saline tomorrow to see the Cheyennes, who are encamped there, and ascertain if possible their intentions. . . .

We celebrated the 4th of July quite extensively here yesterday. We had a horse race—one horse from each Troop—and a foot race, a "sack race" and a "wheelbarrow race." Purses were made up so as to give $5. to the winner in every kind of race, and $20. to the company to which the winning horse belonged. The Suttler was allowed to sell beer and wine at discretion, and whiskey upon approval of company commanders, and in consequence 13 casks of ale disappeared almost immediately and I don't know how many dozens of bottles of other "flooids"—but everything passed off quietly—only one man in the entire command was perceptably under the influence of liquor. He belonged to Company "A"—was a little noisy, and was sent to the guard house in consequence to spend the remainder of his 4th of July! I was officer of the day. Taps did not "sound off" until 11 o'clock, and thereafter all was quiet, except the low sweet music of a violin, guitar, and flute—owned in "I" Troop—which was heard until long after midnight. All the officers, I believe, were serenaded. They have a glee club in "I" Troop too, which is remarkably fine. I believe that I have told you in some former letter about our base ball clubs? They are numerous. The officers had a match game yesterday.

A train laden with a large excursion party (of people from Wyandotte, Manhattan, &c.) which had been up to the end of the track, stopped opposite our camp yesterday, and all the officers rode out, and the men also thronged thither to see, and the excursionists male and female—the latter numerous, but not handsome, in any instance, got out, and "assembled themselves together" while one of the party, a man of care obviously, and apparently an exhorter, or a politician in a small way made a harangue in which the valor of the troops—more especially the 7th Cavalry—the beauties of this country, the detestable character of the Indians, and the growing power and prosperity of Kansas were all recited, to the eminent satisfaction of all parties concerned, and then, after a *brief* response by Major Elliott, (as they were anxious that he should favor them with a speech!)—the crowd reembarked, and the train moved on. . . .

Did I ever tell you that Botzer went and married the young Laundress, Mrs. Brushes' daughter? I believe not. Well, he did, and they kept it a great secret for about six or eight weeks, not even Mrs. Brush, it appears, being aware of their marriage! Poor Botzer, I think he might have done better. I have given Mrs. Brush a wall tent and a couple of "A" tents and she has quite a little village for herself and son-in-law, and daughter, and little boy "Charley" who comes every morning and gets my spurs, sabre, and boots, and keeps them in order for a slight compensation.

Jennie to Albert, East Cleveland, Ohio, July 9, 1868:

I am quite surprised at Gen. Gibbs' thoughtfulness. It is very gratifying to receive a letter from him, written in such a friendly informal manner. Everything he does is so purely military, and mechanical, one would hardly expect anything of the kind. I think you have reason to feel quite flattered by this little attention, but it will be a long time before *I* forget the little grudge I have against him [i.e., the selection of Yates to remain at Leavenworth for the summer].

Albert to Jennie, Camp Alfred Gibbs, Kan., July 8, 1868:

Major Elliott started for the Solomon, and Prairie Dog Creek, and Beaver Creek (northward) yesterday morning, at 6 o'clock, taking Company "A" with him, and left me here in command. . . .

A few hours after Major Elliott started, Lieut. Nowlan received a confidential communication from Col. Keogh, who is at Head

Quarters, informing him that General Sully, (the District Commander) had just received a dispatch from Fort Larned (which is 70 miles or so s.w. of Harker you will remember,) informing him that 2,000 lodges of the Kiowas and Comanches are reported to be moving on that Post—Larned—for the purpose of demanding rations, and other supplies, and that Major Elliott would be ordered to make a rapid movement to that point. . . .

Col. Myers arrived here last night, from Leavenworth, with orders to report to the comd'g officer of Detachment for duty. He could not report to me, as he outranks me, and declines to take command, for a time, at least, so I remain in command—of the four companies and the Band &c.

I have just received a dispatch from Genl. Sully, (addressed to Major Elliott) directing him to hold his command in readiness for a rapid movement to Fort Larned, as trouble is expected there. I have directed the acting Quartermaster, Lt. Nowlan (as Maj. Bell accompanied Maj. Elliott,) to have all his mules shod, with as little delay as possible—further than this we are ready for any movement. I think it more than likely that we may be required to march to Larned—but think that it is not probable that we will have any serious trouble with the Indians. I think that the officer in command at Larned is probably a little "skeery"—it is [Bvt.] Major [and Capt. Henry] Asbury [3d Infantry]. He ought certainly to be able to protect himself there, against all the Indians on the plains, as the buildings are of stone, and well situated.

Albert to Jennie, Camp Alfred Gibbs, Kan., July 9, 1868, 10 A.M.:

We march in an hour toward Fort Larned—leaving only the sick and 3 men and one non-commissioned officer from each company, and one officer in charge of our camp. We take only shelter tents.

I suppose we will await "the logic of events" before we can tell what will result.

10. Fort Larned, July–August 1868

Fort Larned as it appeared to *Harper's Weekly* artist Theodore Davis in April 1867, when visited by the Hancock Expedition. The engraving appeared in the June 8 issue.

The Kiowas, Comanches, Plains Apaches, Cheyennes, and Arapahos had begun to gather near Fort Larned in anticipation of the annuity issues promised at Medicine Lodge. Their temper was somewhat uncertain, and General Sully, the new commander of the District of the Upper Arkansas, ordered a precautionary concentration of units at the fort. The sudden move of Major Elliott's command of the 7th Cavalry from the railroad to Larned was part of this concentration.

Albert to Jennie, camp on Walnut Creek, Kan., July 11, 1868:

The dispatch from Genl. Sully stated that the direction from the point from which we were to send the courier was *south west* of Camp Alfred Gibbs, but we concluded that it must certainly be a mistake, and so we went south 30 degrees east for 25 or 30 miles until we reached a timbered stream unknown to the Geography makers, and not laid down on any map, but which is known to us by the name of Goose Creek. It flows in a deep channel—30 or 40 feet deep—the sides of which are bordered with trees. Here we were sure of finding water—but when we reached it, a little after dark, on the 9th our scouts could find no water. Col Myers, who was at the time commanding the column, (Major Elliott being unwell, and riding in an ambulance) formed the command to go into camp, and only remarked (with his customary shrug of the shoulders) in reply to the suggestion that efforts should be made to find water (as the day had been excessively hot, and the men and animals were very thirsty,) "Vell; you will *tig!*"—The idea of digging in the channel of a stream of that character—pan-clay bottom—was so absurd that I could scarcely refrain from laughing—which would mortally have offended the colonel—but Major Elliott coming up at this time, I agreed to find water in half an hour, and was accordingly sent up the stream with a detail in search of it, while Lieut. Johnson with a detail went down the stream. Riding along the bank, and looking down into the darkness through the tree tops, and the tangled vines and underbrush, I would occasionally see the reflection of the stars in small pools of water, and then I would let two men dismount, one to hold both horses, while the other should climb down, and examine the pool, and bring up a canteen of water. I would then

169

move on until I would again catch a glimpse of the stars, reflected below, when I would dismount two more men. I had not proceeded in this way more than a half-mile before I found an abundance of good water for the whole command—and returning found that Lieut. Johnson, too, had found enough for our Army—two large beaver dams, where the banks were not precipitous, and the water easily accessible. So we moved down and camped. As we went into camp, and the men were busy unsaddling, a large rattlesnake, like a watchman, sprang his rattle in their midst—but the men went on talking, unsaddling &c.—no one paying any attention to him—until I told one of the men to draw his sabre and hunt him up—fearing he might bite one of the men or horses—but the snake could not be found—having probably got into his hole—and no one seemed to care in the least for his presence.

Albert to Jennie, camp near Fort Larned, Kan., July 12, 1868:

We have encamped one mile above the Post, on the south side of the Pawnee Fork. The grass here is excellent, green and delightful. The Post is flourishing—many thousands of Indians are here, but indeed I think there was really no cause for alarm. All the Indians carry revolvers, and look formidable enough, but they appear to be very friendly, and I believe they are, with perhaps the exception of a small number of disaffected ones from each tribe. I have met many of my friends, among the Indians, who recognize me and are glad to see me, since my arrival here. Our camp is constantly surrounded with them but [we] do not admit them. Col. Benteen and [Lieutenant] Hale, and their companies, and Capt. Hamilton and his company are to come here. We are to be here probably 10 days. Michael Sheridan is here, and Dr. Forward, &c. &c.

Albert to Jennie, camp near Fort Larned, Kan., July 13, 1868:

The Indians here are very quiet, and peaceably disposed. Most of the [Kiowa] "Braves" and War Chiefs are off on the War Path, on an expedition against the Utes—Indians who live in the mountains south west of here—and the fact that all the squaws and pappooses and old grandmothers and old men of the tribes are here, with all their teepes, surplus ponies, and other little plunder, and with only enough warriors to guard their camps, and hunt buffalo for the subsistence of the squaws &c is, I think, conclusive evidence that these Indians are friendly, and desire to remain at peace. The Indian agents are to make a distribution of goods to the Indians here soon—in fact they have already done so in part, but it is said that they do not fulfill their promises to the Indians—that they have promised their arms and ammunition, which they now withhold, and the Indians are in a measure displeased in consequence, but perhaps not sufficiently so to go to war. I think whatever promises are made to Indians should be religiously fulfilled to the letter—otherwise bad feeling and trouble ensues.

Col. Benteen and Lieuts Cook[e] & Hale arrived with H & M Troops [from Fort Harker] this morning, and are now encamped with us.

Albert to Jennie, camp near Fort Larned, Kan., July 15, 1868:

I believe that nearly all the other officers of the command are now down at the Post, at a "hop" given by Major Asbury, and to which we were all invited. I did not choose to go, and being Officer of the Day, I had a good excuse—so I sent my compliments and my apology by Lieut. Beecher. Mrs. Scott, the fascinating widow of whom you have heard will be there, also Mrs. Col. Wyncoop, Mrs. Major Asbury and Mrs. Capt. [Nicholas] Nolan, of the 10th Cav. I believe that comprises the female portion of the fandango, unless some of the aborigines are invited! Miss Julia Bent, of the Cheyenne tribe [the twenty-one-year-old daughter of William Bent and Yellow Woman], would be quite an attraction, I am sure, if she could only be persuaded to come—she is really a stately creature, and very handsome. I was invited to dine with Lieut. L. Wesley Cooke of the 3d Infantry, at the Post to day, but did not go, being officer of the day. Sent an apology instead. . . .

. . . I *do* find Major Elliott a very good commanding officer. He has his faults, to be sure, but upon the whole he is an excellent officer, and I like him very well. . . . Apart from my expectations to apply for leave of absence in the spring, I would certainly prefer to be stationed at one of these remote western Posts. Here

one has every thing comfortable, little society to bother him, and a
fair prospect for remaining through the summer. Larned is a very
pleasant Post. It is tranquil and quiet, and something about it gives
it the air of an old Spanish town—as I picture one in imagination.
The officers' quarters are very spacious, and have exceedingly
wide, pleasant porches, extending along the whole front of each
building.

. . . I do not know whether or not Lieut. Godfrey is to be
married this winter. I suppose, however, that he rather con-
templates something of this kind. [He was married in June 1869.]
I do not admire him much. He is of very little account in the
company. He is very slovenly and lazy, and *unmilitary,* and I would
not give one good non-commissioned officer for half a dozen
Lieutenants like him. I have at length resorted to the expedient of
issuing orders affecting him in writing, and furnishing him an
official copy, and have a fair understanding with him that I intend
he shall carry them out to the very letter, and the very first time
that he fails to do so hereafter, why there will be trouble. I know
that you somehow have a measure of regard for him, and perhaps
I should, if I had no official intercourse with him, but as it is, why I
do not immeasurably admire him, I am sure. He presumes a great
deal on his West Point education, and I cannot see wherein it has
benefitted him. In fact, from all I see of West Point graduates, I
am inclined to think that it rests more with the man than with the
Institution whether a course of training will prove an advantage
or not. In the great majority of cases, I think it does not, but that
on the contrary it is a positive detriment to the individual.

I have already told you about the shirts. I think brown linen
ones, or gingham ones with detached collars and cuffs are prefer-
able for field service, such as we have had this summer. I wore one
of the blue woolen ones—with the little leaves on the collar,—on
the march over here, and my felt hat, and trowsers and top
boots—and that was all! The shirt chaffed my skin a good deal
though, and when I arrived here I put on gingham, and brown
linen. When it becomes a little cooler, I think the blue flannel will
be just the thing. Major Inman gave Col. Benteen and Lieuts.
Cooke and Hale each one like mine, with the exception that they
have less pointed, and perhaps wider collars, with a silk embroidered star in the corners.

I finished reading David Copperfield the other evening, and have loaned the book to Col. Benteen. I was delighted with the work to the end. . . .

The Indians have mostly disappeared from our horizon—last night and to day—gone off to follow up the buffalo, or to "make medicine," they said. They keep their religious festivals with quite as much zeal as Christians! "B" Troop [Captain Thompson] is to arrive from Dodge tomorrow.

Albert's journal:

July 16, 1868. Hamilton (with Lieut. Custer and "A" Troop,) has arrived ("A" Troop had started on a scout to the Solomon and perhaps to Beaver Creek from Camp Alfred Gibbs a day or two before we left that camp. Maj. Bell had gone too.) I Troop [Lieutenant Brewster] also returned to day. . . . I placed Lieut. Godfrey in arrest this evening for disrespectfully reporting the Troop &c. We now get a small quantity of ice, daily, from the Post.

July 20, 1868. Released Lieut Godfrey from arrest this ev'g, and directed him verbally to attend all roll and stable calls for the present, and until otherwise ordered, and to inspect the kitchen daily at dinner call.

July 21, 1868. I visited the Arapaho & Kiowa camps on the Arkansas to day, in company with Lieut. [Edward G.] Mathey.* The camps are 9 miles S.W. of here, on the Arkansas. There are about 400 lodges, or 4,400 Indians, and 4 or 5000 ponies and mules there. I found "Little Raven" and other chiefs and head men of the Arapahos taking a vapor bath. Visited *Sittamaw* one of the leading Kiowa chiefs, and had a talk with him, principally by signs, in relation to a defeat which has recently been sustained by a war party of Kiowas and Comanches in an engagement with the Utes. Sit-ti-yaw or "Heap of Bears," the head war chief of the Arapahos, and five other warriors of the tribe were killed, and all the relatives and friends of the deceased are in mourning for them—i.e. having their arms, legs, and bodies scarified, and howling. We were considerably amused at the manner and appearance of one old squaw, who was indulging in a monotonous dance and chant, looking all the while toward the south west, the direction in which the disaster occurred. It seems that the Kiowa war party had gone on an expedition against the Navajo Indians, and finding, on the way, a party of Utes chasing buffalo, attacked them, and followed them two or three miles, into broken country, to the main camp of the Utes, when they were beset by superior numbers, freshly mounted, and driven back fifteen miles, with the loss mentioned. The Kiowa War Party had returned to the other side of the Arkansas, where I saw their Teepes, and Sittamaw said that this afternoon they would cross over to this side of the river. Satanta is in mourning. . . . A horse race is to come off this evening between Col. Benteen's horse and Col. Wyncoops. The day has been very hot.

Lt. Godfrey reported "his presence" to me while I was bathing my face, and declined to receive the report of the 1st Sergeant, which of course has resulted in some "unpleasantness!"

July 23, 1868. Another heavy thunder storm from the north at noon to day. Had to let my "A" tent "down a peg!" It has continued cool and cloudy since the rain up to this hour—11 p.m. There was some rain last night. Lieut. Wallingford arrived from Fort Dodge to day, with "B" Troop. He met with a cold reception from the officers. . . .

July 24, 1868. "Lone Wolf," the Kiowa chief who was wounded in the fight with the Utes was in camp to day, with John Smith, the Interpreter. Lieut. Robbins was placed in arrest to day by Maj. Elliott. His Troop & Self have been on a considerable spree of late! He was up at the Post, all last night, without permission, playing "seven up" and only got back to camp at reveillee! To day it is quite cool and cloudy, and pleasant, like a day in the Fall. . . . The officers are to meet at Capt. Hamilton's tent this evening, to consider the case of Lieut. Wallingford.

Albert to Jennie, camp near Fort Larned, Kan., July 29, 1868:

Major Elliott last evening opened a case of wine which was sent him—or rather for the officers of the regiment, from Washington, by Baron Cussiereau, of the Russian Legation—he informed us that the grapes grew on his "ancestral hills." Col Wyncoop, Indian Agent, commences, to day, to issue arms to the Indians. Is to issue 350 or 375 rifles to them, by order of the Secretary of the Interior, I believe—maybe they will feel very brave when they get those arms, and will begin to turn their thoughts to war again! Who knows. It is certainly very foolish to fight Indians with one hand, and to make presents, and give them arms with the other!

The Cheyennes had refused to accept any of their annuities because the Indian Bureau had withheld the promised arms and ammunition as punishment for the raid on the Kaws. At Wynkoop's urging, however, the Commissioner of Indian Affairs relented, and the Indians at length received issues of pistols, Lancaster rifles, powder, caps, and lead.

Albert to Jennie, camp near Fort Larned, Kan., Aug. 1, 1868:

Major Bell, Lieut. Nowlan, Surgeon Lippincott and myself have been sitting out on the parade ground, in the quiet moonlight for an hour past listening to Col. Myers relate his adventures and experiences among the hostile tribes in Oregon, and indeed some of them were quite thrilling, and all savored of "the dew and damp of meadows," "and the shadows of the forest," "and the thunders in the mountains," and were therefore not a little romantic, but all the while:—

> "Although she may be otherwhere,
> I ever gaze upon her brow
> And hold her fast in silent prayer!"

Yes, dear, my thoughts are always inseparable from you, and so although I sit in the quiet evenings, and listen by the hour to the stirring legends of the army—the usual topic of conversation, for the noise of the outer world does not reach us, and we have a community of interest and fellowship distinct from others,—yet my attention is *never* so wholly absorbed that I cease to think of you, and now as the time approaches when I shall fold you in my arms once more, and be made very, very happy by your charming presence, and your ennobling love, it seems as though I take note of every moment as it passes, and say to quiet my impatience, "fond heart! be still! It is but a little while until she comes!" . . .

[P.S. Aug. 2, 1868.] And now I write a hasty postscript. The review to day was very fine. Mrs. Scott and Mrs. Tappan came up

to witness it—besides others from the post—and about .200
Arapaho and Apache Indians sat on their ponies and looked on in
astonishment—and shortly afterwards the two bands, about 4 or
500 strong, which have been encamped about 3/4 of a mile above
us, on the same stream, passed our camp with ponies, teepe poles,
dogs, pappooses, and as Micawber would say—"in short, *everything*
which an Indian is presumed to possess!" They are going on a
grand buffalo hunt, having just received their arms—elegant
rifles &c. and an abundance of ammunition; a fact of which we
were made fully aware last night, for they kept up a constant yelp,
and discharge of fire arms from midnight until reveille in their
camp, and our horses, in consequence kept up a constant snorting
and pawing, and an occasional effort at a stampede! The magnificence of our Suttler's outfit impressed the "salvages" very
favorably. I showed an Indian "Attig-*caw*-tuh"—an Apache, your
pictures one day, and told him that you were a very good little
squaw, and that I wanted a *little* bow and some arrows for you, and
he said that after one sleep he would bring them for me, and sure
enough he did so—a nice little bow, and seven arrows with sharp
blades, and feathers, and a quiver—which *his* squaw had evidently
just made, (as it was entirely new,) as a present for you! So I will
expect you to excel in archery this fall! . . .

      . . . Brewster is in love with Mrs. Scott they say. In fact Mrs.
Scott is quite a belle. She is about your size and a rather graceful
brunette—possessed of some power of fascination, I suppose, and
graceful enough, though lacking somewhat of culture. She is said
to be wealthy—which may, or may not be true. However, poor
Brewster is undoubtedly head over heels in love—and has not a
ghost of a chance either—and he vainly tries to disguise the ardor
of his "be-smittenness"—but it is quite apparent to all! Alas, poor
Brewster! He is undoubtedly foredoomed to be unhappy, and to
sigh in vain! . . . By the way, Mrs. Scott paid you quite a compli-
ment today. She saw your picture in Major Elliott's album, and
was not aware that it was the likeness of my darling, and upon
turning over the leaf and seeing it, she exclaimed: "Oh! she's
handsome!" and turning to me with "don't you think so?" I of
course acquiesced! She was surprised when she learned who you
were, and congratulated me a good deal!

Albert to Jennie, camp near Fort Larned, Kan., Aug. 5, 1868:

I ran a foot race last ev'g with Lieut. Cooke, 7th Cav., & Capt. [A. E.] Smith, 200 yards for a purse of $150. Cooke won, of course! It appears now that he was a prize racer before the war, and had really distinguished himself somewhat in that line. The ladies and officers of the post were up to witness the race, and all the regiment was out to see, and we were very picturesque, I suppose, in "tights" stockings, and garters. Capt. Hamilton & Lieut. Robbins put up the $50 on me, and took some side bets, amounting to nearly as much more, and lost! Wasn't it too bad! If Cooke could have been induced to agree to run twice as far, I think his prospect would not have been so good. I bantered him to run the race over again, right away, to run back to the starting point, but he wouldn't do it. He ran very fast at the start, but I gained on him rapidly afterwards, but not enoguh to win! I was only running for sport, and was not to have any share in the proceeds in case I won, because I would not put in anything to help make up the purse.

The race was got up mainly as a sanitary measure, to furnish some excitement, and encourage diversions of this kind, among the men, in consequence of the fear of cholera, which was becoming somewhat prevalent, as was supposed, in consequence of the death of one man in "H" Troop with symptoms very like those of cholera.

Last night we had a dance on the parade, in front of Head Quarters, all the ladies from the Post were here. We had the "flys" of a large hospital [tent] stretched on the grass, and staked down for a carpet. The music was very fine. The clog dancers of "E" Troop, in their brilliant costumes, gave an exhibition of their abilities during the evening. Lieut. Godfrey arrived today with the Laundresses.

Albert to Jennie, camp near Fort Larned, Kan., Aug. 10, 1868:

Quite a serious affair occurred at the Post on the night of the 5th inst. Col. Wyncoop, the Indian Agent, was sitting on his porch, with his wife and children, and Mrs. Nolan & Tappan, I believe, and Lieut. [John P.] Thompson of the 3d Infantry, and others, when a mad wolf, a very large grey wolf, entered the post and bit one of the sentinels,—ran into the hospital and bit a man lying in bed,—passed another tent, and pulled a man out of his bed, biting him severely,—bit one man's finger nearly off—bit at some woman, and I believe one or two other persons in bed, but did not bite through the bed clothes—passed through the hall of Capt. Nolan's house, and pounced upon a large dog which he found there, and whipped him badly in half a minute, and then passed the porch of Col. Wyncoops house, and springing upon it bit Lieut. Thompson quite severely in several places,—he then passed on to where there was a sentinel guarding the haystacks, and tried to bite the sentinel, but did not succeed—the sentinel shooting and killing him on the spot! He proved to be of a very unusual size, and there appears to be no doubt that he had the hydrophobia. The Indians say that they have never known any one bitten by a mad wolf to recover.

Word was brought to General Sully yesterday while he was at our camp, that a ranchman in the vicinity of Zara—a man who has been putting up hay, and has a good deal of it ready to sell to the government, shot and killed a Kiowa Indian some where near his ranch on the previous evening. Serious trouble will probably be the result. The nearest male relative of the Indian who was killed will of course kill and scalp some white man before long, at least, and it is not improbable that the Kiowas will commence attacking wagon trains &c. after the old fashion. I do not fear that they will ever venture near our camp, unless it be to attempt to stampede the horses while they are out grazing, or to cut off small parties. It may be, though, that the Indian who was killed was not much respected in the tribe, and that therefore the matter may be compromised in some way. I should feel very sorry indeed if a war were to break out at this season of the year, as in that case we would not probably go into winter quarters at Leavenworth—if any where indeed!—and at all events the orders would not reach us until very late in the season. . . .

I am getting along very nicely with Lieut. Godfrey now. We had a little "wrestle" together, as Lieut. Robbins would say, in which Lieut. Godfrey did not prosper, and since then he has been as good, and as attentive to duty as it is possible for an officer to be. He seems to respect me exceedingly since then, and our relations are very amicable indeed. The fact is Lieuts Godfrey and Johnson had entered the service, presuming a great deal upon their West Point education, and prestige, which was not really very beneficial to them, when put to the test, and it was necessary to teach them their true position before they could become entirely available as subalterns.

Albert to Jennie, camp near Fort Larned, Kan., Aug. 13, 1868:

I am really very discouraged with this kind of life, and if Congress would deem it best to disband the whole army I would not find any fault, I am sure. I am often astonished to hear Major Elliott say that if he were worth a million dollars he would still prefer to remain in the Army—and to hear others express similar opinions. *I* would prefer the quiet and happiness of a rural home, with my own Jennie, to all the honor and magnificence which the world can afford. I am always glad to hear that you are improving your mind, and taste, by reading some favorite author, but, dear one, I do not read much! Indeed, apart from David Copperfield, I have read nothing this Summer! unless it be the Army & Navy Journal, and an occasional newspaper, and works relating to the profession of arms. The administration of a cavalry company, in the field, is an arduous task, requiring constant, and unintermitted attention, and I can not consent to be second to any one, as you well know, so far as the administration of my command is concerned. I like to feel that every thing that the Government expects of me, or that it has been at all possible to accomplish for the welfare, drill, discipline and efficiency of my command has been accomplished.

If you occasionally see the Army and Navy Journal, you may perhaps have observed that Brevet Captain Leavy has been retired for *insanity*—not incident to the service—and that Tom Custer has been brevetted Lieutenant Colonel for gallantry in action at Sailor's Creek—it was at the time when I broke through the enemy's lines, with my regiment, and captured the wagon train of the Army of Northern Virginia—or 400 wagons of it—and 8 pieces of Artillery &c. &c. It appears, from a conversation that I recently had with Custer, that he was with me on that charge (though I had supposed that only one other officer—Lt. Col.

Birdseye, of the 2nd N.Y. Cavalry, who was present—without a man of his command—had got through the lines, and gave up the train with me. The enemy's line was again closed on the rest of the Division, at that time—and the other regiments of the brigade which charged with me were repulsed. [Tom] Custer was wounded at that time.

Albert to Jennie, camp near Fort Larned, Kan., Aug. 16, 1868:

A courier has just arrived from Fort Harker, bringing word that the Sioux and Cheyennes as is supposed—at all events *Indians*— have broken out again. Col. Benteen has had a skirmish with them on the Saline and been driven back about 12 miles. There is a settlement on the Saline north of Harker which the Indians attacked. Col. Myers has just been ordered to Harker to leave with his company within an hour. This whole command was to march for Walnut Creek tomorrow, but now the movement is postponed, and we will shoe up our horses and await further orders. The weather is very hot but cloudy—*sultry*—last ev'g we had foot races, sack races, wheelbarrow races, hurdle races, horse races, &c. &c.—all the officers & ladies of the Post being here to see—it was quite amusing. I write in great haste . . . mainly to say that from present appearances I fear that it will not be best for you to leave home so as to be in St. Louis on the 10th of Sept. as I have heretofore recommended! Things look a little too unsettled dear!

The Indians had indeed "broken out" again. Agent Wynkoop had issued arms and ammunition to the Cheyennes at Fort Larned on August 9. But several days earlier a war party of about 200 Cheyennes, unaware of the government's decision to lift the arms embargo, had ridden north to raid the Pawnees. En route, for reasons still not entirely clear, they ravaged white settlements on the Saline and Solomon rivers. Between August 10 and 12, they robbed and burned cabins, ran off stock, ravished 5 women, and killed 15 men. Thus the Indian war of 1868–69 burst over the southern plains. For Barnitz it was to be the final episode of his active military career.

11. The Sully Expedition, September 1868

The junior major of the 7th Cavalry, Joel H. Elliott was an able and ambitious young officer. He commanded the regiment in the field during the summer of 1868, while Custer sat out the suspension from duty decreed by court-martial. Elliott died at the Washita, under circumstances that brought criticism of Custer and opened a wound in the regiment that remained unhealed until the Little Bighorn eight years later.

The Cheyenne raids on the Saline and Solomon were followed by others. As summer turned to autumn, war parties continued to strike at settlements and travel routes in western Kansas and eastern Colorado. Generals Sherman and Sheridan planned a winter campaign to punish the offenders in the season when they were most vulnerable. Meantime, the 7th and 10th Cavalry and a company of civilian frontiersmen specially recruited by Maj. George A. Forsyth* (the other Forsyth on Sheridan's staff) marched and countermarched in a largely futile effort to divert the Indians until the onset of winter. The Sully Expedition of September 1868, in which Barnitz participated, was part of this effort.

Albert to Jennie, camp near Fort Larned, Kan., Aug. 19, 1868:

We broke camp yesterday morning and marched to a point about 2 miles below the Post—Larned—and went into a permanent camp, as we supposed—but last night got orders from General Sully—who appears to be up on the Solomon fighting Indians (in his imagination, probably!) to change camp immediately, to a point north or north east of here, on Walnut Creek. . . .

. . . *General Sully is anxious for a war.* N.B. He does his fighting in an ambulance!—N.B. furthermore, I do not believe that any great degree of reputation is to be achieved by fighting these Bedouins of the Plains, and if I run after them very much hereafter, and that voluntarily, it will be because my horses need exercise!

Albert to Jennie, camp on Walnut Creek, Kan., Aug. 27, 1868:

We are ordered to make strenuous efforts to discover Indians, and in the event of our discovering any, we are to utterly destroy them! It is an easy matter to plan this whole thing out, and "organize victory" after a fashion, on paper, but I doubt whether we will accomplish much. Indians are difficult to catch at any time, when in sufficient force to whip them, and I think it is quite as probable that they will manage to catch a few recruits in the mean time.

Albert to Jennie, camp on Walnut Creek, Aug. 31, 1868:

I suppose you will be glad to hear that I have received a commission as Brevet Lieutenant Colonel U.S.A. to rank from March 2, 1867, "for gallant and meritorious services in action at Sailors Creek, Va."

Albert's journal:

Aug. 24, 1868. . . . Decided to day never to drink any intoxicating liquor hereafter with officers or others while in the Army, and I have formed this resolution not because I have been inclined to intemperance at all myself, but because I have witnessed the effects of liquor on others, and am persuaded that it is mentally and physically injurious, in almost every instance, and therefore not to be indulged in even moderately, if one would attain and preserve the best physical and intellectual conditions. Besides, the example of an officer who does not drink at all is much needed in the regiment, and I might almost say in the Army at large! . . .

Aug. 31, 1868. . . . We mustered to day at 1.30 p.m. Just as the command fell in for muster we were surprised to find the whole heavens filled with locusts, or grasshoppers, and the ground, wagons, horses and everything covered with them, they came from the North, or North west. Must have been above the rain clouds, during the heavy rains. What was not a little surprising, too, was that last year on the 31st day of August, just as we were about to muster on the Saline River, north west of here, a cloud of locusts appeared, swarmed over every thing, and for weeks afterwards continued to devour every thing upon which they alighted, even the blouses of the men were in some cases eaten full of holes!

The Sully Expedition formed at Fort Dodge, Kansas. Consisting of more than 500 men in nine troops of the 7th Cavalry under Major Elliott and Captain Page's company of the 3d Infantry, the column crossed the Arkansas River on September 7 and struck south toward the Cimarron River, where the main body of Cheyennes was thought to be located. Barnitz's journal continues:

Sept. 10, 1868. Continued the march 8 miles in a southernly direction, and crossed the Cimarron, where we found Major El-

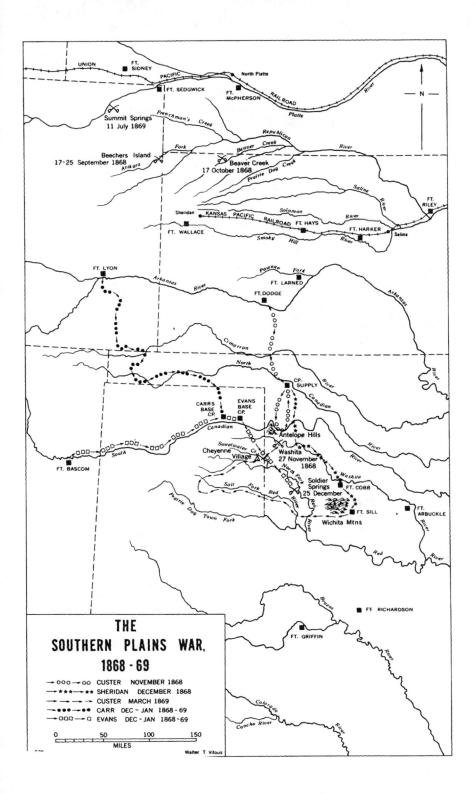

FT. SIDNEY

UNION PACIFIC

FT. SEDGWICK

North Platte

FT. McPHERSON

RAILROAD

Platte

River

N

Summit Springs
11 July 1869

Frenchman's Creek

Republican

Beaver Creek

River

Beechers Island
17-25 September 1868

Arikara

Fork

Beaver Creek
17 October 1868

Prairie Dog Creek

Saline River

FT. RILEY

Sheridan

KANSAS PACIFIC RAILROAD FT. HAYS

Solomon

River

FT. WALLACE

Smoky Hill River

FT. HARKER

Salina

FT. LYON

Arkansas River

Pawnee Fork

FT. LARNED

FT. DODGE

Arkansas

River

Cimarron

North

CP. SUPPLY

River

Canadian

CARRS BASE CP.

EVANS BASE CP.

Canadian

Antelope Hills

Cheyenne Village

Sweetwater Cr.

Washita
27 November
1868

Washita

River

FT. BASCOM

South

Salt Fork

Red River

North Fork

Soldier Springs
25 December

FT. COBB

FT. SILL

FT. ARBUCKLE

Prairie Dog Town Fork

Wichita Mtns

Red River

FT. RICHARDSON

Brazos

FT. GRIFFIN

River

THE
SOUTHERN PLAINS WAR,
1868-69

→ ooo → oo CUSTER   NOVEMBER 1868
→ ★★★ → ★★ SHERIDAN   DECEMBER 1868
→ → → → →   CUSTER   MARCH 1869
→ ●●● → ●● CARR   DEC - JAN 1868-69
→ □□□ → □   EVANS   DEC - JAN 1868-69

0   50   100   150
MILES

Walter T. Vitous

Colorado River

Concho River

liott awaiting us, he having found a trail, leading eastward and then continued the march for a distance of 18 miles, eastward, along the stream, following Indian trail. In the afternoon and evening skirmishes occurred with a small party of Indians. A few men of the company engaged. Grass good all day along the Cimarron. Evidences of many animals having been recently grazed, by the Indians, along the stream.

Sept. 11, 1868. As we were breaking camp this morning, a party of Indians dashed down and captured and carried off on their ponies, at full speed, two men of "F" Troop [Captain Yates's cook and his striker], one of whom, severely wounded, they were obliged to drop in consequence of immediate and vigorous pursuit. With the others they escaped, although pursued a distance of three or four miles. The Indians also succeeded in driving off, at the same time, 3 public horses of "F" Troop, and one private horse, which were not recovered. (James Curran of "F" Troop was the man who was carried off, and not recovered, and John [Alexander] Kennedy was the man wounded, shot through the left lung, and carried off, and subsequently recovered.) Continued the march, skirmishing, 10 miles eastward, along the stream, to deserted Indian village, which was found at point where some stream from the south (or south west) unites with the Cimarron. Here we had an exciting engagement of three or four hours duration, with a force of several hundred Indians, who charged repeatedly, but were as often disconcerted, and driven off, among the bluffs, with apparent loss, bu the superior range and accuracy of our guns.—Continued the march, following Indian trail, and skirmishing constantly for a distance of 14 miles in a south-easternly direction, to North Fork of the Canadian, which we crossed, and then went into camp on the right bank. Camp fired into at night.

Sept. 12, 1868. Continued the march for 2 miles in a direction nearly due east, (bearing a little south) along the right or southern bank of the stream, (which is timbered and contains an abundance of water.) About 11 o'clock, as we approached Wolf Creek, (a timbered tributary of the north fork of the Canadian,) the Indians appeared in force, in our front, and made a vigorous and determined charge on the company, which had the advance, but were repulsed by a volley at close range, (the company acting on foot, and occupying the crest of a ridge,) and dispersed among the sand hills, but soon reappearing in front, and on our flanks, the action became general, and lasted about half, or three quarters of an hour, when the command moved on, skirmishing continually, crossed North Fork of the Canadian, and encamped on the right bank of the stream. Camp fired into at night.

Sept. 13, 1868. Continued the march for 20 miles in an easternly direction, to the middle fork of the Canadian, when crossing the stream, and becoming involved in the Sand Hills, the fighting, which had been kept up all day, became more determined on the part of the Indians: Private Cyrus W. Corbet, of "F" Troop was here killed: Train unable to proceed: Command recrossed the stream, and marched 3 miles in a northern direction, and encamped on the North Fork of the Canadian.

Sept. 14, 1868. Command crossed North Fork of the Canadian, and continued the march 20 miles in a northernly direction through a mountainous, beautiful country: The Indians continually harrassing our rear for 10 miles of the march, until we had arrived on the summit of a mountain, when the Indians made a great smoke, on a summit in our rear, assembled their forces and apparently withdrew. Encamped this evening on right (south) bank of Buffalo Creek, a wide, shallow stream which flows eastward through red earth and sand, amid bluffs composed of gypsum.

Sept. 15, 1868. A man of "I" Troop was mortally wounded on picket last night. Continued the march 8 miles in a direction N. 10° W. to the Cimarroon, which here flows through a sandy channel a mile wide, though the stream is only a few yards wide at present. It is bordered by grand bluffs of gypsum. A few Indians appeared as the last files were descending from the bluffs to the stream, and some shots were exchanged when the Indians withdrew. Having crossed the Cimarron, our course (still N. 10° W.) lay for 3 miles among sand hills, covered with wild sage, and then 21 miles along high "divides," through an exceedingly broken, red earth country, abounding with grass, and also with buffalo,

many of which we killed. We encamped in the evening on some
unknown stream, which flows S.E. and contains at present but
little water and much sand.

Albert to Jennie, camp on Bluff Creek, 45 miles southeast of Fort
Dodge, Kan., Sept. 16, 1868:

I know how anxious you are to hear from me, and upon no
other consideration could I be induced to write to you at
present!—for all day yesterday we marched northward over a
mountainous country—or constantly on the high "divides" or
ridges of a mountain, (scarred every where with deep gullies and
ravines, with myriads of buffalo grazing on the summits) and
under a cloudy drizzly sky, with a cold wind blowing in our faces,
without any cessation from day break till dark, when we reached
this stream, (a tributary of the Cimarron—which flows eastward,
and empties into the Arkansas) and encamped. We found some
scattering trees here, and are keeping large fires, but the cold
wind continued all night, and is still blowing, and it is almost
impossible to keep warm. So it is difficult to sit in a little "A" Tent
and write letters—giving, at the same time, directions about estimates for clothing, ammunition, lariat ropes, horses &c. &c. which
must go off at once, by the same courier who takes this. I suppose
we are having a touch of the equinoxial storm at present, and
that after it is over we will have pleasant weather again.

When I last wrote you on the 7th from camp north of Fort
Dodge, we were just starting southward after the Indians. Immediately after finishing my letter we mounted, marched 7 miles
to Fort Dodge and were there joined by "B," "C," & "K" Troops 7th
Cav. ("L" did *not* join us) and "F" Company (Brevet Major [John
H.] Page, and "Tommy" Wallace) 3d Inf., with a little howitzer—a
supply train of about 30 wagons also joined us, and the whole
force, under Genl. Sully (Lieut. Col. 3d Inf.) moved across the
Arkansas, and marched 35 miles that night in a South Westerly
direction. Genl. Sheridan witnessed the crossing of the river, and
saluted us all as we passed, and was undoubtedly very anxious to
accompany us, but was compelled to remain behind to attend to
other duties. (He is still at Dodge, we presume, awaiting tidings
from us.) Well, we continued to push on, in the direction we had

started, day after day, until we had crossed the Cimarroon when the trails of Indians began to grow distinct, and numerous, and at length, on the 10th inst. a party of our buffalo hunters were fired into, and quite a lively chase of the Indians ensued, and thereafter we had daily and constant fighting, in front and on our flanks and rear, as we moved onward on the trails of their teepes, making about 25 miles a day until the evening of Sunday the 13th inst. when having followed the trails and Indians into the Sand Hills between the middle and south Fork of the Canadian River, it was impossible to move the train further, and after consultation Genl. Sully determined to move back to this point (65 miles to the north or north east—toward Fort Dodge) and send in to that point for additional troops, and supplies for say *two months*, and a pack train, and then return and follow the Indians into the Wichita Mountains, to which point they will doubtless retreat, after a protracted fight in the sand hills. The Sand Hills cover a tract probably 10 miles square, and are coarse sand, overgrown with wild sage (which is a shrub which grows in bunches about two or three feet high) and bunch grass—and there are occasional clumps of wild plumb bushes, and even stunted cottonwood trees growing through these sand hills. The Hills afford an admirable field for the display of an Indian's resources of strategy! I only wish you could witness the Indian mode of fighting; it really is amusing sometimes! The Indians maneuver so much like wolves! They always ride at full speed, whooping, and with their tall war bonnets (of feathers) careening from right to left, like the mast of a ship in a storm, and they are no sooner driven from one sand hill, than they pop up on another, always passing around its base, and ascending it from the far side, and always watching for a chance to make a dash, and cut off some straggler, or drive through some thin part of a line! One morning, just as we were breaking camp, a party dashed down suddenly and cut off two men of "F" Troop, and 4 horses and were off like a flash, carrying off the men—whom they had wounded—on their ponies—a vigorous and immediate pursuit forced them to drop one of the men, who although badly wounded will probably recover, but the other could not be rescued, and if he lived long enough they doubtless had a war dance around and tortured him to death. The horses were not recovered. On the 13th another man of "F" Troop was killed. I was directed to advance directly through the sand hills, and had forded a stream and gone forward some distance, when "F" Troop was directed to cross and advance as skirmishers, dismounted. I was moving forward a skirmish line mounted with a platoon in reserve, and had dislodged the Indians from several hills in my front, when they at length, about a hundred of them, occupied a hill on my right, and a little to my rear, and made a stand and succeeded in killing the man I have mentioned, besides inflicting some other damage, until a cross fire from my skirmishers hurried them out of their position. Some of the sand hills are shaped like inverted tea cups, having depressions on top sufficient to screen the Indians and their ponies from a fire in any direction. We do not know exactly how many Indians we have killed or wounded, but probably not less than 10 or 15 have been killed, and twice as many wounded. One morning, as I was in advance, about 15 or so Indians made a desperate charge on my company, or rather perhaps on myself, as I had gone to the top of a sand hill in advance, but I quietly rode back, dismounted my company, and moved the men to the crest of the sand hill, and did not allow them to expose themselves until the Indians were ascending the hill and in point blank range, when I rode back over the crest of the ridge to induce the Indians to follow me, and gave the word "ready! aim! fire!" and there was a lively tumbling among the Indians!—but as they all clung to their ponies—or were fastened to them they were carried swiftly around a sand hill, out of view—but we shortly afterwards killed two that we know of, and one pony. A man of "E" Troop [Pvt. C. H. Tares] was seriously wounded on the 12th, a man of "I" Troop [Pvt. Charles Kreiger] was mortally wounded by an accident night before last—or rather yesterday morning at daybreak—shot by one of his party on picket, he having carelessly gone to the front, and been mistaken for an Indian. He died last night, and has just been buried. Our route has been through a diversified country, and in some places the scenery has been truly sublime. We have been in the Indian Territory, and below the north western line of Texas—probably *in* Texas for a short time. We killed not less than 75 buffaloes yesterday, and last evening there was a general feast on fat buffalo humps, tongues, and marrow bones! When we started northward the Indians followed us fighting constantly until day before yesterday afternoon, when finding that we were really giving up the pursuit of their families they built a large fire on the summit of a mountainous hill, and collected together their forces, and returned, as was supposed, to the sand hills,—but yesterday, when crossing the Cimarroon, (a shallow stream, which flows through a sandy channel half a mile wide, between tall bluffs of pure gypsum) a party of 7 Indians made a dash upon some stragglers, who fortunately looked around and discovered them in time to act on the defensive, and the Indians were driven off. I saw yesterday a grove of summack trees some of which were two feet in diameter. You know the summack is usually a shrub, about one *inch* in diameter. The summits of the hills which we traversed yesterday abound in places with sea shells, and the old red sand stone, and quartz rock, and petrified wood.

General Sully goes in to Fort Dodge tomorrow, with the train, for supplies. If this campaign is prosecuted, it will occupy two months, I suppose, and maybe even longer, so there is no prospect of our seeing one another for a long time, is there dear!

I do not mind the hardships of the campaign though I know they will not be slight, nor the danger to be incurred, but oh, I do grieve to endure this cruel separation. But, dear, I have two or three books with me, and some papers and magazines will probably reach us from Dodge, and I will try to bear with patience and fortitude the *unmitigated* evil of a protracted campaign. My men have behaved splendidly, under some trying circumstances of late, and now the care and patience which I took and endured last winter, and summer in their instruction begins to be rewarded. I can go with my company almost anywhere. All the hostile Indians, it is thought, or nearly all, have been assembled below to protect their villages, and we will doubtless find their trails, without difficulty when we return.

12. Winter Campaign, September–November 1868

Before the Washita. This picture was taken in camp near Fort Dodge, Kansas, in the fall of 1868 shortly before the 7th Cavalry marched for the Washita. Officers identified by Barnitz are himself (fourth from left, seated), Major Elliott (sixth), General Custer (eighth, with dog), and Lieutenants Bell (last, with dog), Robbins (seventh, second row), Cooke (eleventh), and Hale (twelfth).

The troops of the Sully Expedition, Major Elliott now commanding, re-
mained in camp on Bluff Creek until September 23, then marched
eighteen miles to the northwest and, on the twenty-fourth, laid out a new
camp on a stream known as Cavalry Creek. For more than a month, while
General Sheridan tried to get his winter campaign organized, the 7th
Cavalry operated from bases at various locations on Cavalry Creek.

Albert to Jennie, camp on Bluff Creek, Kan., Sept. 22, 1868:

A supply train—containing only partial supplies however, arrived from Fort Dodge to day escorted by a troop of colored
cavalry, bringing the mail—only a small mail though, and word
that Genl. Gibbs is at Dodge—"sick"—with [Adjutant] Myles
Moylan, and that when he recovers he will come on, and take
command of his regiment! I am not at all anxious to see him. He
will go with us a few days, until the weather begins to grow very
disagreeable, or hardships rather in excess of what were anticipated, and then it will take a least a squadron of cavalry to escort
the old gentleman back to Fort Dodge. . . .

And you are glad to know that I have given up tobacco! Yes, it is
really so dear. I have not smoked at all for upwards of a month—
about six weeks, I believe, and have not tasted tobacco since
sometime in May, and I do not taste any kind of liquor, just
because I know that it will be gratifying to you, dear, more
perhaps than for any other reason,—and yet my own judgment is
rather in favor of this course—and more especially in the army.
Only think, dear, the Suttler sold (6) *six barrels of whiskey,* besides a
quantity of wine, and other liquor between the time of our leaving
the camp on Walnut Creek, and arrival here!—and most of that to
officers, too,—as the men could not get any without a special
order! Of course, there is a good deal of happiness in six barrels
of whiskey, and some of the officers were very happy a good deal
of the time! This had one result, of which you may not be pleased
to hear—whenever anything looked serious at the front or on
either flank or in rear, my company was always ordered immediately to that point! I considered it complimentary, of course,
and yet it was sometimes not a little amusing. I had the advance in
the sand hills, and when I saw the train going into "park" away in

the rear, I sent word to Genl. Sully that I could easily advance, and was quite mortified to find that it was determined to retreat "for rations" as it was said—though we had enough to last us till the end of this month—of everything except forage, and I was very sanguine, from all indications, that within two or three days more we should have overhauled their villages, and ended the campaign—whereas to retire then was only to protract the matter and render it more tedious as well as difficult.

Albert to Jennie, camp on Cavalry Creek, Kan., Sept. 27, 1868:

Capt. Weir comes on to take command of his company—"D"— that hitherto commanded by Lieut. Robbins—(who *always* wishes to be remembered to you—and who always insists that you are to select a wife for him!) By the way, did you hear that Capt. Weir had unaccountably lost all his hair last Summer? Fact! He wore a wig for a long time, but his hair is now growing out again nicely. . . . I am rather glad to see Weir here. He is very well read, and social in his disposition. He brings some news of interest to us, shut out as we are here from communication with the outer world—some sad news too—though you may have had fuller details through the newspapers. He says that "Sandy" (Colonel) Forsyth's company of scouts—Kansas Volunteers—was attacked one morning some where north of Fort Wallace, and a number of the scouts were killed, and many others wounded. Lieut. Beecher of the 3d Infantry was wounded in seven places—mortally—a second dispatch to General Sheridan stating that he was dead. He was at Wallace last summer, and I thought a great deal of him. He was a nephew of Henry Ward Beecher, was lame, having been wounded at Gettysburg. Col. Forsyth was also severely wounded in the engagement, and his recovery, it is said, is doubtful. He had one thigh broken, and the other wounded. A number of Indians were killed in the fight, it is reported—11 bodies, I believe, falling into the hands of our troops.

Barnitz refers to the Battle of Beecher's Island, which occurred on the Arikara Fork of the Republican River in eastern Colorado. On September 17, 1868, Forsyth's scouts (not Kansas Volunteers) were attacked by 600–700 Cheyenne Dog Soldiers and Sioux led by Bull Bear, Tall Bull, White Horse, and Pawnee Killer. The whites took refuge on a small island

and withstood several mass charges followed by a week-long siege. Half were killed or wounded, including Lieutenant Beecher and Surgeon John H. Mooers killed and Forsyth badly wounded. The Indians withdrew on September 25 upon the approach of a relief column from Fort Wallace. Here, rather than in Barnitz's fight near Fort Wallace the year before, the famed Cheyenne warrior Roman Nose was killed. Barnitz's letter of September 27 continues:

The weather is *delightful* here now. The days are tranquil and hazy, and just warm enough, and not too warm. I fear that the weather is *too* delightful to continue so, long! We have a beautiful camp, amid timbered streams. We kill numerous buffalo every day. They are now fat. I wish I could send Pa a present of two or three! Some of them are of *enormous* size! Yesterday a party of men of "I" Troop found a flock of wild turkeys near here and shot 11 of them, and afterwards Serg't Harris went down and shot three, and sent one to me. I had it nicely roasted for dinner, it was young, and very tender. I shot a couple of sage hens just close to camp—they are much like prairie chickens. Will have one roasted tomorrow. Had raccoon for breakfast! . . . The groves along the stream are well filled with turkeys. I have an excellent cook now—and a little mess chest—which however I may not be able to take along on a màrch, if transportation is limited. . . . I hope that the campaign may be prosecuted vigorously now, and that we may keep on until we really accomplish something. I am not at all satisfied to lead this kind of life forever. I wish either peace or else war, and if war, then I am in favor of the most vigorous and persistent measures until the Indians are so thoroughly whipped, and killed off that they will be glad to remain at peace for our generation, at least!

Albert to Jennie, camp on Cavalry Creek, Kan., Sept. 30, 1868:

On the 17th day of the month, when at our first camp of repose, after the Indians had ceased to hover upon our horizon, Captains Thompson & [Lee P.] Gillette* and Lieutenant Nowlan & Brevet Major Bell got permission to go in with the train to Fort Dodge, and subsequently Lieuts. Wallingford & Berry—only Capt. Gillette & Lieut. Wallingford have as yet returned. The others seem to have become attached to the Post, and doubtless find it very pleasant to remain there. Lieuts. Robbins & Custer have permission to go in with the train in the morning—it will start at daybreak. Lieut. [H. W.] Smith—'"Salty" has been sent on there to take charge of disabled horses &c. He has generally been in arrest all summer and fall—he was seldom out of arrest more than two or three days before he was in again! He says being in arrest appears to be his normal condition! Nearly all the dwellers at Fort Larned are now at Dodge,—including the charming widow Scott!—I believe that several of the officers of the regiment were or are more than half in love with her! Captain Gillette 7th Cav. has a wife—a very pleasant, rather good looking woman, and two or three children at Dodge.

Albert to Jennie, camp on Cavalry Creek, Kan., Oct. 18, 1868:

On last Saturday a week ago General Custer arrived (with his hair cut short, and a perfect managarie of Scotch fox hounds!) bringing H & M Troops (Col. Benteen & Lt. Hale & Cook[e]) and on the very evening of his arrival sent out three columns in search of Indian encampments! He appeared to think that because his arrival here was immediately succeeded by an Indian attack, on a small scale (which resulted in the untimely death of an Indian pony,) and because we had had a considerable skirmish the day before with a party of about 75 Indians, who had got after Capt. Brewster, while out riding alone, and had run him into camp, (and whom we subsequently chased for about 15 miles,) that therefore Indians were plentiful hereabouts, and could easily be found! But none of the columns succeeded in finding any Indians, and so on last Monday Genl. Custer broke camp here, and marched with the whole command for Medicine Lodge Creek, which we followed for a distance of 60 miles without finding any very recent traces of Indians but found a lodge—a big "medicine lodge" 60 feet in diameter and perhaps 40 feet high, containing 30 scalps and numerous trophies, which we brought away and burned the lodge—also captured 4 ponies, we then—rather my troop & E & I Troops—marched northward 30 miles to Rattlesnake Creek, and for a distance of 30 miles along the stream, and then returned to the encampment of the regiment, when the whole command returned to this camp, arriving here this afternoon. We have been almost constantly in the saddle since leaving here. We habitually arose at 4 a.m. and marched at 6 a.m. while it was still a little dark. I am really tired—very tired this evening, and do not feel at all like writing, and yet I must write hasty letters to my mother and others—as the train & escort will start in to Fort Dodge at 4 a.m. tomorrow, for supplies, and will take in the mail. On the return of the train—say in 4 days—we will march on the long contemplated expedition toward the Wichitaw Mountains, and the sand hills, and will in all probability see a great many Indians before we return. Some of us may never return, but as you say the Good Man is regardful of us here as elsewhere!—but I am not a believer in special dispensations of goodness you know, and doubt not that the supreme being is just as careful for our welfare as he is for that of a blade of buffalo grass—and no more! I don't know but that it might be a slight satisfaction to believe as you do that the Good Man is particularly concerned about us, but I don't, nevertheless! . . .

We will take a large supply train with us, and may be gone a long time, and may be I will not have an opportunity to send another letter to you, after this one, until we return. It is whispered dear, that we will not be expected to accomplish much against our red brethren further than, by keeping them constantly on the move, to wear down their ponies, until March, and that then we will proceed against them in earnest! How do you like the prospect? I do not like it. I try to bear all calamities with fortitude, but to be deprived of your society through all the dreary months of the ensuing winter is a calamity which I know not how to endure with any patience. . . .

I have a new 2nd Lieutenant, whom you will probably like,—he is a graduate of West Point, and a native of Chester County Pa. His name is Thomas J. March.* He appears to be a young man of good habits—neither drinks, smokes nor chews. Appears to be zealously devoted to his profession and anxious to learn, and withal to have good common sense, more than I can say of some graduates of West Point whom I have seen! . . .

The Indians made their appearance here as we were leaving this camp for Medicine Lodge Creek, and charged on our rear guard, which resulted in their having one of their ponies killed— and the saddle and equipment, blankets, a shield &c fell into our hands. The Indians also dropped two fine revolvers in their flight, one of which I got, and one of my men got the other. Genl. Custer's dogs caught & killed a wolf to day as we were coming into camp.

Generals Sherman, Sheridan, and Sully had united in an appeal for the remission of the remaining weeks of Custer's sentence in order that he might participate in the coming campaign. He assumed command of the regiment on October 10 at the camp on Cavalry Creek.

Sheridan's plans were by now well advanced, even though logistical problems delayed their execution. Old Fort Cobb, deep in Indian Territory, had been reactivated as agency for the tribes that wanted to accept the reservations set aside in the Medicine Lodge treaties and remain at peace. Bvt. Maj. Gen. William B. Hazen was appointed military agent at Fort Cobb. All Indians not associated with Hazen's agency were to be regarded as hostile. Against these Sheridan would make war. He organized three columns to converge on the area west of Fort Cobb where the hostiles were thought to be laying out their winter camps. One would come east from Fort Bascom, New Mexico, one southeast from Fort Lyon, Colorado, and the third and largest south from Fort Dodge, Kansas.

Albert to Jennie, camp on Cavalry Creek, Kan., Oct. 21, 1868:

A small train arrived this evening from Fort Dodge, bringing some rations, and the mail. We have been on half rations for several days, and fully expected a large train, with at least a month's supplies this evening, but were disappointed. There are no supplies at Fort Dodge, and so the Expedition must be postponed until they arrive! Isn't it really disheartening! We must break camp at daylight tomorrow morning, and march back to the vicinity of Fort Dodge, to await the arrival of rations, and other supplies, and then we will have to march back here again, of course, on our way to the Indian country. It is really a pity that we are so excessively economical in this Department! Rations and all manner of supplies sufficient to last a force of this size for six months, at least, should have been stored at a post like Fort Dodge, at all times, but false notions of economy would not permit the keeping of an ounce of any thing on hand, in excess of the current want of the garrison, and now we see the result! An Expedition of some magnitude is indeffinitely delayed, and an opportunity afforded for the Tribes to form additional alliances, and finally we will get started I suppose in a season when operations will be exceedingly difficult, and *costly* to the Government, and so in the end all these strenuous efforts for "economy" will have availed nothing, and on the contrary will have only been productive of harm.

On October 22–23, because of the supply shortage, the 7th Cavalry marched back to Fort Dodge and went into camp twelve miles below the post, on the south bank of the Arkansas River.

Albert to Jennie, camp near Fort Dodge, Kan., Oct. 28, 1868:

Day before yesterday a party of Indians made a dash upon some animals lariated in the vicinity of Fort Dodge, and succeeded in stampeding and driving off a few horses and ponies, besides doing some other damage, whereupon General Sully wrote a personal letter to Genl. Custer telling him that they *"didn't feel safe* at the Post, without some cavalry" and requested that a Troop should be sent up "to protect them!" It is really amusing, isn't it?—when you reflect that there are *seven companies* of Infantry here, armed with the finest guns in the world, and having in their possession, in addition to their ordinary arms, 3 or 4 pieces of Artillery, with men detailed to operate them! General Custer says that he is going to hold onto the letter, to show, if there is any dispute about it, i.e. that the cavalry was wanted here to *"protect"* the Infantry! Well, I was sent up yesterday with my Troop, to protect them, and here I am, encamped about 3/4 of a mile below the Post. It has been arranged with General Sully that I am not to report to either the commanding officer of the Post, Major Douglass (3d Infantry) nor to the commanding officer of the Infantry camp near the Post, Brevet Major Page, 3d Inf. but am to be entirely independent, and use my own judgment in all cases. I expect to be stationed here until the expedition starts, and will then accompany it, in command of a squadron composed of "G" & "L" Troops—"L" Troop is soon to arrive here from Puebla. It is Col. Sheridan's Troop. A change was recently made in the composition of the squadrons, so that "I" Troop was put into another squadron. To day it is very windy, and I have seen no Indians yet,

and suppose that they will hardly make their appearance until the
wind subsides, as they cannot shoot their arrows with much accuracy except when the air is comparatively still.

The Indians who approached nearest the Post the other day
were all *little boys*—only 8 or 10 years of age it appears!—A large
band of warriors, however, was collected in the hills, in rear of the
Post, watching them, and ready to make a descent if they had been
closely pursued. One of the boys, a son of "Big Mouth" a noted
chief, was wounded by "Romeo" a half-breed Arapahoe boy who
is acting as guide and scout, and who recognized many of the
Indians in the attacking party. Romeo's horse was wounded—in
the encounter, and he himself made a narrow escape, as his horse
fell just as he reached a point from which he was covered by the
fire of the Infantry. . . .

Genl. Gibbs is expected here from Harker with a detachment of
150 recruits for the 7th Cavalry in a few days. I become very much
exasperated occasionally, when I think of the old gentleman, and
wish him all manner of unhappiness! . . .

. . . Concerning all the other columns of cooperation there
may be some doubt, but there appears to be no doubt whatever
that *we* are to go down at the appointed time, and spend the
winter in harrassing the Indians, and in operations calculated to
wear down their ponies, so that in the spring—say in March, when
their ponies are poorest, we can easily overtake them, and their
"villages" and teach them such lesson as they will not be likely to
forget soon! However the President of the society for the preven-
tion of cruelty to animals might regard the matter, I do not think
that any mercy will be shown to the Indians when we overtake
them! If we fall into their hands, we expect to be tortured to
death, and any that fall into our hands may expect to die very
speedily. . . .

I suppose you are anxious to know who are at the Post. Well,
there is Lieut. Stouch, 3d Inf. & A.A.Q.M., and wife—Major
Douglass, Lieut. "Tommy" Wallace, Capt. [William] Mitchell, all
of the 3d Infantry, and also [Bvt.] Maj. [and Capt. William M.]
Beebe [38th Infantry] and several others whom you do not know.
Lieut. Wallingford & family, and Capt. Gillette & family are also
here, Wallingford and Gillette having received permission to

come up here and remain because their families are here. So much for being stationed at a little western Post! Lieut. Wallingford's babe died day before yesterday, and was buried yesterday. Capt. Gillette and Major Beebe are confirmed inebriates, and the same may be said of Col. Keogh—they are seldom sober. The same is true of Col. West. He was drunk all the time that we were on the late expedition, and had to be hauled in an ambulance. He has been drunk for a week past, and having become sick in consequence, was sent up here, by the surgeon for medical treatment! I might name a good many others who are addicted to intemperance!—Sam Robbins and "Salty" Smith are not always duly sober, and Captain Hamilton winks with unusual rapidity at times!—I cannot say that I ever know him to be more seriously affected by liquor. Brevet Major Asbury 3d Inf. who is here, is drunk nearly all the time! The fact is Jennie, there appears to be a premium offered for drunkenness in the army! Almost *all* the old officers drink a great deal. Indeed I do not know any one except General Hoffman who does not, more or less, and a man is not regarded as sociable who does not keep a sort of open house and have something for his friends to drink, and he has a very small chance of becoming popular with the drinking class, unless he indulges a little himself—in fact, they are rather inclined to regard him with some distrust, I think, as one who may be intolerant of their vices!—At all events, I have observed that about nine out of every ten of those who are selected for staff duty are of the drinking class, and as a consequence are most sociable with those who drink and are always ready to lend their influence to have good companionable fellows selected to fill any position that may become vacant on the staff! What I deduce from all this is, that I am never likely to be selected for any staff duty, but will have the pleasure of riding about on these plains so long as there is an Indian left to cause a feeling of uneasiness along the borders. If that is any consolation, dear, why you may as well avail yourself of it!

I can not conceal from you that I do become dreadfully discouraged. Not because of the hardships which I endure, and dangers which I undergo, but because of the necessity of being forever separated from you. I dare not tell you how unhappy I am at times, when I think of the dreary prospect. All my philosophy is of no avail, and my only relief is in tears. The companionship of those about me is irksome to me, and I long, oh, with an *unutterable* longing for the society of my own, dear wife! So wretched do I become, at times, in spite of all efforts to prevent it, that I could wish to die, if it were not a selfish wish.

By early November the Fort Dodge column had begun to take shape. It was to consist of eleven troops of the 7th Cavalry under Custer (actually twelve, for Lieutenant Cooke organized a company of picked marksmen as "sharpshooters"), five companies of infantry under Captain Page (three of the 3d, one of the 5th, and one of the 38th), and the 19th Kansas Volunteer Cavalry commanded by Col. Samuel J. Crawford, who had left the governor's chair to take the field. Major Inman had charge of the train of 450 wagons. The infantry was to build and man a supply depot on the Canadian River to serve as a base for cavalry operations. As district commander, General Sully commanded the expedition. Although the Kansans had not yet appeared, he set forth for the Canadian on November 12.

Albert's journal:

Nov. 10, 1868. General Custer is requiring all the company commanders to exchange horses, so as to secure a uniformity of colors in each company. I have bitterly opposed the scheme, but must comply I suppose. All my old horses were well trained, and very carefully trained, and the men were much attached to them, and now, just as we are to march on the campaign, every thing is to be turned topsy turvy!—There is much dissatisfaction among the men, in consequence which will result in numerous desertions hereafter. Had the change not been insisted upon until after the campaign, and just as we were going into garrison, it would have been far better. I am to have chestnut colored horses, Col. Myers Greys, Col Weir Blacks, Capt. Hamilton Browns, Capt. Gillette Sorrels &c.

Have received 13 recruits (of whom 12 are here) and 6 attached men of L Troop of whom 5 are here, to day. Have received 17 new horses, and been required to transfer 7 Greys to Col. Myers—2 sorrels to Col West, 3 do [ditto] to Capt. Gillette and 3 do to Capt Brewster—total 15.

Nov. 11, 1868. Wrote Jennie two letters to day, and sent her an extract from a paper. We march tomorrow morning on the long contemplated expedition against the Indians. The train moved over the river to day, 5 companies of Infantry are with it. The weather has become settled once more, and quite pleasant. General Sully, who is to have command of the expedition arrived from Fort Dodge this evening. Genl. Sheridan was expected but was unable to come. Will probably join us on the Canadian.

Nov. 12, 1868. The command broke camp this morning, crossed the Arkansas, and marched nearly 5 miles in direction a little east of south, to Mulberry Creek, where it encamped, without grass but at a point where there are wood and water, at 10.30 a.m. I lost my Remington pistol, Breech-Loader, on the march. Will go back in the morning to look for it. General Custer has ordered that all my chestnut colored horses I have in all, shall be placed upon one end of my picket lines, and shall all be formed together at the head of the column on a march! This will necessitate the breaking up of the squads, as at present organized, or necessitate a reissue of my horses, and will cause renewed dissatisfaction. Drew overshoes & gloves this evg. Am detailed as commander of the advanced guard tomorrow—my own troop to form the advance. Have felt very indignant and provoked all evening in consequence of General Custer's *foolish, unwarranted, unjustifiable* order with regard to the new horses, which will necessitate the placing of them all together, whereas they should be scattered among the old horses, and in the front rank, (as well as rear rank) where no recruit nor uninstructed horse ought to be! I could write objections by the page, such as only an experienced company commander can fully understand, had I time, but it is sufficient to say that I am thoroughly *disgusted* and *disheartened.*

> "Let school taught pride dissemble all it can
> These little things are great to little man!"

Nov. 13, 1868. I rode back about 3½ or 4 miles this morning to look for my pistol, but did not find it. Saw great droves of wolves prowling about our old camp, howling dismally. Had command of the advanced guard to day, and am field officer of the day,—my own company and B Company (which was rear guard to day) furnishing the pickets. Our course to day was at first south east, for perhaps 10 or 15 miles, and then due south. . . . We are encamped on one of the branches of bluff creek. When nearing the creek we saw some herds of buffalo in the distance, and our Osages & guides put off in pursuit, and some killed three or four. As I rode along I came to a small hackberry tree, in the branches of which I found some fine pieces of meat, attached to which was a small paper bearing the legend—

"Col. Barnet, G Troop
Capt. Barry (Berry) "C" Troop
California Jo"

—from all of which I inferred that "California Jo" [Moses Milner*] one of our scouts, had placed the meat there, (where he thought it would attract my observation as I came along,) with his compliments, which I afterwards found to be the case.

Nov. 15, 1868. Camp on the Cimarron. We marched 10½ miles today in a direction about due south, or perhaps one or two degrees east of south, crossed the Cimarron, where there was some quicksand, and went into camp on its right bank. Sand hills south of the stream. Water quite salty. Had conflict with McGinness, which resulted in his being "squelched," and being tied up, and afterward sent to the guard house. He was mutinous, and mean as usual. As we approached the Cimarron some small herds of buffalo were seen in the distance. General Custer and the guides set off in pursuit. On going into camp General Custer came in with 12 quarters strapped upon the horses. The General gave me a very fine hind quarter of a young cow.

Nov. 19, 1868. . . . Here, as General Sully announces (see Genl Field orders No 8) a camp of supply for the troops operating south of the Arkansas is to be located, and until further orders it is to be designated "Camp Supply."* A log structure is to be erected here for the protection of the Infantry about 150 men, who are to remain here, and as a magazine for supplies, while two columns of Cavalry, one (comprising 11 companies of the 7th Cavalry) under Genl. Custer, and the other (comprising 10 companies of the 19th Kansas Vol. Cav.) under Col (Governor) Crawford are to march southward, with 25 or 30 days supplies, to punish the Indians. This is the programme as set forth in General Field Orders No 10 of this date from Hd. Qrs. Dist. of the Upper Arkansas. . . .

A large number of hospital tents erected. Well begun, and dug 10 or 12 feet, to quicksand, on site of new Post. Maj. Inman begins to unload his vast supply of axes, spades, shovels, grindstones, doors and casings, window casings sashes, boards &c &c—a large pile of paulines being among the latter. The Osages look on in wonder—Lieut. Jackson smoking a ponderous meershaum, and seeming to reflect deeply, and with great solemnity, as he superintends the construction of a sod chimney for Major Inman's tent! The Infantry have cut 600 logs to day, and the mowing machines have done well. The prospects are that we will be obliged to stay here for a couple of weeks, before we will be allowed to go, for the Infantry have no idea of being left "unprotected" before the new Post is completed. Our Osages have discovered a trail, leading northward, which has recently been traversed by a war party of 4 or 500 Indians, and General Custer has applied for permission to leave two companies of Cavalry here to "protect" the Infantry, while he follows down the Indian trail in search of their villages! His request will scarcely be complied with. . . .

Nov. 20, 1868. Hitherto I have refused for several months to sign any "whiskey orders" as they are called (permits for the men to purchase whiskey from the Camp Trader) but having been so frequently importuned of late by both privates and non-commissioned officers of the company for permits, and finding that by some means they obtain whiskey at any rate, probably by inducing acquaintances in other companies to procure permits for themselves from *their* officers, and get the whiskey and then paying them for it at a great advance on its cost, I have therefore endeavored to reconcile matters in some way so that the temperate men of the company may not be entirely debarred from the privilege of paying the Trader $12 a galon for an inferior article of whiskey, while at the same time the intemperate men will be restrained from excesses, and all will feel an interest proportionate to their love for the "inebriating drink" to preserve a proper state of sobriety in the Troop. I have agreed to sign a permit for *not to exceed one quart per day* for *each squad*, making one galon for the entire company. The chiefs of squads are to hand in on a slip of paper before guard mounting the names of all the men of their squads who wish whiskey, and the amount required. I then write one order for the entire amount, and after the order, or permit, has been approved by General Custer one non-commissioned officer selected by the chiefs of squads, goes to the Trader with the money (contributed pro rata by the men concerned,) and procures (in four canteens) the entire amount. This arrangement is intended to prevent the counterfeiting of orders, or permits, as only one will be signed per day, and that never for more than a galon, and I know just what men obtain the liquor. In case any man becomes intoxicated, he will not be permitted to have any more liquor during the present year, and no permit will be signed for the squad to which he belongs for 10 days. I think that the tendency of this arrangement will be to restrain men from excesses, or at least if it does not accomplish this, the allowance will be diminished or shut off entirely.

This evening Major Elliott and Genl. Custer had all the chestnut colored horses that could be found in any of the Troops led out and allowed me to exchange other horses for them, provided I could match the color of the company to which the horse belonged. I got eight of my own color—chestnut.

The foundation logs of Fort Beecher laid to day—went down and sat on a log and talked with General Sully concerning the contemplated structure. He told me of how one of the Osage Indians to day had kicked and spit at, and cursed, in his own tongue, a small whirlwind which came by from the north, and which he (the Osage) believed to be the ghost of one of the Arapaho warriors who went northward three or four days ago, and who has been killed; the ghost being, as the Osage said, on his way south to the Arapaho village, to inform his relatives of the fact of his death.

Albert to Jennie, Camp Supply, Indian Territory, Nov. 21, 1868:

I wrote you a *very* hasty letter this afternoon . . . and handed it to Bradley, the scout, as he sat upon his horse, waiting, while a detachment of 150 mounted men were moving out to escort him 40 miles on his way toward Fort Dodge to night. He had just deposited the letter carefully in the pocket of his hunting shirt, when a cloud of dust was discovered some miles away to the westward, and at the same time the picket reported a wagon train approaching, and presently Col. Moore of Genl. Sheridan's staff arrived, and reported the General and General Forsyth, Surgeon [Morris J.] Asch, Col. [Andrew J.] McGonnigle, Col. Crosby &c &c just behind, escorted by a squadron of the 19th Kansas Vol. Cav!

Judge of our surprise! We had expected that Genl. Sheridan would come down, but not so soon. We expected the Kansas companies from Dodge to come down escorting additional supplies, which it appears they have not done. Well, of course the letter previously written (it was written in General Sully's tent, on the instant that I learned that a scout was in readiness to start, and while he was at the door, readjusting his saddle,) did not go out . . . .

Shortly after dark this evening Officers Call sounded at General Custer's quarters, and he informed us that he was going down presently to make an informal call upon General Sheridan, and requested all the officers who desired to do so to accompany him, stating that he was going to take the Band along, and give the General some music. . . .

Well, we all went up and called upon General Sheridan. He received us in his good, genial way, shaking hands with all, and seemed well pleased to see us. He received us in the open air, around a big camp fire. Like Grant, Sheridan is a man of few words, but he always *looks* very animated, and although he really does not say much, you come away with the impression that you have had quite a prolonged and interesting conversation with him! He evidently is a little disappointed with our failure to meet with Indians; and perhaps he would have preferred that General Sully should have allowed us to proceed at once in search of the Indians, upon our arrival here, instead of delaying to aid and protect the Infantry while they are constructing sort of a permanent fortification for their own security and comfort, quite as much as for the protection of our supplies. Paulins would have sufficed to cover *them,* and rifle pits or hastily constructed stockades would have probably answered all purposes for a short campaign very well. At least if it had become necessary to construct more permanent works here, there would have been ample time hereafter. As it is, the Infantry all have an abundance of "A" Tents along, while the cavalry have only little shelter tents, which they carry on their horses, and one wall tent for the officers of each company, and an "A" Tent for each 1st Sergeant.

. . . It has commenced to snow since I have returned from General Sheridans camp, (which is five or six hundred yards distant,) and if it continues I suppose it will greatly facilitate the tracking up of our "Indian Friends" when we start after them. We are all in readiness to move now, and only await the arrival of the Kansas Cavalry (which is under the immediate command of Colonel Crawford, the Governor,) when we will at once move southward with 25 or 30 days rations and forage.

Albert's journal, Nov. 22, 1868:

Considerable snow fell last night, and sleet, alternating with snow and rain to day. Wrote to Brother Mack, Mother, Jennie (a postscript) and the Cleveland Herald to day. I hear this evening that Genl. Sully has been relieved, and is to start northward toward Harker, with the train in the morning. The 7th Cavalry is to march southward tomorrow at 6 a.m. with a months supplies, in search of the Indian villages. Reveille to be at 4 a.m.—two hours before daylight! The officers who are junior to him in rank propose to raise $1500 for Capt Gillett, if he will resign! He is a confirmed inebriate, and all are anxious to get rid of him.

Ever the man of action, Sheridan doubtless perceived that the aggressive Custer would be more likely to run down the Indians than the slow, cautious Sully. The approach of Colonel Crawford and the Kansas regiment had prompted Sully, a regular army lieutenant colonel, to issue orders assuming command of the expedition by virtue of his brevet rank of brigadier general. Custer, of course, immediately pointed to his own brevet of major general. Sheridan mediated in Custer's favor, ordering Sully back to his headquarters with the scarcely consoling explanation that the expedition was leaving the District of the Upper Arkansas.

13.   The Battle of the Washita, November 1868

Camp Supply, Indian Territory, base for Custer's Washita campaign of November 1868. Here Captain Barnitz underwent surgery and convalesced after suffering a near-fatal wound at the Battle of the Washita. From *Harpers Weekly,* February 27, 1869.

Albert's journal:

Camp on Middle River. Nov. 23, 1868. The regiment broke camp at "Camp Supply" this morning, at the hour designated, 6 a.m., and marched through a blinding snow storm, with the wind in our faces, and through the soft snow a foot in depth to this point, where we arrived about 1.30 p.m. and went into camp. During the march it was impossible to see more than a few hundred yards in any direction, on account of the falling snow. Ravines ran off to our left, apparently. Distance marched to day was 16 miles, direction S. 30° W. Sand hills as we approach this stream. Grass excellent, apparently, but snowed under. Started up a Jack Rabbit as we approached the stream. "I was too lively for him!" He couldn't run in the snow, and a dog which happened to be near quickly caught him. We had him for supper. There is plenty of timber here. . . . General Sheridan will remain at Camp Supply until we return, and General Sully has been relieved, and will go to Fort Harker, I am told. I pity Genl. Sully, for I believe that he has tried to hurry forward affairs as fast as possible, whereas his being relieved just now appears to reflect discredit upon him. We are all glad however that Genl. Sheridan will await our return. This has been a *very* disagreeable day. I wore buffalo overshoes and lodge-skin leggings.

2nd Camp on Middle River. Nov. 24, 1868, 9 p.m. Snow and occasional sleet & rain all last night. So dark this morning, while at stables, that I could not distinguish the horses. The driver of "G" Troop train slow, did not commence harnessing until "forward" had sounded. "G" Troop marching on left flank opposite rear of train. Col. Benteen in rear. The drivers of supply train not awake in time, and had not fed or harnessed mules. "G" Troop remained in camp until all had moved out. Found 8 prs spurs, nose bags, &c. in camp. Morning very cold. Snow a foot deep. Horse of "K" Troop gave out, and I ordered him to be abandoned, which was done. Two young deer started and a lively chase ensues. Came down, on horseback, and caught rabbit. Osages & sharp shooters & Genl. Custer kill numerous buffalo. I go out with Harris and [Pvt. Edward] Shebrosky & get steak & ribs. A good many mules are about "played." Teams had to be doubled repeatedly at sandy crossing. High peaks off on our right. Sand hills probably. Sand hills on our left, all along the stream. Artemesia grows everywhere, stream well timbered, water plentiful & excellent. Driver broke a 2nd tent pole & lost both my stoves, which were afterwards recovered. Genl. Custer has buffalo meat issued after going into camp. After marching 16 miles up right bank of Middle River in south westerly direction went into camp on right bank of stream, in woods. Had [Pvt. Joseph B.] Morris make me a new tent pole. Dug away snow and pitched tent on sandy bottom. Teamsters cut cottonwood trees for browsing their mules & men cut same for their horses, as they cannot get grass on account of the snow—fine buffalo steaks for supper. Weather has moderated this ev'g—no wind. We are feeding, *nomily*, 2/3 forage (9 lbs.) but in fact only about *half* forage or 6 lbs per day! How horses & mules are to keep up at this rate is more than I can say.

Camp Supply, Ind. Ter. Jan. 7, 1869. I will now attempt to make some notes in my journal, from memory. Nov. 25. Command broke camp at the usual hour, and marched south all day, through deeper snow than hitherto encountered, over the great "divide" between the "middle River" and the [South] Canadian. About dusk, we crossed a tributary of the Canadian, a stream of considerable size, and after marching about 2 miles further (a distance of perhaps 35 miles during the day,) we reached and encamped upon the north bank of the Canadian at a point where there is considerable dead timber—oak, walnut, and coffee-tree principally,—very suitable for fuel. This was the first time we had encountered oak and walnut since leaving the vicinity of Fort Riley. Beyond the Canadian at the point where we encamped, are some stupendous summits. . . . They can be seen for a distance of 15 or 20 miles, approaching from the north. Had some difficulty to feed the horses in the darkness, so as to ensure each horse getting his allowance of grain (3 lbs!)—but had all the horses formed in line, and counted, and then held while feeding, a place being tramped in the snow in front of each horse, in which to place the grain—(as nearly all the nose bags on hand were full of holes,—many having become unserviceable, and been abandoned on the march.) Made an attempt to graze the horses after they had eaten their grain, but found that they would not paw through the snow for grass, (although it was quite good along the slope leading to the river,) and finally had to give up the attempt, put up the picket line, and fasten the horses to it, as they were becoming restless, and could not be herded with safety. Digging away the snow to make a space for my tent, and for the shelter tents of the men, a laborious operation in the darkness.

On Thursday morning, Nov. 26, reveille was, as usual, two hours before daylight, and just before daylight we marched, "G" [Barnitz], "M" [Hale] & "H" [Benteen] Troops, marching up-stream (westward) under Major Elliott, while the other portion of the regiment, together with the train, under Genl. Custer pro-ceeded down stream, with the intention of going into camp about 10 miles below, and awaiting our return. We were to march about 25 miles before rejoining the other portion of the regiment. The morning was excessively cold, and a dense fog prevailed. It was necessary to dismount very often, and walk in order to prevent our feet from freezing. As the snow was a foot deep, with a hard crust, which broke beneath our feet, walking was exceedingly difficult and tiresome. After proceeding about two miles I saw a bear track, the first I had seen, and shortly afterwards the Osage Indians who were with us called our attention to a trail resembling a "buffalo path" which was covered with snow, but which had evidently been missed during the prevalence of the snow storm, as the snow in the path was not so deep as elsewhere, whereas it should have been deeper, if the path had been made by buffaloes. Besides the path was parallel to the stream, and buffalo paths always lead direct to water, and after having drunk the buffalo scatter out, and proceed to grazing. Moreover buffalo do not move about much during a storm, but remain huddled together in sheltered places. From all these considerations it was obvious that we were in close proximity to Indians, or at least that the valley had recently been traversed by a considerable body of them, but whether a war party or a hunting party we could not tell. After proceeding about a mile further we came to a timbered tributary of the Canadian and proceeding cautiously up its bank for a short distance we found where the Indians had encamped, during the storm, and had cut down cottonwood trees, to browse their ponies—all traces of their camp were snowed over, except the broathes [?] of branches, which were still standing. We now crossed the stream, and returned to the Canadian, whither the paths led, and after continuing up the stream for a mile further we came suddenly upon a plain, fresh trail, which had obviously been made in the afternoon of the day previous, by a war party of from one to two hundred Indians. It was known to be a war party from the fact that the Indians had no dogs with them, whereas hunting parties are always accompanied by dogs. The trail led south east. The command was now formed by fours, (it had previously marched by twos, on account of the difficulty of breaking a path through the snow,) stoppers taken from the muzzles of the carbines, magazines loaded, levers tested, to see whether they were frozen fast, as was often the case; and then a couple of couriers (from my troop,) were started back to General Custer, with intelligence that we had found a trail, and would follow it rapidly until we received further orders; we then pressed forward along the trail, crossed the Canadian, (a wide stream with a deep, rapid current in the centre, and filled with floating ice,) and entered a strip of timber on the southern bank, in which we found a large, broken down pack mule, which had been abandoned by the Indians. Beyond the stream the trail led up a steep, mountainous ascent, which was in places quite precipitous; so much so that we found it necessary to dismount, and lead our horses, for a distance of a mile, or further. Having passed the summit of the ridge we continued to press forward until about 11 oclock, when coming suddenly upon a ravine in which we found a quantity of dry oak wood (as well as some small green trees, in the top of one of which was an eagle's nest) we halted for an hour, to rest, put out pickets, and built up good comfortable fires. Having rested, we moved on and about 2 or 3 o'clock were joined by a courier from Genl. Custer, with orders to continue pursuit, and with intelligence that he, (Genl Custer) would follow us with all the other mounted men of the command, and with the ambulances and a few wagons lightly loaded with forage and rations. Just after dark, after having marched a mile or two through the timbered sand-hills along a stream or rather dry sandy "arroya" which is probably a tributary of the Washita, we were overtaken by a courier from General Custer with orders to halt and build fires for the command, as he was going to hurry forward with forage and rations, so that we

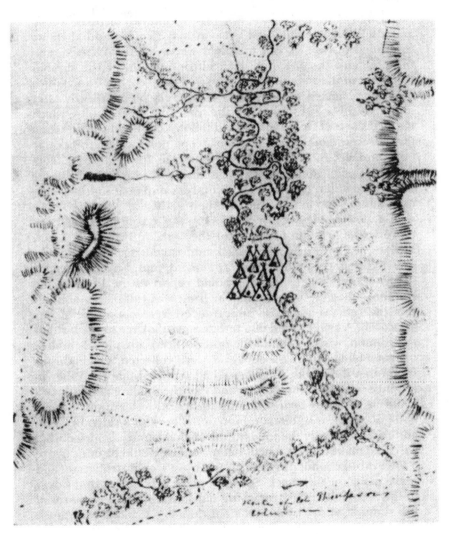

MAP 3. Barnitz's sketch map of the Washita Battlefield.

might feed, and get something to eat, when we would continue the pursuit. The wagons having arrived the horses were all fed— receiving full forage for the first time within two or three weeks, and the men were allowed time to make coffee and then we continued pursuit. About midnight we struck the Washita, and the trail now became quite difficult on account of the sinuous character of the stream, which runs in a deep channel, and which we were obligated to cross and recross very often. Shortly after midnight we began to discover the traces of "teepe" poles, which entered the trail from the left, and followed down in the direction that we were going. The traces of teepe poles at length became quite numerous, always entering our trail from the left, from which it was obvious that a village, traces of which Genl. Custer had found about ten miles below our encampment on the Canadian was moving in the same direction as the war party which we were following. About 2 or 3 o'clock in the morning, just as I was crossing the Washita for perhaps the 10th or 15th time, Lieut. Moylan, the Adjutant, rode back and stated that Genl. Custer directed that I should halt my command, and, accompanied by Lieut. March, my lieutenant, should report at the head of the column,—that the whole valley in front was full of ponies, and that the Indians, (from all appearances) were not aware of our approach. A rapid gallop of a few minutes took me to the head of the column, where I found the other officers already assembled, or assembling, and as soon as all were collected, Genl. Custer stated that the scouts, in advance had reported that the valley in advance was filled with ponies, and that the tinkling of a little bell could be distinctly heard; that he wished us to leave our horses, and go quietly, with him, on foot, to the crest of a ridge in front, and carefully study the topography of the country, and see what we could make out; he stated that no talking would be done above a low whisper, until our return, when we would deliberate, and make plans for the attack. So we all crept very quietly and slowly to the top of the ridge, removing our hats, or caps as we neared the summit, and I could not help thinking that we very much resembled a pack of wolves, and that if the Indians should discover us they would very likely mistake us for wolves, and so take no notice of us. One thing however was against us. The snow was about a foot deep, and the surface was frozen hard, so that when crushed beneath our feet the noise could be heard for a considerable distance. Having gained the crest of the ridge, we could see, though not distinctly, the course of the Washita, on our right, with what appeared to be tributaries entering from the left and possibly from the right, and the summits of steep bluffs were seen looming up on all sides of the valley, but the herds of ponies, and teepes were not visible although the tinkling of a little bell could be distinctly heard at times, and some of the officers who looked through a night glass were of the opinion that they could discern herds of ponies. Having made our observations, we returned to the point where our horses were left, when the following plan of attack was announced by General Custer.

The command was divided into four columns. The first, Companies G [Barnitz], H [Benteen], & M [Hale], under Major Elliott was to pass around the hills to the left (of the position at the time the plan was adopted) and reach the Washita below the village, and then move up the stream to the attack at the proper time. The second Co's B [Wallingford] & F [Yates], under Col. Thompson was to countermarch, recross the stream which we had just crossed, and march, under cover of the bluffs that skirted the right bank of the stream, to a point opposite the village, and there await the signal to charge down upon the village. The third column, E [Myers] & I [Brewster], under the command of Col. Myers, was to move directly down the right bank of the stream, keeping within the timber which skirted it, until within view of the village, and there await the signal for attack.

The 4th column, Companies A [Hamilton], D [Weir], C [Berry], & K [West], & the Sharp Shooters [Cooke] under Genl. Custer was to move directly toward the village, from the ridge upon which the officers had crept to make their observations, previous to the announcement of the plan of attack. The attack was to be made at day break, and in the meantime each column was to get as close as possible to the village without giving any alarm. If however, in spite of all precautions, the Indians should discover our advance, and endeavor to escape, or fire upon any portion of the command, the attack was to be made at once; otherwise, the signal of attack was to be sounded, at daybreak by the band, which was to play on the summit of the ridge from which Genl. Custer's column was to advance, and instantly, at the appointed signal, or at the firing of a gun, the advance was to be made from all directions—all were to go in *with a rush* and this was particularly enjoined upon all the officers, by Genl. Custer, as he fully realized the importance of concentration.

The plan of attack having been announced, the columns were ordered to move at once to their respective positions, as only about an hour remained until daybreak. As Major Elliotts column moved out, a number of dogs, belonging to the command, followed, and as it was feared that they would alarm the Indians, prematurely, some of the men were directed to catch them and strangle (or muzzle) them, with lariat ropes, and dispatch them with knives. After the column had marched a few hundred yards, toward the bluffs (to the left) we crossed several distinct and well-beaten trails leading toward the point where, from all indications, we had previously concluded that the village must be located, and subsequent events proved our conclusions to be correct. Attempting to ascend the bluffs at one point, Maj. Elliott was fearful that we were too close to the Indian village, and that the Indians would either hear our horses crushing through the snow or else see us outlined against the sky, and so he countermarched the column (no orders were given, except by signs, or in a low tone) and ascended the bluffs at a point more remote from the village. We now moved on until we were behind a towering bluff, which rose on our right, about, as we supposed, opposite the point, on the stream, where the village was located. Here Major Elliott halted the command, and requested me to go with him to the summit, to make observations; we dismounted, and leaving our horses with an orderly, climbed to the top of the bluff, and lying down on the snow, looked down into the valley below, and endeavored to make out the location of the village (which, as we afterwards found, was directly in front of us, on the stream below, and no more than half a mile distant) but the night was so dark that we could see nothing except the dark outline of the timber along the stream.

Here, abruptly and unaccountably, Barnitz's journal account of the Washita campaign ends.

Custer's target, hidden by the predawn darkness of the Washita Valley, was a Cheyenne village of fifty-one lodges belonging to Chief Black

Grandson of Alexander Hamilton, Captain Louis M. Hamilton was one of the ablest as well as youngest officers of the 7th Cavalry. He commanded Troop A and was killed at the Battle of the Washita at the age of twenty-four.

As regimental quartermaster, Lieutenant James M. Bell brought up the wagon train with boldness and dispatch after Custer's charge at the Washita. He retired in 1901 a brigadier general.

A big-framed Canadian, Lt. William W. Cooke commanded the company of picked marksmen at the Battle of the Washita. Succeeding Moylan as adjutant in 1871, he penned Custer's famous last message at the Little Bighorn and died near his commander on Custer Hill.

Custer named "California Joe" (Moses) Milner chief of scouts for the Washita campaign, but strong drink quickly lost him the post. The fall from grace, however, did not deprive the army of his vast treasury of frontier lore and skill.

Kettle. Unknown to Custer, it was but one of a series of villages of Cheyennes, Arapahos, Kiowas, and Comanches dotting the valley downstream toward Fort Cobb.

Black Kettle was a peace chief. There can be little doubt that he and other Cheyenne leaders desired peace. Only a week before he had conferred with General Hazen at Fort Cobb and asked to make peace. But Hazen, knowing that Sheridan had taken the field to punish the Cheyennes, declined. And indeed, Black Kettle admitted that his young men did not want peace and that he could not restrain them. Some were even then raiding in Kansas—those whose trail led Custer to his objective—and in the village when Custer attacked were four white captives and numerous trophies of the Kansas raids.

Thus the question has been heatedly debated ever since whether Black Kettle's village was peaceful. There is no wholly satisfactory answer. Like so many issues of our Indian relations, there is only ambiguity.

About 1889, apparently for an Atlanta newspaper reporter, Barnitz wrote a lengthy account of the Battle of the Washita. Scrawled in part on stationery of the Kimbell Hotel and in part on lined note paper, it adds important details to his other accounts. We here pick up the narrative at the point where the journal ended:

We lay down on the snow, on the summit, and peered into the darkness, but it was like looking into a well—only the tops of the trees could be distinguished, but as the barking of a multitude of dogs could be heard in the woods, we conjectured that there, without doubt, was the village, and this view was confirmed by finding, as we proceeded, many distinct trails, where teepe poles had been dragged through the snow, and these all converged toward the large grove which we had fixed upon as the location of the village, or main camp of the Indians. As we reached the base of the hill, after our observation, judge of our surprise and consternation as we were beset by half a dozen of large fox hounds belonging to the [Indian] band, and their baying might, without doubt, have been heard for miles in the still air, and we now had no longer any hope that our approach was unheralded to the Indians. We found to our surprise, that the [regimental] band, which should have remained with General Custer, was through some misconception of orders, following us, and that Col. Benteen's squadron, which should have accompanied us had not yet

come up. The band was at once sent back, and we pressed forward, and soon came to a deep, rocky cañon, which crossed the
direction of our march and seemed to forbid further progress.
We however found a place where we could enter it, in single file,
and following down its level bottom for some distance, toward the
village, at length found a steep trail where by holding firmly to
our horses' manes, and applying spurs vigorously, we succeeded
in climbing once more to the upper air. Here we found a large
number of ponies, tethered with lariats, in a grove of second
growth white oak trees, to which the dry leaves still clung, and
these were diligently pawing through the snow to obtain the grass
beneath it, and paid not the slightest attention, at our approach, as
they were evidently famishing for food. We here expected,
confidently, to be fired upon by Indians who might be in charge of
the herd, but to our surprise moved forward unchallenged, and at
length reached the stream, below the village, at a ford, the approach to which was much trampled by ponies. We were halted,
without crossing, and facing up the stream dismounted to fight on
foot. I however selected ten picked men, who were expert shots
on horseback, and placed them, under charge of Sergeant [Fran-
cis] McDermott, on the prolongation of the left flank. As Colonel
Benteen's squadron had not arrived, and as it was still an hour or
two until dawn, and the whinnying of multitudes of ponies could
be heard among the bluffs beyond the stream, Major Elliott and
myself crossed over and made a prolonged reconnoissance, to
ascertain if possible, if other villages were located in the cañons,
where the ponies were heard, but our observations only
confirmed our belief that the entire village lay above us on the
stream. Having completed our reconnoissance, and indications of
approaching dawn appearing in the east, and Col. Benteen having
at length arrived, I forded the stream with my command, and
then dismounted, as before, placing the ten mounted men on the
left flank, and having the horses of the dismounted men led in
column behind us, set forward, with my right resting on the
stream. Benteen at the same time moved forward, mounted, on
the right (left bank) of the stream. As we proceeded, it became
necessary for my men to repeatedly ford the crooked stream, the
water of which was about knee deep, and as cold as ice, but
notwithstanding this, they preserved their alignment, as though

on dress parade, and pressed forward with zeal, for day was breaking rapidly, and we were anxious to gain our position at the appointed time. As we moved forward, we soon came to ponies and mules, tied beneath cottonwood trees, with piles of branches piled in front of them, and which they were eating with evident relish. An Indian wrapped in a red blanket, presently sprang up from among the animals, and ran rapidly in the direction of the camp. Others quickly followed him, until we appeared to have started a numerous covey. Some of my men raised their carbines to fire upon them, but wishing to prevent alarming the camp until the last moment, I forbade them to fire, and we pressed forward with increased speed. We had just reached the edge of a shallow ravine beyond which we could see the clustered tepees, situated among wide-branching cottonwood trees, when a shot was fired in the village, and instantly we heard the band on the ridge beyond it strike up the familiar air "Garry Owen" and the answering cheers of the men, as Custer, and his legion came thundering down the long divide, while nearer at hand on our right came Benteen's squadron, crashing through the frozen snow, as the troops deployed into line at a gallop, and the Indian village rang with unearthly war-whoops, the quick discharge of fire-arms, the clamorous barking of dogs, the cries of infants and the wailing of women.

As we afterward found out, other villages were situated lower down the stream, and a natural impulse incited the Indians in the village we had surrounded to rush in that direction. As they did so they encountered my line, and were either killed, or driven back into the ravine, where some of them for a time made a determined stand. A moment later I discovered a large party running from the village over some sand hills on our left, in the direction of herds of ponies which had attracted the attention of Major Elliot and myself, and I directed the fire of my men upon them for an instant, without apparent effect, and fearing they would escape, I sent Sergeant McDermott, with his mounted men, to head them off, and drive them toward where Col. Thompson's squadron was expected to come down the bluffs, and join in the fight; and in order if possible to ascertain where that squadron was, and be able to co-operate with it, and at the same time lay out a few of the Indians myself, I put spurs to my horse and dashed among those nearest my position, but on riding into their midst, I discovered that they were all old squaws, some with papooses astride of their necks, and leading others by the hand, and not caring to waste ammunition on them, though to tell the truth, I was not at all sentimental about it, for they were always fiendishly cruel in torturing captives, I was about to rejoin my command (not seeing anything of Thompson's squadron), and had driven them some distance in that direction, where they were eventually captured, by my men—forty-eight squaws in all—when looking in the direction in which they had been running, I saw the warriors running, and now distinctly outlined against the sky, and dashing forward I soon rode into the rear of them, and quicker than I can tell converted two of them into very good and harmless Indians, though their feathered arrows just singed my neck, and then seeing an Indian aiming at me with a gun, I made a dash for him, with head depressed behind my horse's neck, intending to have him on my right side, when I reached him, so as the better to use my revolver; but when I reached him, he wasn't there. He knew too much about war, and preferred to be on the other side of my horses neck, but instantly turning my horse I made another dash for him, and again he jumped to the left, and was aiming at me, as before. I now closed my right leg back of the girth, and carrying my bridle hard to the left, caused my horse to passage, as it is called, to the left, so as to close up nearer to the Indian, as I did not wish to take any chances of failing to dispatch him with one shot, for I had need of all the others. I suppose the Indian felt the same way, for he still held his fire, and adroitly avoiding my maneuver fell back so as to be partially covered by my horses head, but still on my left side, where he again aimed at me, but still did not fire on the instant, but as I aimed at him threw up a dressed buffalo skin, which he had about him, with the apparent design of causing my horse to jump, and thus disconcert my aim. He had aimed at my heart, but I had fired just an instant sooner than he did, and my horse bounded slightly when I fired, and this alone saved my life. He stood so near me that the blaze from his gun burnt my overcoat. His ball appears to have struck the lower edge of a rib, and then glancing downward, as I was leaning forward at the time, cut the next rib in two, and a piece out of the next rib below, where it was reflected, and passed through my body and out through the muscles near the spine, passing again through my overcoat and cape. You see he was loaded to kill.

. . . Perhaps that shot would have ended [the Indian's] career, but as the smoke cleared a little, I was surprised to see him still on his feet. He had dropped the butt of his gun to the ground, and stood holding the muzzle with his left hand, with his right hand thrust beneath his buckskin garments, and was leaning forward with a horrible grimace on his face, as though about to drop his scalping knife and make a rush for me. I thought at the time that was his intention; but perhaps he had placed his hand where my ball had passed through him, and I never knew how it was, but acting on the first supposition, I turned my horse to the left, cocking my revolver as I did so, and leaning on my horses neck, as though about to fall off, until I had the Indian directly on my right side, and very near me, when quickly raising my pistol I fired, and the Indian turned and fell headlong over his gun, just as two of my mounted men reached the spot. I endeavored to speak to them as they passed me, riding toward the remaining Indians, but could not utter a sound. So I turned about, and rode slowly, and painfully toward the village, until becoming [passage missing] . . . and my hands up my overcoat sleeves, and lay down in a little depression on the hill, in the expectation that I would very speedily die, but that some of my men might be attracted to the spot and thus be apprised of my fate.

Thus ends this narrative. At Camp Supply on December 5, 1868, Barnitz dictated to Lieutenant Nowlan a letter for Jennie giving a briefer but timelier account of the battle:

When the appointed moment had arrived, the Regimental Band struck up "Gari Owen," and the squadrons moved forward with a rush, and all was activity; the Indians were completely taken by surprise. Yet they were instantly up and around. The fighting was severe but I am unable to say how many were killed. The bodies of one hundred and three warriors were found in and around the village, but many more must have been killed whose bodies were carried off by their friends. It was surprizing to see how soon, when once the action had commenced, how all the hills were alive with mounted warriors, armed and equipped with their shields, and war bonnets. These as it was afterwards ascertained had come from other villages in the valley, having heard the firing. Shortly after the firing commenced I observed a large body of Indians running off towards the left. I at once dashed in among them, passing through a large drove of Squaws and children who were screaming and very much frightened. I came upon the warriors who were ahead and striking out as hard as they could run for their ponies. Riding up close along side of the first I shot him through the heart. He threw up his arms, by the same movement drawing his bow from the scabbard let fly an arrow at me. This was the last act of his existence. I passed on to the second and shot him in the same manner. There was yet another close to me. He was armed with a large Lancaster rifle given to him by the peace commission. He took aim, while I was closing upon him and about to fire, but was several times disconcerted by my acting as if I were about to fire upon him myself, until finally I had some doubt if his rifle was loaded. When however I got quite close to him to fire, he returned my fire at the same instant, both shots taking effect. Mine I believe must have passed through his heart, as he threw up his hands frantically and as I was told by others of my company died almost immediately.

I rode back toward the village, being now unable to manage my horse, and the pain of my wound being almost unbearable. I dismounted and lay down in such a way that I would not bleed internally. As soon as the fight was nearly decided I was placed upon a buffalo robe and carried down the hills a few hundred yards further, where I was allowed to rest in a place of comparative security until Doctors Lippincott and [William H.] Renicke arrived. Both were so blind, from the effects of snow, that they with difficulty could attend to the wounded, and pronounced my case truly hopeless, but made every effort for my comfort for the short time it was supposed I had to live. All the officers gathered about me, as the progress of the fight permitted, and endeavored to cheer me with their condolences; in the meantime the Indian village was burned together with a quantity of stores, supplies, gun powder, &c—and all the ponies that could be gathered together, were driven in. Two were selected for each of the Squaws, who were captured, and two for each officer; the remainder, some eight or nine hundred, were shot to prevent them falling into the hands of the Indians. We now awaited the arrival of our ambulances, which were toiling towards us through the intricate labyrinths where our horses could hardly proceed by file. When at length these arrived the wounded were loaded in, and we commenced our return march towards this point.

Lt. Edward S. Godfrey to Jennie, Camp Supply, I.T., Dec. 5, 1868:

From our camp on the Washita River I telegraphed you that Col Barnitz was badly wounded—to be candid was thought at the time to be mortal—yet delicacy impelled me to leave the word "mortally" out; now I am glad I did so. Your husband has every indication of recovering. His color is good, almost as well as before his wound was made. The wound was made by a ball from a Lancaster rifle (supplied by the Interior Dept.) fired by a Cheyenne warrior. The ball entered his left side on a line with the left groin and about four inches above the navel; coming out on the left side of the spine cutting the top of his pants. The wound is one that rarely occurs without cutting the intestines, and that was what was at first appeared to be the case. Happily recent indications have shown that not to be and all the surgeons (Drs. Ash [Asch], Sternberg, Lippincott, [Elias J.] Marsh, and Renick) agree that he will recover though twill be some months before he will be for duty. 'Twas a terrible shock on his system yet his cool and heroic conduct during his affliction has saved his life. After the battle was over the Drs. gave him up and delegated me to inform him. I very reluctantly did it in as delicate terms as possible. He received it with some emotion and gave me messages for you, yet insisted that his case was not hopeless.

I transcribe here the notes I took down. "Tell Mrs B. that I don't regret the wound so much as I do leaving her. It has been so long since we met, that the expectations of the happiness we would enjoy upon our reunion is more than I can bear."

"I am glad she is not here to see my suffering as she could do me no good. Tell her not to grieve for me, that I love her."

Then his suffering and emotions became so great that nothing was audible or could be understood. After resting a time he gave me his mother's address also his brother. Then he talked about the possibilities of his recovery if he could only be where he could remain quiet and not be moved. Such a thing was out of the question however, as we had a train of over a hundred wagons, guarded by Lt Mathey with only 80 men, and should the Indians find him all our supplies would be lost.

Col. with his troop was under Maj. Elliott to attack the village from the east side. Col with the troop was posted so as to cover a neck of woods. Moving along a ravine, he took the left of the line mounted and Lt March the right dismounted. When the attack began the Indians poured out of the village upon Col's flank. Col killed two Indians, he is sure of, and the third he was aiming at, when he would dodge behind his pony. This continued a short time when both took aim and both fired at the same instant and both were wounded. The Indian reached for his scalping knife when he saw that the Col was wounded, but was too weak to carry out his intention of scalping. Col thinks he has gone to the happy hunting ground. Col then rode back of the lines and was taken in charge. He described the yell of despair given by the first Indian he shot, the wicked, vindictive and malicious look of the third, while skirmishing for the shot.

By the time Barnitz received his wound, the troops had seized the village and driven out the inhabitants. Black Kettle and his wife and Chief Little Rock were slain, and the few pockets of resistance that developed were quickly eliminated. Warriors from the lower villages, however, rode to the aid of their kinsmen, and Custer had to defend his position throughout the day.

Shortly after Barnitz fell, Major Elliott saw some Indians attempting to escape downstream and with Sgt. Maj. Walter Kennedy and seventeen troopers he gave chase. An Indian force riding from the other camps cut off the detachment and wiped it out to the last man.

As Barnitz writes, Custer destroyed the village and killed about 800 Indian ponies captured early in the fight. Then, with band playing and banners flying, he boldly feinted toward the other villages. As the besieging Indians hastened to defend their homes, he quickly reversed his march and under cover of night withdrew from the battlefield. He thus left without knowing or attempting to learn the fate of Elliott and his men—an act, however militarily defensible, that severely exacerbated the tensions that already beset the officer corps of the 7th Cavalry.

Military losses were Major Elliott, Captain Hamilton, and 19 enlisted men killed, and Captain Barnitz, Lieutenants Custer and March, and 11 enlisted men wounded. Custer reported the bodies of 103 Cheyenne men counted on the battlefield and 53 women and children taken prisoner. His report is silent on the number of women and children killed, and his count of slain warriors has been disputed. Donald Berthrong [Southern Cheyennes, *p. 328*] *cites three reliable sources for the estimate of between 9 and 20 men killed and 18 and 40 women and children killed.*

14. Epilogue

Albert, Jennie, and baby Bertha on porch of Fort Leavenworth quarters in May or June 1870, on the eve of Albert's disability retirement.

On December 2, 1868, the 7th Cavalry proudly marched into Camp Supply under the approving eye of General Sheridan. First came the colorfully bedecked Osage trailers, firing their rifles, shouting, and brandishing Cheyenne scalps. California Joe and the white scouts came next, followed by the Indian prisoners mounted on ponies. Then Cooke's sharpshooters and all eleven troops of the 7th Cavalry passed in review before Sheridan and his staff as the regimental band gave forth the rollicking air of "Garryowen."

Sheridan had already issued a general order congratulating the 7th and its commander in fulsome language. And in fact the Battle of the Washita was a significant action in the history of plains warfare. Not only did Custer devastate a band of Cheyennes, inflicting casualties and destroying food, shelter, transportation, and other possessions at the beginning of winter, he also validated Sheridan's strategy by demonstrating that troops could operate in the winter and by serving notice on all the tribes that winter no longer afforded safety from attack.

The Washita battle opened a campaign destined to last until the following spring. Another of Sheridan's columns, commanded by Maj. Andrew W. Evans, clashed with Comanches at the Battle of Soldier Spring on Christmas Day, but no other actions were fought. Instead, Custer marched deep into Indian Territory and west into the Texas Panhandle in operations that kept the Cheyennes on the move and contributed importantly to their surrender the next summer. They and the other southern plains tribes then settled on the reservations established under the Medicine Lodge treaties, but not until after another war, in 1874–75, did they accept the reality of their conquest.

Albert Barnitz, of course, did not participate in these events. He had reached Camp Supply on December 1 after a jolting ride of 100 miles in an army ambulance, as he told Jennie in the letter of December 5 quoted in the last chapter:

You may judge that my ride for five days was a very tedious one. During the whole time I could not eat one morsel of anything and for every spoonful of water that I ' drunk I vomited up two. Immediately upon my arrival here General Sheridan came to see me attended by his chief Medical Officer, and greeted me very kindly, placing me in quite comfortable quarters for the field. His cook has been directed to furnish me with any thing I might desire.

Perhaps you would like to know just how I am situated at present. Well, first as to the bed, it is a small cottage bedstead with two comfortable matresses. All the officers who were possessed of such luxuries as feather pillows have placed them at my disposal, so that I am now very sumptuously furnished in that line, and can vary my position at will. I am almost entirely free from pain, and have a good appetite for such small diet as I am permitted to eat. My principal diet consists of beef tea and farina. As to my furniture, my tent contains a comfortable little stove, and improvised table and a chair or two, and you can perhaps imagine the rest.

Lieutenant Godfrey added in a letter of December 8: "I went down to see the Col. last evening. Botzer and Mullin are waiting on him. You doubtless remember them as very faithful men, and fully devoted to their charge."

Albert to Jennie, Camp Supply, I.T., Dec. 24, 1868:

And would you like to hear how I am getting along, dear? I am doing *very* well indeed. I am able to sit up all day, and to walk around a little in my tent—can get up and dress myself without assistance. Have an excellent appetite, and am gaining strength every day. The ball entered just in front of the short ribs, and passed out *below* the ribs, and just above the hip bone, and nearer to the spine than where it entered, a mass of tissues about the size of a man's fist protruded from the anterior wound and looked exactly like one of the sausage balls which are sometimes exposed at Butcher's stalls; this the surgeon, Dr. Sternberg, removed, by an operation with a curious instrument of recent invention, shortly after I wrote you last. Since then the anterior wound has nearly healed up—it is entirely closed, and has grown almost full, and the posterior wound is closing daily, although it still continues to discharge somewhat. Upon the whole I am recovering very rapidly. I have no pain whatever. I have not taken a particle of medicine of any kind, except one grain and a quarter of morphine—scarcely one full dose. I think I will entirely recover from my wound in time—so that I will not realize that I have ever been wounded.

Dr. Sternberg and Lieut. Nowlan mess together, and their cook prepares any thing for me that I desire. The Commissary Department is now quite a perfect "Institution"—it contains nearly every thing that can be desired, twice as many things as used to be kept, and every thing of the very best. Even Orange County butter—the genuine article, sweet and good, in small 8 or 10 pound kegs is now furnished. Maj. Inman brought down 1100 pounds, I believe, this trip. We have all kinds of Jelly, and preserves &c. When Genl. Sheridan went away he left some chickens for the Hospital, two of which I have had. Some of the officers go out hunting daily and always send me a share of the game, if they get any. I have received 13 quails, and some rabbits which I have had nicely broiled and relished greatly.

Dr. Sternberg judged Barnitz's case unusual enough to warrant description in the Surgeon General's Circular No. 3 *of 1871, pp. 250–51, from which Barnitz later copied the following extract:*

After receiving the wound the Colonel rode about two hundred yards, dismounted, and laid down, holding his horse until some of his company came to him. About half an hour afterward he was examined by Assistant Surgeon Lippincott, U.S.A., who found a mass of omentum [tissue connecting the stomach to the other visceral organs] protruding from the anterior wound, about the size of a man's fist. The doctor supposed, from the position of the wound, that the intestine must be wounded, and that the injury must necessarily prove fatal. The Colonel was brought to Camp Supply in an ambulance. . . . I found him very much fatigued by the journey, but having a good pulse, and presenting no bad symptoms. . . . On the 8th I removed the protruding mass of omentum. I commenced the operation with a wire ecraseur, but before it was completed the loop of wire broke, and I severed a small portion which was not yet cut through, with scissors. . . . December 12th the Colonel is able to sit up an hour or two at a time, has a good appetite, sleeps well, and may be considered out of all danger.

Today Barnitz's granddaughter remembers a traumatic visit, at the age of fourteen, to the Army Medical Museum in Washington, D.C. There she

viewed the mortal remains of Grandfather Albert—the ball of omentum preserved in a jar of formaldehyde and placed on display courtesy of George M. Sternberg, late Surgeon-General of the U.S. Army.
Meantime, Jennie had been having adventures of her own.

Jennie to Albert, Fort Dodge, Kan., Dec. 28, 1868:

What joy to see you dear handwriting once more! Oh Albert, I hardly know how to write to you again, and what to say to you! And yet I have so many things to tell you that I despair of ever being able to finish. The past four weeks seem to me like some terrible dream from which I have just awakened—the recollections of which make me shudder. How did I ever endure those two weeks of agonizing suspense! I have wondered over and over that my reason did not leave me—or that I was not utterly prostrated, and yet darling I never gave you up for one moment—it seemed to me you would *not* die—that when you thought of *me*, you *would* live, and then it seemed too, that the kind Father, in whose tender care we always are, would not make my life so wretched. My hope and faith sustained me. Had it not been for this I must have given up. I received the dispatch Wednesday morning, and do not blame Mr. Godfrey dear, for sending it, for I can see now that it was so fortunate. The hope implied cheered me through all those dreary days, and nights. Mr. Godfrey wrote me a very kind sympathetic letter. I left home the day I received the dispatch. Nothing could have kept me at home an hour. Mamma felt as if she could not have me come, in such a state of mind, fearing I would be sick on the way & no one to take care of me, but she did not try to detain me. It was a terrible journey. From the moment I left our house people seemed to know who I was and *why* I was coming West. I wish I could give you some idea of the kindness and attention I received all along the way. At Leavenworth I met Col [Thomas] Anderson, who did everything for me. Sent dispatches ahead announcing my coming, broke open the Baggage Room for my trunk, and sent me all the news he could hear while at Harker. Col Stein was also on the train, and was so kind. Good old man! I shall never cease to remember him. I stopped at the hotel at Ellsworth where I was directed by Col Anderson. Found the proprietor a very cultivated eastern man, who has been in better circumstances. Was there two days. The severe snow storm occurred the night I reached there, and imagine my feelings when I was told that there would be no trains for a number of days! but now as I look back I can see that every thing was so kindly ordered, I was better there. As soon as the officers heard that I was in Ellsworth, they sent for me to come to the Post [Fort Harker]. I was invited to Maj Inmans, and to a number of other places, but accepted the first. Everybody came to see me often, but you know I did not want to see anybody, only that I might ask them questions about you. Gen. Sully and Gibbs were determined that I should come no farther West, but remain at Harker, and Gen Sully sent dispatches for me obtaining all possible information, which was of course nothing only as it showed the kindness of his heart. Of course I could not stay at Harker, & had to say very emphatically that I was going to Hays before it was listened to. I was at Maj Inmans not quite a week. Came to Hays with a lot of recruits, in care of Capt. [Thomas B.] Hunt, having a special car sent through for me. As a dispatch preceded me Col. [Michael V.] Sheridan [the General's brother] met me at the Depot & took me to Col. [Anderson D.] Nelsons, commanding the Post, where I was nicely entertained for one week. They did everything for my happiness but as I could hear nothing from you, I was wretched, however the Wednesday after I arrived Col Sheridan came in bringing Mr [Lt. William I.] Reed [5th Infantry] from Dodge, who had news from you. I had looked forward to this moment with so much dread, feeling that be the news good or bad, I could hardly endure it, but I heard it calmly, though I felt like throwing my arms about the neck of the one who had brought me the news. I shall never forget him. It is a fortunate thing to be the bearer of good news. The officers & ladies came running in to congratulate me. There was a great deal of feeling manifested. Could you have witnessed it, I am sure you would have felt gratified. They had no hope of you, as they have since told me, but they would not tell me when I first arrived. Friday I received your dear letter, written by Lieut No[w]lan, also a kind letter from Mr Godfrey. Since that time I have been *happy*. Capt & Mrs [Amos W.] Kimball insisted on my spending the remainder of my time with them, which invitation was accepted, and it seems to me they are the kindest persons I ever saw. Had she been my own mother she could not have done more, and her

sympathy for me was so real. We have an invitation to spend a
little time there as we go East. Col Nelson has also invited us. By
the way, Gen. Easton came to Hayes, & came to see me at once,
bringing a very urgent invitation from Mrs. Easton for us to stop
there when we go to Leavenworth & remain as long as convenient.
Now he says "I shall tell Mrs Easton that you promised to do so,"
which I did at last. He is a dear old man! At Harker & Hayes the
officers were opposed to my coming farther West, but of course I
was determined to do so. Col Nelson gave a Hop while I was there,
which I was obliged to attend, as I was told it was given for me. It
was very pleasant, though there are only five ladies at the Post. Mr
Stouch came there with his wife en route for the east, & of course
had his ambulance very comfortably arranged, & he very kindly
offered it to me if I would come to Dodge, which opportunity I
gladly accepted. Maj [Lewis C.] Forsyth—just ordered to Dodge
from Vicksburg, & cousin of Gen Forsyth—very kindly took me in
his care. We had not a large escort but I had great confidence in
Mr Stouch, Maj Forsyth & brother, & we came through all safe, in
one day & a half. Wasn't it a rapid journey? When within about a
mile of the Post, we met five or six officers who had ridden out to
meet us. It was very pleasant to be so warmly welcomed. I came to
Mrs. [Chancellor] Martins, & occupy rooms with her, though we
take our meals with Mr Stouch. The officers here are "wondrous
kind" They are in all the time, three or four times a day. They are
so delighted to have a lady arrive, they have been so long without
them. I reached here Sunday evening. Last night we gave [Bvt.]
Maj [and Capt. Andrew] Sheridan [3d Infantry, post commander]
a surprise. The evening was spent in dancing. I went with Mr
Reed, whom I like much principally because he seems so interested in you, & seems to think so much of you. He is cultivated
& very delightful in conversation. The very night I reached here I
received your last letter, and it has made me oh so happy, only
that I *was* disappointed in not seeing you with Maj Inmans train
which came in yesterday—however I did not want you to run any
risks, & yet it seems as if I should fly to you. Only a hundred miles
apart! That is a sweet thought, & I can wait, for I feel that you are
safe, and that is enough. With that assurance nothing can make
me unhappy. We have been over this morning to see the fifty
squaws [captured at the Washita] start for Hayes. Mr [Lt. Thomas]

Wallace takes them & it seems a dangerous trip as of course the Indians are watching. Since I came Mr Wallace has presented me with a beautiful little work box made here of black walnut. It seems as if the officers could not do enough for us. I had fully intended to go to Camp Supply, when I came here, but of course it would not be wise for me to do so under the circumstances, & yet I dont know how to wait, but I will be patient. How can you come here if Maj Inman does not go back to Camp Supply? That makes me a little anxious. Mrs Martin would have gone with me had I gone I think. Of course as soon as I heard of your safety, I informed your friends & my own—indeed I was writing letters two days. . . . You can hardly imagine in what haste I am writing as [Bvt.] Col [and Capt. James F.] Crilly [A.Q.M.] came before we were up this morning saying that the courier would go in a short time, but Maj Sheridan said he would keep the couriers till this letter was finished. When can I hear from you again. Oh! I have so much more to say to you, but I cannot. How much you have endured my precious one, & how brave & heroic you have been through it all. May God bless & keep you.

P.S. Mrs Benteens baby died while I was at Harker. She was in very low spirits. Her own health was miserable & she was constantly anxious about her husband.

Jennie to Albert, Fort Dodge, Kan., Jan. 11, 1869:

You will be surprised to hear that Gen. Gibbs is dead. He went to Leavenworth to spend the holidays, went out Christmas evening to a little party, and the next morning was dead. He died of Appoplexy. Gens. Easton, Morgan, and some others have gone to New York with his remains. Poor Old General! With all his faults he had a kind heart! The morning I left Harker, I was detained at the Depot two hours, and the Gen. went down & sat with me, and we had a very pleasant familiar talk. Never shall I forget how his eyes filled with tears when he spoke of you. He told me about his long army life, talked to me about Mrs Gibbs—indeed I am glad my last recollections of the Gen. are so pleasant. Just as I started he sent a dispatch to Gen McKeever saying what time I would arrive at Hayes, and as he shook my hand he says, "dont forget to *remember* me to the Major, and when you come back let me know, that I may send an ambulance for you, and when you reach Fort Leavenworth, go right to Mrs Gibbs." and added "Mrs B you cannot ask too much of me." Notwithstanding all his unpleasant ways he will be missed in the Reg.

Jennie to her mother, Fort Hays, Kan., Feb. 10, 1869:

I can only say that the reason I have not written to you for the past two weeks is, that Albert was with me, and though I have thought every day that I would write, still day after day would go by, & I would not write. Two weeks ago last Sunday, Albert came from Camp Supply. Couriers came in advance, saying that they would arrive on Sunday so the Commanding Officer of the Post, Maj Sheridan, very kindly took a company of Cavalry, about twenty scouts—the Maj accompained me. We crossed the Arkansas river and went out about twelve miles to meet them. You can imagine it was a most exciting ride and [we] met them at the place where we expected. Albert is looking very well. His wound is nearly healed. He has a most excellent appetite, & weighs 166-1/2 lbs, but oh, he was fearfully wounded. I tremble every time I look at him. We left Fort Dodge Sunday morning, came to Fort Hayes in an ambulance, with a good escort, about a hundred miles, reaching here yesterday, Tuesday. Think of it: not a house to be seen, all that long distance, hardly a tree, nothing but the buffalo & wolves. I took a severe cold coming over but think it will be better soon. We will be here a few days, will go from here to Leavenworth, and do not know what arrangements we shall make—that is what time we shall start east, but you will see us some time in the early spring. I inclose a picture taken at Dodge. It is miserable but thought you would like to see it. I am very happy now. Can see that Albert improves every day.

Escorted by a detachment of Kansas cavalry and accompanied by Captain Asbury, Barnitz had left Camp Supply in an ambulance on January 21 and reached Fort Dodge on the twenty-fourth. The same caravan carried the remains of Captain Hamilton. From Dodge Albert and Jennie journeyed to Fort Hays and took the train to Fort Leavenworth, arriving on February 18.

An extended leave of absence for convalescence gave the Barnitzes, at last, the leisure they had so long anticipated, and they returned to East Cleveland. En route, they paused in Cincinnati to visit Murat Halstead, the celebrated journalist for whose paper Barnitz had written occasional dispatches during the Civil War. As Barnitz recalled in an interview published in the Atlanta Constitution, *Jan. 12, 1889:*

[After the Battle of the Washita] the word went forward, as usual, that I was dead again, and so my old friend, Murat Halstead, of the Cincinnati Commercial, wrote up my obituary in good style, and for the third time, recounting how I had written poetry in my youth, and had corresponded for his paper during the war, and how I had distinguished myself as poet, journalist and warrior. He may even have shed a tear or two, as a parting tribute. Then when a few weeks later I surprised him by calling upon him to pay my respects, as I passed through Cincinnati on leave of absence, I thought he appeared a little disgusted to be again confronted by the apparition of one whom he had so often glorified as dead! At all events, he said, on parting, "Barnitz the next time you are killed, I am just going to say, 'Barnitz is dead.' I am tired of writing obituaries of you—and all to no purpose."

The Barnitzes passed a pleasant, relaxed summer and autumn with the Platts in East Cleveland before returning to Fort Leavenworth. They were back on October 19, 1869. A week later the 7th Cavalry marched in from a summer of scouting, patrolling, escorting, and simply drilling at various posts and camps in Kansas and Colorado. Lieutenants March and Law had commanded Barnitz's Troop G since the Washita. Custer was still lieutenant colonel of the regiment, but Bvt. Maj. Gen. Samuel D. Sturgis had replaced A. J. Smith as colonel and now commanded the post of Fort Leavenworth while Custer retained command of the regiment.

The usual garrison routine characterized life at Fort Leavenworth that winter of 1869–70. Albert, however, could not perform troop duty and served instead on detached service as instructor of cavalry recruits. Also, Jennie was pregnant. Bertha arrived on March 26, 1870, and kept the household in turmoil for weeks afterward.

A bill in Congress to authorize an enlarged army retired list gave promise of passage. Barnitz knew that he could never again perform field duty, and he decided to apply for disability retirement. On June 21, 1870, the family closed out its army home for the last time and entrained for Ohio. In October Barnitz appeared before an examining board in New York City, and on November 30 the ·mail brought War Department orders placing him on the retired list.

Crowning his military honors, Barnitz was awarded a brevet of full colonel for "distinguished gallantry" at the Battle of the Washita. But perhaps more satisfying as testimony to his military worth was a letter he received shortly before leaving Fort Leavenworth. Dated "G Troop 7th Cavalry, Camp near Forks Solomon River, Kan., April 1, 1870," it was from Pvt. Francis S. Gordon. Gordon's long and creditable service as Barnitz's first sergeant had ended unhappily on March 25, 1868, when he deserted following arrest for drunkenness. But he had repented and with Barnitz's help had been restored to duty with relatively light punishment. Gordon had reported to Fort Hays, where G Troop was stationed, on February 3, 1870. "Of course I visited the quarters of the troop," he wrote, "before proceeding to my own quarters, the Guard House, and am happy to say, met with a very flattering reception from all the old members of the troop; and it gives me great pleasure, Col., to state, that they made many and earnest inquiries, in ragard to the state of your health, and if you were going to come out in the spring, and take command once more. They all earnestly wish you would. The troop has been commanded during the past year by at least 7 officers, but they say that 'the Col. was worth them all' to look after the welfare of the men. So it is the earnest wish of the troop, one and all, that as soon as your health permits, you assume command."

At the age of thirty-five, Barnitz's active military career had ended. A pension of $175 per month furnished a reliable income. He and Jennie built a big house in East Cleveland a few blocks from the Platts. Albert read law, dabbled in Republican politics, wrote poetry, and devoted himself to keeping Jennie contented. Two more daughters followed Bertha in quick succession—Maidie in 1873, Blanche in 1875. Then the Barnitzes became afflicted with the wanderlust, and for the rest of their days they traveled ceaselessly from one end of the country to another. Albert wrote long travelogues for the Cleveland Morning Herald *and* Daily Leader, *which won him free or discounted railroad tickets and hotel accommodations.*

Although retired, Barnitz never lost interest in the army or pride in his military record. As he grew older he reveled in the status of scarred war hero, participated with great zest in the affairs of veterans' organizations, and attained a modest reputation as a conversationalist, raconteur, and

Albert in retirement, about 1876.

246   EPILOGUE

public speaker. As many a reporter discovered, the colonel could always be counted on for exciting, colorfully recounted reminiscences of military adventure.

One hot July day in 1876 the Barnitz family was stunned and saddened by news from Montana. Sioux and Cheyenne warriors had wiped out five troops of the 7th Cavalry in a disastrous action on the Little Bighorn River. The roster of dead evoked many a memory of Kansas in 1867–68: George and Tom Custer, Yates, Keogh, Cooke, "Fresh" Smith. McIntosh, the part-Indian lieutenant who commanded Albert's old troop in Major Reno's valley action, had died. So had Edward Botzer, the faithful little German bugler who had fought by Barnitz's side at Fort Wallace in 1867 and nursed him to recovery after the Washita. Now a sergeant in G Troop, he had been cut down at the ford as Reno retreated across the Little Bighorn. Other comrades had narrowly escaped—Benteen, Moylan, Weir, Godfrey, Mathey. Barnitz's journal noted the gloom that settled over the home in East Cleveland, and Bertha remembered it the rest of her life. Years later Albert remarked: "Jennie, if I had stayed in the Army, by this time I would have been general." No, replied Jennie, "You would have been an angel."

Renewed association with the army came in 1892, when Bertha married Lt. Bernard A. Byrne, a likable young Irishman who was adjutant of the 6th Infantry. Ben Byrne won a Medal of Honor for gallantry in the Philippines in 1899 while serving as lieutenant colonel of a volunteer infantry regiment, but contracted a tropical disease from which he died in 1910, shortly after his retirement. Maidie died at the age of thirty-eight, in 1911, after a shattering emotional experience in the San Francisco earthquake of 1906. Blanche, after an unsuccessful marriage, lived with her parents.

During the decades of restless travel interrupted by brief sojourns in East Cleveland, Albert and Jennie fell into a relationship that seems best described as affectionate mutual toleration. Jennie grew more and more strong-willed, devoted to comfort and self-gratification, and preoccupied with external forms and appearances. Albert grew more and more easy-going, affable, philosophical, unconcerned with the trivial, and beloved by an ever-widening circle of friends. Granddaughter Betty, today the Marquesa de Zahara, vividly recalls the contrast—Jennie, possessed of "the soul of a Major General," who "ran everyone, and ran them ragged"; Albert, "just plain beautiful," whom Betty "adored," who "managed to give a child a sense of comspiracy shared." Of Jennie's disapproval of his 1857 volume of poetry, which she did not think her grandchildren ought to be permitted to read, Albert wrote revealingly to Bertha in 1908 that Jennie was "like the 'W.C.T.U.' women, who have never 'fit the wars' and know nothing of what they are talking about, and are nonetheless 'much sot in their way.' I will venture to say that Jennie has never read, and seriously considered, half a dozen poems in that juvenile volume." But they admired, respected, and surely loved each other for all their differences of temperament, which gave each the strength to tolerate the other's eccentricities.

Death came to Albert Barnitz on July 18, 1912, at Asbury Park, New Jersey, in his seventy-seventh year. An autopsy revealed that a growth around his old wound had caused death. Also discovered was a fragment of his army overcoat, driven into his body forty-four years earlier by a ball fired by a Cheyenne warrior from a Lancaster rifle. Jennie and Bertha took the colonel's body to Washington, D.C., where the War Department furnished a chaplain and firing squad for the last rites in Arlington National Cemetery. Jennie followed in death in 1927, at the age of eighty-six (or thereabouts), and Bertha was ninety-one when an automobile accident took her life in 1961.

Appendix A

People Identified in the Text with an Asterisk

BASSETT, BRADFORD L. Bassett was born in Pennsylvania in 1836 and moved to Kansas in 1857. He served inconspicuously throughout the Civil War, emerging a captain. With the support of Kansas Governor Samuel J. Crawford and other political figures, he secured a commission of second lieutenant in the 7th Cavalry in 1867. Bassett went home to Illinois on sick leave in the fall of 1868 and remained there until his death on March 11, 1869, of chronic dysentery and abscess of the liver.

BEECHER, FREDERICK H. Born in New Orleans in 1841, Beecher was reared in Massachusetts. As Barnitz notes, he was the nephew of the famed cleric Henry Ward Beecher. He was mustered as a sergeant in the 16th Maine Infantry in August 1862 and commissioned second lieutenant in February 1863. He was severely wounded at Fredericksburg but fought at Chancellorsville and was again wounded, almost mortally, at Gettysburg. Transferred to the Veteran Reserve Corps early in 1864, he served until the close of the war with the Freedmen's Bureau in North Carolina. He received a regular army appointment as second lieutenant in the 3d Infantry in November 1865 and was promoted to first lieutenant six months later. Beecher suffered severely from his wounds and was attempting to obtain an appointment to the Quartermaster Department when killed in the Battle of Beecher's Island, Sept. 17, 1868.

BELL, JAMES M. A well-educated and competent officer, Bell served as the 7th Cavalry's efficient quartermaster from 1867 to 1869, and is remembered for the dispatch with which he got needed supply wagons to Custer after the charge at the Washita. Born on Oct. 1, 1837, in Williamsburg, Pa., Bell obtained a master's degree at Wittenberg College in 1862. He served brief military tours in the summers of 1862 and 1863 before finally mustering as a captain in the 13th Pennsylvania Cavalry in October 1863. He participated in sixteen major engagements, including Mine Run, the Wilderness, Spottsylvania, North Anna, and Ream's Station. Regular army brevets up to major later recognized his battle record. Appointed a second lieutenant in the 7th Cavalry in 1866, he was promoted to first lieutenant in 1867. He was on leave of absence during the Little Bighorn campaign of 1876 but received his captaincy as a

result of Yates's death. Bell fought at Canyon Creek against the Nez
Percés in 1877 (and later received a brevet of lieutenant colonel for his
part) and performed a variety of frontier duties all over the West for the
next twenty years. In the Spanish–American War he commanded a
regiment in the Cuban campaign of 1898 and in 1899, as a brigadier general of volunteers, led a brigade in the Philippines. In 1901
he was promoted to brigadier general in the regular army and retired.
He made his home in Pasadena, Calif., where he died on Sept. 17, 1919.

BENTEEN, FREDERICK W. One of the 7th Cavalry's foremost officers,
Captain Benteen commanded Troop H from 1866 to 1882. With a
character and temperament fully as positive as Custer's, he immediately
formed an acute distaste for the regimental commander, and he
emerged after the Washita as the leader of the anti-Custer faction. He
had written a letter criticizing Custer for the abandonment of Major
Elliott. It was published anonymously in a St. Louis newspaper. Custer
threatened the author with a horsewhipping but backed down when
Benteen stepped forward to claim the distinction. For the next eight
years, until the Little Bighorn, Custer and Benteen were bitter enemies.
    Born on Aug. 24, 1834, at Petersburg, Va., Benteen moved to St.
Louis in 1849. He entered the volunteer service in September 1861 as a
first lieutenant in the 10th Missouri Cavalry, in which he rose to captain
in October 1861, major in December 1862, and lieutenant colonel in
February 1864. He fought creditably in eighteen major engagements,
including Wilson's Creek and Pea Ridge, and participated in the siege of
Vicksburg. He was with Gen. A. J. Smith at the fight with Forrest at
Tupelo. After the war brevets up to lieutenant colonel in the regular
army came to Benteen for the Battle of Osage and the charge on
Columbus, Ga. From July 1865 to January 1866 he served as colonel of
the 138th U.S. Colored Volunteers. Benteen applied for a regular army
commission in September 1866, submitting recommendations from
Generals S. R. Curtis, W. S. Rosecrans, Alfred Pleasanton, Emory Up-
ton, and Clinton Fisk, as well as the governor of Missouri and mayor of
St. Louis.
    Despite a preference for easy assignments, Benteen was widely ad-
mired in the army as an almost ideal cavalry troop commander. Stocky,
with thick gray hair, intense eyes, and a ruddy, smooth-shaven, cherubic
face, he made H Troop one of the consistently best in the 7th. Lt. Hugh
L. Scott, later Army Chief of Staff, testified that "I found my model early
in Captain Benteen, the idol of the Seventh Cavalry on the upper
Missouri in 1877, who governed mainly by suggestion; in all the years I
knew him, I never once heard him raise his voice to enforce his purpose." Benteen did well at the Washita. His coolness and bravery prob-

ably saved Major Reno's command from Custer's fate at the Little Bighorn. And he distinguished himself at Canyon Creek in 1877. A brevet of colonel was awarded him in 1868 for an action against the Cheyennes a year earlier, and a brevet of brigadier general in 1890 for the Little Bighorn.

Even so, Benteen was capable of consuming hatreds, as his relations with Custer attest and as his correspondence with Theodore Goldin amply demonstrates. The latter, recently published, shows Benteen to have been a man of monumental vindictiveness and cancerous bitterness toward almost all his old comrades.

He also, like so many other frontier officers, had a well-developed fondness for the bottle. This at last proved his undoing. As a major, to which rank he was promoted in the 9th Cavalry in 1882, he commanded Fort Duchesne, Utah, in 1886, and was charged with repeated offenses of drunkenness on duty. In one instance, he did "conduct himself in a scandalous manner in the post trader's store, using obscene and profane language; taking off his clothes, to quarrel with citizens, and exposing his person. This to the dishonor and disrepute of the military service." Then at the court-martial he comported himself in an insubordinate manner that did not help his cause with the court's president, Barnitz's old Civil War commander, Col. August V. Kautz. The court found Benteen guilty and decreed dismissal from the service. President Cleveland, noting his long and honorable service, softened the sentence to suspension for a year. Benteen repaired to Atlanta, where he had established residence, and requested disability retirement to take effect at the end of his suspension. This was granted, and he retired in June 1888. He died on June 22, 1898, of paralysis and was buried in Arlington National Cemetery.

BLACK KETTLE (Cheyenne).   One of the most prominent chiefs of the Southern Cheyennes, Black Kettle was known throughout the 1860s as the principal advocate of peace and accommodation with the whites. He signed the Treaty of Fort Wise in 1861 and the Treaty of Medicine Lodge in 1867. Black Kettle was the victim of the infamous Sand Creek Massacre of 1864, when Colorado militia under Col. John M. Chivington, the "Fighting Parson," attacked and almost wiped out his village. Black Kettle, who thought he was under military protection, narrowly escaped with his life. He was not so fortunate four years later, when Custer surprised his village on the Washita. Black Kettle fell early in the fighting. He was approximately fifty-one years old at his death.

BREWSTER, CHARLES.   Born in New York in March 1836, Brewster clerked for a mercantile firm, a bank, and a law office before volunteering for the Union army in 1862. In 1864 he served as captain and commissary of subsistence on the brigade staff of General Custer. Captured in the Shenandoah Valley by the Confederate partisan John S. Mosby, Brewster and twenty other prisoners were forced to draw lots for the selection of seven to be executed in retaliation for executions of Confederates by Custer. Twice Brewster drew blanks. Subsequently he escaped and served in New Orleans until mustered out in July 1865.

Both General Custer and Quartermaster General M. C. Meigs, for whom Brewster worked as a civilian private secretary in 1865–66, endorsed his application for a regular army commission. He was appointed a second lieutenant in the 7th Cavalry and promoted to first lieutenant in February 1867. When the army was reduced in 1870, Col. S. D. Sturgis, regimental commander, referred Brewster to the Hancock Board, which was paring down the officer corps, as "constitutionally inefficient inasmuch as he is a very trifling character and brings neither energy or industry into play in the execution of his duties and besides all this is unreliable and untrustworthy never hesitating to tell a lie when it suits his purposes." Rather than face the board, Brewster requested discharge, which was granted in November 1870.

For the next thirty years he brought political influence to bear to secure reinstatement in the army, but each time he failed. Upon one such occasion, in 1878, Benteen, Mathey, Godfrey, Moylan, and Bell signed a letter to the Senate Military Committee stating that Brewster "is totally unfit, in every way, to be an army officer. He lacks decision, force of character, self-respect, and indeed everything that is noble and manly, and fails utterly to command the respect of troops. . . . We can recall nothing in Lt. Brewster's military career, in the 7th Cavalry, that would at all redound to his credit, but many things to the contrary."

Brewster died at Milford, Neb., July 20, 1904.

BULL BEAR (Cheyenne). Prominent chief of the Dog Soldiers, Bull Bear usually was mentioned along with Tall Bull and White Horse in Dog Soldier relations with the whites during the 1860s. He signed the Medicine Lodge Treaty of 1867, fought at Beecher's Island, and finally, after the death of Tall Bull at Summit Springs, drifted with his people into the new reservation set up for the Cheyennes in Indian Territory. He apparently took his band north to roam with the Sioux in 1870 but was back in 1871 and thereafter lived uncomfortably under reservation restraints. Bull Bear and his people participated in the Red River War of 1874–75 and thereafter accepted the reservation.

COMMAGERE, FRANK Y. Commagere seems to have been one of the 7th Cavalry's most ineffective officers, constantly in trouble of one kind or another and, though a social fellow, scarcely of officer caliber. Born in Ohio on April 8, 1844, he was a midshipman at the U.S. Naval Academy briefly in 1861, then served a year in 1862–63 as a second lieutenant in the 67th New York Volunteers before being dismissed. For a year in 1865–66 he was a major in the 6th U.S. Colored Cavalry. Despite this undistinguished record, Commagere won an appointment as first lieutenant in the 7th Cavalry in 1867. As Jennie notes in her diary, he resigned in January 1868. He left Fort Leavenworth abruptly, without permission and without turning over public property. Later he sought reinstatement, alleging that he had resigned in a "reckless moment" after being refused leave to visit his mother, who was in "distressing circumstances." Failing in reinstatement, he petitioned for renomination to his old rank. Again, in 1876, immediately after the Little Bighorn, he applied for appointment to the 7th Cavalry—without success. He died on July 25, 1892.

COOKE, WILLIAM W. An able and energetic officer, one of Custer's favorites, Cooke is remembered as commander of the picked company of sharpshooters at the Washita and for an impressive growth of whiskers. Born in Canada on May 29, 1846, he moved to New York in 1860 and was mustered as a second lieutenant in the 24th New York Cavalry in 1864, at the age of eighteen. He fought at the Wilderness, Spottsylvania, and Cold Harbor, was wounded in the leg at Petersburg, and returned from convalescence in time to participate in the Appomattox campaign. Appointed second lieutenant, 7th Cavalry, in 1866 he was promoted to first lieutenant a year later and also received brevets for Civil War services up to lieutenant colonel. Custer made him regimental adjutant in 1871 to succeed Myles Moylan. As adjutant on June 25, 1876, Cooke scrawled the famous last message from Custer and shortly afterward died near him in the "last stand." His body was subsequently interred at Hamilton, Ontario.

COOPER, WICKLIFFE. Born at Lexington, Ky., Oct. 19, 1831, Wickliffe Cooper spent two years at Dickenson College, Pa. In 1861 he enlisted in the 20th Kentucky Infantry and was soon commissioned second lieutenant and assigned to staff duty. He fought at Shiloh and Corinth, was captured at the Battle of Richmond, Ky., and subsequently exchanged. Commissioned lieutenant colonel of the 4th Kentucky Cavalry in March 1863, he was promoted to colonel a month later and commanded his regiment at Chickamauga the following September. While on sick leave at Lexington in June 1864, he assumed command of assorted local forces and repulsed the Confederate cavalry raider Gen. John H. Morgan.

Later Cooper participated in the operations against Gen. John B. Hood and in Gen. James H. Wilson's expedition through Alabama.

With this distinguished record—subsequently reinforced by regular army brevets of lieutenant colonel and colonel—Cooper easily obtained a commission in 1866 as second major of the 7th Cavalry. Already, however, he was so far afflicted by alcoholism as to have little impact on the regiment before his tragic death on June 8, 1867. This occurred on Medicine Lake Creek, Neb., as Custer's command approached the Platte River on its foray in search of Cheyennes and Sioux. Cooper had exhausted his supply of whisky and, in a fit of delerium tremens, shot himself in the head with his pistol. Of him Custer wrote, on the same day (Merington, *Custer Story*, p. 205): "But for intemperance Col. Cooper would have been a useful and accomplished officer, a brilliant and most companionable gentleman. He leaves a young wife, shortly to become a mother."

In the spring of 1868 an effort was made to establish that Cooper had been taking morphine for heat stroke and died by accident rather than suicide. Custer, Major Elliott, and Surgeon Coates refuted this contention in persuasive official reports. Attempting to obtain a pension, Mrs. Cooper later induced friends in Congress to seek redress, and in 1875 a Senate committee concluded the "the habits of his life, the location of the wound of which he died, and all the attendant circumstances are inconsistent with the theory of suicide." Finally, in 1885, an act of Congress directed the Secretary of War to "correct" Cooper's record to show that he had "died by hand of person or persons unknown"—which of course was not true but conveniently disposed of the vexing problem.

Cox, Charles G. As Barnitz intimates, Cox was a highly political officer. Born in Portland, Me., in 1841, he compiled a creditable Civil War record, then went to Colorado, where he became Adjutant General of the Territory. Through political influence, he sought a Regular Army appointment, brevets up to colonel, and easy staff duty. He turned an appointment of second lieutenant of infantry in February 1867 into a transfer to the 7th Cavalry in May into an appointment of captain, 10th Cavalry, in August and a detail to General Hancock's staff in November. At the same time, however, General Grant blocked his petition for a brevet of colonel on grounds that his highest Volunteer rank had been major, and he had to content himself with a brevet of major. In 1870 Cox was cashiered following conviction on charges of drunkenness on duty and misappropriation of public property. He died on Jan. 14, 1886.

Custer, Elizabeth Bacon. As indelibly and almost as deeply as her husband, Libby Custer stamped her mark on the 7th Cavalry. Like

Jennie Barnitz, she was a tiny, slender, dark-haired beauty, well educated, socially adept, and completely devoted to her husband. However
they regarded George Custer, most acquaintances liked and admired
Libby. She in turn, conscious of her obligations as wife of the commanding officer, worked hard at promoting harmony, solidarity, esprit, and
simple good times in the regiment.

Born on April 8, 1842, in Monroe, Mich., Libby enjoyed an early life
of comfort and quiet refinement as the daughter of one of the town's
leading citizens, Judge Daniel Bacon. As youths, Libby and George
Custer, an Ohio boy who lived occasionally with his half-sister Lydia
Reed, did not come to know each other, because the Reeds were far
beneath the Bacons' social level. But Captain Custer of General McClellan's staff was another matter, and the courtship, conducted furtively in
1862–3, finally overcame Judge Bacon's resistance, especially after Captain Custer became General Custer. They were married in Monroe on
Feb. 9, 1864.

The thirteen-year marriage of Elizabeth and George Custer is one of
history's great love stories. She submerged herself completely in him and
his career. Unlike most army wives, she followed him wherever the flag
took him, to muddy bivouacs in Virginia, remote and vermin-infested
frontier forts, and tent homes in Kansas and the Dakotas. Indeed, she
went places where she should not have gone and where her presence
interfered with or even endangered the conduct of military affairs. In
return, Custer lavished on her a love approaching worship, placing her
at the center of almost every thought and act and devoting himself
tirelessly to her happiness.

Widowed by the Little Bighorn at the age of thirty-four, Libby spent
the balance of her long life—fifty-seven years—extolling Autie and de-
fending him against critics. In three books (*Boots and Saddles* [1885], *Following the Guidon* [1890], and *Tenting on the Plains* [1893]) she wrote
vividly of frontier life in the 7th Cavalry while also glorifying its commander. As Jane R. Stewart has written of these books: "They projected
the Custer image that she wanted the American people to accept." And
most people did—until other interpretations began to take root.

Elizabeth Custer died in New York City on April 6, 1933, two days
short of her ninety-first birthday, and was buried beside her husband in
the post cemetery at West Point Military Academy.

CUSTER, GEORGE ARMSTRONG.   Custer is one of the most controversial
figures in American history. In his associates he inspired either love or
hate, rarely indifference. History reflects this disagreement. Some histo-
rians have characterized him as reckless, brutal, egotistical, selfish, un-

principled, and immature. Others have viewed him as portrayed by his first biographer: a model of "truth and sincerity, honor and bravery, tenderness, sympathy, unassuming piety and temperance." In fact, he was all this, and more—repository of a host of baffling contradictions, paradoxical combination of virtue and vice.

Custer was born on Dec. 5, 1839, at New Rumley, Ohio. He passed his early years here and with his half-sister, Lydia Reed, at Monroe, Mich. Graduating from West Point in 1861 at the foot of his class, the young lieutenant plunged into the Civil War with an aggressive fighting spirit that quickly brought him to the attention of his superiors. In 1863 Maj. Gen. Alfred Pleasonton selected him and two other youthful officers for promotion to high rank. At the age of twenty-three Custer became a brigadier general. Two years later he won his second star. From Gettysburg to Appomattox, the flamboyant, gold-bedecked horseman with the flowing yellow hair led first the Michigan Cavalry Brigade and then the Third Cavalry Division from one triumph to another. The explanation for this record lies in a mixture of inexhaustible energy, driving ambition, incredible good fortune, courage of a high order, and rare combat talents and instincts. On swift perception and almost instant reaction, he built his success. By the close of the war he was a trusted lieutenant of General Sheridan and a widely admired national hero. The white towel that signaled the surrender of Lee's army at Appomattox came to General Custer, and to Mrs. Custer General Sheridan presented the table on which the surrender terms were signed by Grant and Lee.

Although a major general of volunteers and a major general by brevet in the regular army, Custer's rank in the army line had by 1865 advanced only to captain. With the reorganization of the regular army in 1866, however, and with Sheridan's help, he won appointment to the lieutenant colonelcy of the 7th Cavalry. For the next ten years, while the colonel of the regiment (first Smith, then Sturgis) remained on detached service, Custer led the 7th in campaigns against the Sioux, Cheyenne, Arapaho, Comanche, and Kiowa Indians of the Great Plains. His baptism in Indian campaigning occurred in General Hancock's operations of 1867, in which he learned how little he knew about unconventional warfare. This was followed in 1868, however, by the immensely successful Washita campaign, which lifted him from the disgrace of his 1867 court-martial and gave him fame as an Indian fighter. After an interlude in Kentucky, the 7th Cavalry went to Dakota Territory in 1873 and, under Custer, participated in the Stanley Expedition of that year, which protected surveyors of the Northern Pacific Railroad and skirmished with Sioux on the Yellowstone; the Black Hills Expedition of 1874, which opened this remote corner of the Sioux hunting grounds to white gold-seekers; and finally the Little Bighorn campaign of 1876.

On June 25, 1876, Custer led the 7th Cavalry in an attack on Sitting Bull's huge encampment in Montana's Little Bighorn Valley. Five troops under his immediate command perished to a man at the hands of several thousand Sioux and Cheyenne warriors. The other seven troops dug in on bluffs four miles distant and held out until help came. In this dramatic and hotly controversial clash, one of the nation's most spectacular military disasters, Custer achieved an immortality that a dozen brilliant victories could not have earned him. He enjoys today a prominent and enduring place in the history and folklore of America.

CUSTER, THOMAS WARD. Like Mike Sheridan, Tom Custer's career prospered under the influence of a distinguished older brother. Born in Ohio on March 15, 1845, he enlisted in the 21st Ohio Infantry at the age of sixteen and fought with distinction at Stones River, Chickamauga, Missionary Ridge, Kennesaw, and Atlanta. In November 1864 he was commissioned a second lieutenant in the 6th Michigan Cavalry and promptly appointed to the staff of General Custer in the Shenandoah Valley. At Namozine Church on April 4, 1865, Tom captured a battle flag; then, two days later, at Saylor's Creek, he joined Barnitz in the charge of the 2d Ohio and wrested another battle flag from the hands of its bearer, in the process receiving a musket ball through his cheek. For these two events he became the proud bearer of two Medals of Honor. With General Custer's help, he received a regular army appointment of second lieutenant in February 1866 and, after passage of the Army Act in July, of first lieutenant in the 7th Cavalry. Brevets up to lieutenant colonel honored his war record. Tom was an energetic, fun-loving youth, eternally, with his brother, perpetrating practical jokes on others of the Custer entourage. Unlike his brother, he occasionally drank heavily. Promoted to captain in 1875, Tom commanded C Troop at the Little Bighorn and fell next to his brother in the famous "last stand" on June 25, 1876.

ELLIOTT, JOEL H. The third major of the 7th Cavalry, Elliott received his commission in March 1867. Because of Cooper's death and Gibbs's ill health, Elliott found himself the senior officer in the field during the year of Custer's suspension from duty, 1867–68. A year younger than Custer, he was younger than most of the captains and some of the lieutenants. Nevertheless, he was a dedicated, conscientious, ambitious soldier with a wealth of combat experience in the Civil War, and he performed creditably, if not entirely beyond the criticism of Barnitz, as a field commander. The Washita cut short a promising career. Pursuing fleeing Cheyennes down the valley, he exclaimed: "Here goes for a brevet or a coffin." As Benteen put it, he "was 'pirating' on his own hook," and it won him a coffin instead of a brevet.

Born in Wayne County, Ind., on Oct. 27, 1840, Elliott enlisted in the 2d Indiana Cavalry at the outbreak of the war and fought as a private at Shiloh, Perryville, and Stones River, in the last two as orderly to Gen. A. McD. McCook. Commissioned in the 7th Indiana Cavalry in June 1863, he served as a company commander under Col. F. W. Benteen and Gen. A. J. Smith. He was twice severely wounded. In December 1864 he commanded his regiment in Gen. B. H. Grierson's famed raid through Mississippi. In December 1865, while a member of General Custer's staff in Texas, he decided to apply for a regular army commission. Custer endorsed the application: "Capt Elliott is a natural soldier improved by extensive experience and field service. He is eminently qualified to hold a commission in the Regular Army."

It has been generally believed that Elliott, despite his youth and lack of previous service in any grade above captain, won a major's commission in the regular army because, as Gen. E. S. Godfrey recalled it years later, "he passed such a perfect mental examination that the board recommended his appointment as major of cavalry." There can be no question that he possessed unusual intellectual endowments as well as a superlative combat record. But the appointment came about because the application of December 1865, despite repeated follow-ups, kept getting lost among all the paper in Washington. Finally, in March 1867, after most of the vacancies in the postwar army had been filled, the powerful wartime governor of Indiana, Oliver P. Morton, called in person on Secretary of War Edwin M. Stanton to urge Elliott's candidacy. Queried by the Secretary, the Adjutant General reported that two vacancies existed for which the young man might qualify: captain, 9th Cavalry, and major, 7th Cavalry. The Secretary at once issued an appointment to the latter post. Only then did Elliott appear before the Hunter examining board, which routinely confirmed the Secretary's appointment.

FORSYTH, GEORGE A. "Sandy" Forsyth, one of the two Forsyths closely associated with General Sheridan, was born at Muncy, Pa., on Nov. 7, 1837. He fought with distinction in the 8th Illinois Cavalry through the Civil War, participating in sixteen major battles and more than sixty minor ones, including those of the Shenandoah and Appomattox campaigns. He was wounded four times and emerged a major. Regular army brevets up to colonel later honored this record. Appointed a major in the 9th Cavalry in 1866, Forsyth was assigned by Sheridan in 1868 to organize a picked company of civilian frontiersmen for Indian duty. In the Battle of Beecher's Island, Sept. 17–25, 1868, the company was badly mauled by Sioux and Cheyenne warriors and Forsyth was wounded three times, almost mortally. For this action he was brevetted brigadier general. He served as military secretary to General Sheridan in 1869–73 and as aide-de-camp to him in 1878–81. Forsyth retired in 1890 as lieutenant colonel of the 4th Cavalry. He wrote two books, both published in 1900: *Thrilling Days of Army Life* and *The Story of the Soldier*. He died in Massachusetts on Sept. 12, 1915.

FORSYTH, JAMES W.   The other of General Sheridan's Forsyths, James W. was born in Ohio on Aug. 26, 1836, and graduated from West Point in 1856. He served through the Civil War principally in staff positions, first with General McClellan, later with General Sheridan, and ended the war a brigadier general of volunteers and with a regular army brevet of brigadier. Appointed a major in the 10th Cavalry in 1866, he continued his close association with Sheridan, whom he served as lieutenant colonel and aide-de-camp (1869–73) and military secretary (1873–78). He became lieutenant colonel of the 1st Cavalry in 1878 and colonel of the 7th Cavalry in 1886. He commanded the 7th at the Battle of Wounded Knee in 1890 and, although severely criticized by Gen. Nelson A. Miles, was absolved of blame by a court of inquiry. Forsyth retired in 1897 a major general and died at Columbus, Ohio, in 1906.

GIBBS, ALFRED.   More than any officer save Custer, Major Gibbs placed his mark on the newly formed 7th Cavalry in 1866–68. Poor health, the result of an Apache lance wound sustained near Cooke's Spring, N.M., in March 1857, kept him in garrison more than the field. But it is a measure of his skill and perseverance that, even in the presence of so forceful a personality as Custer, Gibbs left his stamp prominently on the regiment. "His influence in shaping our regiment in social as well as military affairs was felt in a marked manner," recalled Elizabeth Custer. Barnitz came to regard Gibbs as a petty tyrant, and Jennie thought Mrs. Gibbs an iceberg, but Mrs. Custer's view was softer: "General Gibbs was a famous disciplinarian, and he had also the quaintest manner of fetching every one to the etiquettical standard he knew to be necessary. He was witty, and greatly given to joking, and yet perfectly unswerving in the performance of the most insiginificant duty." "General Etiquette," his associates labeled him. The regimental band, destined to become a bright ornament of the 7th, was largely the creation of Major Gibbs.

Born on Long Island on April 22, 1823, Gibbs belonged to a family prominent in the nation's scientific and political affairs. After attending Dartmouth College, he went through West Point, graduating in 1846. As a lieutenant in the Mounted Rifles, he participated in Scott's advance on Mexico City and so distinguished himself as to earn brevets up to captain. In the years between wars he saw hard frontier service in California, Texas, and New Mexico. Captured by Texan troops with a command of regulars at San Augustine Springs, N. M., in July 1861, Captain Gibbs was paroled immediately but not formally exchanged for a year. Thereafter he served as colonel of a New York volunteer regiment until October 1864, when he was promoted to brigadier general. Under Sheridan he ably led a cavalry brigade in the Shenandoah Valley and in the Appomattox campaign. Brevets up to major general in the regular army recognized his Civil War services.

Bad health kept Gibbs at Fort Leavenworth during the winter campaign of 1868–69. There, on the day after Christmas 1868, he died suddenly of "congestion of the brain." He was buried in Portsmouth, R.I.

GIBSON, FRANCIS M.   Gibson was born in Philadelphia on Dec. 14, 1847. After clerking for a time in the army Pay Department in Washington, he applied for a regular army commission in October 1867. Within three days he received an appointment, promptly passed the examination, and found himself in the 7th Cavalry. Gibson participated in all the field operations of the regiment from 1868 to 1877. At the Little Bighorn he was Benteen's lieutenant in H Troop. He retired in 1890, a captain, on disability caused by chronic gastroenteritis and died in 1919. Katherine Gibson Fougera's *With Custer's Cavalry* is an account by his daughter of her mother's life in the 7th Cavalry.

GILLETTE, LEE P.   Born in Kingsville, Ohio, on April 21, 1834, Gillette served through the Civil War as an officer of the 1st Nebraska Cavalry, fought at Fort Donelson, and was wounded at Shiloh. He received a 7th Cavalry appointment in 1867 and a year later was made captain. As Barnitz notes, however, he had become a hopeless alcoholic and, on the eve of the Washita, was induced by a purse of $1,500 taken up by his fellow officers to resign his commission. (This remedy, which was not uncommon, reflected a measure of self-interest by the subscribers; it not only eliminated an undesirable associate but also advanced all his juniors one step on the seniority list.) Gillette's resignation, "immediate and unconditional," is dated Camp Supply, Nov. 22, 1968, the day before the regiment marched. The endorsement by Custer, same date, reads: "Approved and respectfully forwarded with the recommendation that this officer's resignation be accepted. He is utterly worthless as an officer and unfit to hold a commission in the army." Gillette died on May 13, 1894.

GODFREY, EDWARD S.   Born at Kalida, Ohio, on Oct. 9, 1843, Godfrey served a brief enlistment in an Ohio regiment in 1861, then won appointment to West Point, and was commissioned in the 7th Cavalry after his graduation in 1867. Tall and lanky, with piercing eyes, a big nose, and a mustache of incredible dimensions, he became one of the regiment's most prominent officers and remained with it for twenty-five years. He fought at the Washita in 1868, marched with the Yellowstone Expedition of 1873 and the Black Hills Expedition of 1874, commanded K troop in Benteen's battalion at the Little Bighorn in 1876, received a severe wound at Bear Paw Mountain in 1877 (and later a Medal of Honor and brevet of major), and led his troop at the Battle of Wounded Knee in 1890.

Godfrey is usually viewed as a thoroughly competent professional officer who resisted the frontier temptations that enervated or ruined so many of his contemporaries, and who held the respect and confidence of officers and soldiers alike. Against this reputation, it is interesting to come across Barnitz's criticism of Godfrey the subaltern as lazy, undisciplined, and snobbish about his West Point education. But note, too, that under Barnitz's stern discipline Godfrey seems to have begun to outgrow these youthful flaws. Even so, in 1870 Colonel Sturgis recommended Godfrey to appear before the Hancock Board, which was reducing the officer corps, stating that he was inefficient and complained that cavalry life interfered with his domestic comfort and convenience. Sturgis himself apparently recognized the frivolous character of this indictment and withdrew it. Thereafter, only Benteen among the 7th's officers has left any serious criticism of Godfrey, and he had good words for almost no one.

Godfrey achieved considerable repute as a historian of the Little Bighorn. His article, "Custer's Last Battle," in the *Century Magazine* for January 1892 quickly became, and remains, a basic source for the campaign and battle. Subsequently he published other contributions relating to the Custer fight and other frontier military episodes in which he participated. He also became a warm friend of Elizabeth Custer.

Godfrey was promoted to colonel of the 9th Cavalry in 1901, following service in Cuba and the Philippines. His friends, including the army Chief of Staff, urged his promotion to brigadier general. It was delayed, however, because of the opposition of President Theodore Roosevelt, who held Godfrey responsible for the killing of women and children at the Battle of Wounded Knee. The President finally relented in 1907 and allowed him to retire as a brigadier.

A railroad accident after the Battle of Wounded Knee left Godfrey with injuries from which he never entirely recovered, but he lived an active life for twenty-five years after his retirement and died at Cookstown, N.J., on April 1, 1932.

HALE, OWEN. "Holy Owen" is often mentioned as a personification, in appearance and conduct, of the ideal cavalry officer, and his descent from patriot Nathan Hale reinforces the image. Born in Troy, N.Y., on

July 23, 1843, he did well in the Civil War, first as sergeant major, then as an officer of the 1st New York Mounted Rifles. He was appointed a first lieutenant in the 7th Cavalry in 1866 and advanced to captain in 1869. On detached service in 1876, he missed the Little Bighorn. At the Battle of Bear Paw Mountain, Sept. 30, 1877, Captain Hale was killed while leading his squadron of the 7th Cavalry in the first charge on Chief Joseph's Nez Percé encampment.

HAMILTON, LOUIS MCLANE. Hamilton was a scion of a distinguished and influential family. His father, Judge Philip Hamilton of Poughkeepsie, N.Y., was the son of Alexander Hamilton. Louis was named for his maternal grandfather, Louis McLane, United States senator and member of President Andrew Jackson's cabinet. Born on July 21, 1844, Hamilton entered the regular army 3d Infantry in September 1862, at the age of eighteen, as a second lieutenant. The appointment came to him through the influence of his cousin's husband, Gen. Henry W. Halleck. Hamilton distinguished himself at Fredericksburg, Chancellorsville, and Gettysburg and fought at Petersburg and Appomattox. He was promoted to first lieutenant in May 1864 and, with the expansion of the regular army in 1866, received one of the captaincies of the 7th Cavalry. He was said to be the youngest captain in the regular army. Hamilton was a good troop commander, energetic, ambitious, able, and popular with his fellow officers. The Washita (Nov. 27, 1868) cut short a promising career at the age of twenty-four.

HANCOCK, WINFIELD SCOTT. Of General Hancock at the time of his ill-starred Indian expedition of 1867, reporter Henry M. Stanley wrote: "He is a tall, stately figure, in the prime of life, with a commanding appearance, and excites admiration and respect wherever he goes." Hancock boasted a superb Civil War record, and indeed correspondents had dubbed him "Hancock the Superb." His honors included Antietam, Fredericksburg, and Gettysburg (for which he received the formal thanks of Congress), and Spottsylvania Court House. Of his Civil War services, General Grant wrote: "Hancock stands the most conspicuous figure of all the general officers who did not exercise a separate command. He commanded a corps longer than any other one, and his name was never mentioned as having committed in battle a blunder for which he was responsible. . . . His genial disposition made him friends, and his personal courage and his presence with his command in the thickest of the fight won him the confidence of troops serving under him."

Hancock was born in Pennsylvania on Feb. 14, 1824. Graduated from West Point in 1844, he distinguished himself in the Mexican War and received a brevet for his conduct at Contreras and Churubusco. Between wars he served chiefly in quartermaster capacities, and although he performed frontier duty he lacked much direct experience with Indians. His 1867 operations against the southern plains tribes were an exception to an almost uniformly successful military career.

After 1867 Hancock commanded various departments and divisions, most notably the Division of the Atlantic (1872–86). In 1880 he was the Democratic candidate for President but was defeated by James A. Garfield. Hancock died on Feb. 9, 1886, at the age of sixty-two.

HICKOK, JAMES B. Plainsman, scout, lawman, and gunfighter, "Wild Bill" Hickok has become one of the most colorful figures in the legend and folklore of the frontier. Born in Troy Grove, Ill., on May 27, 1837, he went west in 1855, participated in the strife of Bleeding Kansas and the bloody border warfare of the Civil War years, and became a deputy U.S. marshal in 1866. By 1867, when he signed on as a scout with General Hancock, Hickok had acquired the sobriquet of "Wild Bill" and had attained prominence as a gunman. Affecting shoulder-length hair and immaculate if gaudy clothing, he attracted attention wherever he went. Hickok served creditably as an army scout for two years. In 1869 he was U.S. marshal of Hays City and in 1871 of Abilene. After touring the East with Buffalo Bill's theatrical troupe in 1872–73, Hickok joined the Black Hills gold rush. He was shot in the back and killed by Jack McCall in a Deadwood saloon on Aug. 2, 1876. The standard biography is Joseph G. Rosa, *They Called Him Wild Bill: The Life and Adventures of James Butler Hickok* (Norman: University of Oklahoma Press, 1964).

Barnitz and Wild Bill crossed paths before the Hancock Expedition. In July 1865, in a famous duel arising from a gambling dispute, Hickok shot and killed Dave Tutt in the public square of Springfield, Mo. Major Barnitz, commanding in Springfield, had Bill arrested and turned over to the civil authorities. A jury later found him not guilty. Barnitz's diary for July 21–22, 1865, tells of the episode.

INMAN, HENRY. An energetic and popular quartermaster officer, Inman so efficiently managed the logistical support operations for the winter campaign of 1868–69 that he won a brevet of lieutenant colonel. Nevertheless, his military career can scarcely be pronounced a success.

Born in New York City on July 3, 1839, Inman enlisted as a private in the 9th Infantry in 1857 and served until appointed a second lieutenant in the 17th Infantry in May 1861, shortly after the outbreak of the Civil War. He spent most of the war in quartermaster assignments, emerging a captain with a brevet of major. In Portland, Me., in 1865, he became embroiled in a dispute over pay accounts that was only settled years later when the amount at issue, $500, was simply withheld from his pay. As quartermaster at Fort Union, N.M., in 1867 he was tried on charges brought by General Hancock.

In 1870–72 Inman was again tried on a variety of charges including embezzlement, misappropriation of public property, making false returns, disobedience of orders, neglect of duty, giving false receipts, and other offenses. In the midst of these proceedings, the Quartermaster General wrote of him: "He is reported active and energetic in the field but extravagant in organizing his business and unable to keep his employees within reasonable numbers." Also, he was said to be lax in paying his personal debts. "All of this has led to a voluminous record in regard to him in this office," concluded the Quartermaster General.

Cashiered from the army in 1872 as a result of three trials, Inman subsequently attained some note as a writer on frontier historical topics. Also, with the aid of former Governor Samuel J. Crawford of Kansas, he spent the rest of his life vainly trying to clear his military record. He died on Nov. 13, 1899.

JACKSON, HENRY.   Jackson's career paralleled that of Nowlan. Born in England on May 31, 1837, he served as an officer in the British army before coming to the United States. From 1863 to 1865 he was an enlisted man in an Illinois cavalry regiment and sergeant major of the 5th U.S. Colored Cavalry. In 1865 he received a first lieutenancy in this regiment and was mustered out in March 1866. Appointed a second lieutenant in the 7th Cavalry, Jackson served steadily and competently in the regiment until 1896, when the workings of seniority made him a major in the 3d Cavalry, from which he retired as colonel in May 1901. Jackson died of cancer of the esophagus at Leavenworth, Kan., on Dec. 9, 1908.

KEOGH, MYLES W.   An aura of romanticism has settled over Keogh, daredevil soldier of fortune, troop commander at the Little Bighorn, and owner of the celebrated horse Comanche, the only living thing found on the Custer Battlefield after the battle. Of his foreign antecedents, he wrote the following in his application for a commission in one of the new regular army regiments, Oct. 25, 1866: "Born in Orchard House, Carlow Co. Ireland, on March 25, 1842. Was educated at Carlow College & resided at my home or college until I was sixteen years of age. I then traveled over Europe & in six months afterward entered service in Italy, where I served as 2d Lt. in an Infantry Regiment for two years & half. I was then joined by two other officers of my Regt & having sent in our resignations & acquiring our Passports came to New York & on the 9th of April 1862 I was mustered into the U.S. Service."

Keogh's Civil War record was outstanding. Although he served throughout the war in staff positions, he sought out combat and was invariably cited for bravery and gallantry in action. He was aide-de-camp, successively, to Generals James Shields, John Pope, John Buford, George B. McClellan, George Stoneman, and John M. Schofield. Among the battles in which he fought were Port Republic, Second Manassas, South Mountain, Antietam, Aldie, Beverly Ford, Culpepper, Brandy Station, and Gettysburg. He participated in the Atlanta campaign, fought at Kennesaw and Resaca, and was captured on the Stoneman Raid near Macon, Ga., on July 31, 1864, but was exchanged two months later.

Mustered out of the volunteers a major in September 1866, Keogh had already obtained a regular army appointment of second lieutenant in the 4th Cavalry as a result of glowing testimonials from Generals Meade, Stoneman, Schofield, Thomas, and Cox. Before joining his regiment, however, Keogh was appointed captain in the new 7th Cavalry and soon received brevets up to lieutenant colonel for Civil War achievements.

Keogh was captain of I Troop from 1866 to 1876. He missed the Washita because, as Barnitz mentions, he had accepted a detail to General Sully's staff. But he was at the Little Bighorn and died there, just over the ridge from Custer.

Keogh was the "Irish officer" of whom Mrs. Custer wrote in *Following the Guidon* (p. 150) as turning himself over to his striker "for safe-keeping. Literally, he had given himself up to be directed as Finnigan willed—not, of course, in official affairs, but in every-day doings. He even enjoyed declaring that he had no further responsibility in life. Finnigan kept track of his purse, his clothes, his outfit, his debts. He did not know where anything was, and he did not propose to inquire. . . . This captain, proud as Finnigan was of him, sometimes became so hopelessly boozy, the man concluded that the safest place for the valuables and the family funds was in his own quarters."

After the Custer Battle, Keogh was buried in Auburn, N.Y.

KICKING BIRD (Kiowa). A chief of great force and ability, Kicking Bird was the leader of the Kiowa peace faction, in distinction to Lone Wolf, the principal spokesman for the war faction. Kicking Bird signed the Treaty of Medicine Lodge in 1867 and tried to persuade his people of the futility of resistance to the white advance. Through the troublous years of 1869–75 on the Fort Sill Reservation, Kicking Bird held firm for peace, and in the Red River outbreak of 1874 he quickly brought most of his people back to the reservation. He died suddenly on May 5, 1875, probably poisoned by a member of the war faction.

LAW, EDWARD. Born into a leading Philadelphia family on Nov. 30, 1847, Law was educated in private schools, toured Europe in 1860–61, and for a time attended Heidelberg College. This was followed by Harvard and the University of Pennsylvania. The family intended him to enter a profession, but Law preferred the military and in August 1867 was appointed a second lieutenant in the 7th Cavalry. His services were creditable, but in 1870 he resigned his commission to study law. Admitted to the bar in 1872, he practiced his profession in Philadelphia and was elected to the state legislature in 1880. On Oct. 5, 1881, he drowned in the Schuylkill River in a boating accident.

LEAVENWORTH, JESSE H. The son of Gen. Henry Leavenworth, for whom the fort was named, Jesse Leavenworth was born at Danville, Vt., on March 29, 1807. He pursued his father's profession, graduating from West Point in 1830, but finding military life not to his liking, he resigned his commission in 1836. For the next two decades he practiced civil engineering in Chicago. Commissioned colonel of the 2d Colorado Infantry in 1862, he commanded troops along the Santa Fe Trail, with headquarters at Fort Larned. In October 1863 he was dishonorably discharged for enlisting a unit without proper authority. Later, the discharge was changed to honorable, and in 1864 he was appointed Indian agent to the Kiowas and Comanches. In this post he lacked effectiveness. Both whites and Indians criticized him constantly, frequently with hints at corruption. Correspondent Henry M. Stanley's characterization of him during the Hancock Expedition is interesting: "Colonel Leavenworth is now a cripple, and his head is silvered by age. He has an astute look, and is devoted to red tapeism. His coat pockets are always full of official documents, and the ends of said papers can be seen sticking out an inch or so, and on each one will be found legibly inscribed, 'Leavenworth, Indian Agent.'" He resigned his post in May 1868 and returned to his family in Milwaukee, where he died on March 12, 1885. A biographical sketch is Carolyn Foreman, "Col. Jesse Henry Leavenworth," *Chronicles of Oklahoma* 13 (1935): 14–29.

LEAVY, JAMES T. Born on Feb. 4, 1841, at Lexington, Ky., Leavy served for two years during the Civil War as second lieutenant in the 3d Kentucky Cavalry, later receiving brevets of first lieutenant and captain for services at Shiloh and Savannah. Appointed a second lieutenant in the 7th Cavalry, he joined in May 1867 and served almost a year before appearing before a retirement board that found him incapacitated by reason of insanity and had him confined in the Government Hospital for the Insane. His wife secured his release in October 1868, and in 1872 he enlisted as a private in the 4th Artillery under an assumed name. After service in the Modoc War, he was discharged on petition of relatives and thereafter lived in Harpers Ferry, W.Va. In 1887 the mayor of Harpers Ferry made strenuous efforts to have the War Department recommit Leavy as "insane and a terror to his family and neighbors." He died of heart failure on July 8, 1893, leaving a wife and fifteen-year-old daughter, and was buried in Rock Creek Cemetery, D.C.

LIPPINCOTT, HENRY. Born on Sept. 22, 1839, at New Glasgow, Nova Scotia, Dr. Lippincott studied medicine and in 1863 entered the army as an acting medical cadet. In 1864 he was ordered to California and served as regimental surgeon of the 6th California Volunteers at Forts Humboldt and Grant. Appointed assistant surgeon and 1st lieutenant, U.S.A., in February 1866, he was assigned to the 7th Cavalry as regimental surgeon in March 1867 and served in that capacity until November. Again in October 1868 he was attached to the regiment for the winter campaign against the Cheyennes. At the Battle of the Washita, he attended the wounded Barnitz, but, afflicted with snow blindness, judged him mortally wounded. Lippincott continued with the 7th until March 1871. Thereafter, he rose in the Medical Department to the rank of colonel and Assistant Surgeon General in 1901 and retired in 1903. In his last years he suffered chronic illness and died at Brooklyn, N.Y., on Jan. 24, 1908.

LITTLE ROBE (Cheyenne). A major chief of the Cheyennes, Little Robe usually stood with Black Kettle in seeking accommodation with the whites. Incensed like all Cheyennes by the Sand Creek Massacre in 1864, he figured prominently in the warfare of 1865. He participated in the council with General Hancock at Fort Larned in April 1867 and signed the Treaty of Medicine Lodge in October. Initially he was among the hostiles in the uprising of 1868. After the Washita, however, he surrendered to General Sheridan at Fort Cobb and thereafter exerted his influence among his people, in opposition to the Dog Soldier leaders, to secure a general surrender. On the reservation Little Robe continued to speak for peace and acquiescence and was included in a delegation of Cheyenne chiefs given a tour of eastern cities in 1871 and another that conferred with President Grant in Washington in 1873. In the Red River War of 1874–75 Little Robe counseled peace and remained at the agency when most of his people went out.

MARCH, THOMAS J. A graduate of West Point, March was appointed a second lieutenant in the 7th Cavalry in June 1868 but resigned his commission in 1872.

MATHEY, EDWARD G. "Bible-thumper," Mathey was called in the 7th Cavalry because of his distinction as the "star blasphemy-hurler of the regiment." He explained this trait as the result of an early experience in

France, where he was born on Oct. 27, 1837: his family forced him to study for the priesthood; in revolt he embraced agnosticism and in 1845 fled to America. He served through the Civil War in Indiana volunteer regiments, emerging a major and veteran of fourteen major engagements, including Stones River, Chickamauga, Kennesaw, Atlanta, Franklin, and Nashville. Appointed a second lieutenant in the 7th Cavalry in 1867, he spent the next three decades in the regiment, until retired on disability with the rank of major in 1896. Afflicted with snow blindness on the eve of the Washita, Mathey took Captain Hamilton's place with the supply train, thus freeing the latter to fight, and die, in the battle. At the Little Bighorn, too, Mathey had charge of the pack train. He does not seem to have been more than a mediocre officer but probably did not deserve Benteen's indictment: "Of all the non-entities with which a troop of cavalry could be damned, head and front, Capt. E.G.M. fills the bill." Mathey died in Denver on July 19, 1915, following a prostate operation.

MILNER, MOSES (California Joe). One of the most famous frontier scouts, California Joe is remembered chiefly for his services in the Washita campaign of 1868 and for his prominent mention in Custer's book *My Life on the Plains*. Born in Kentucky on May 8, 1829, Moses Milner had gone west at the age of fourteen and become a skilled trapper and mountain man. Milner scouted for Kearny and Doniphan in New Mexico and Chihuahua during the Mexican War years of 1846–48, prospected for gold in California in 1850–52, and established a cattle ranch in Oregon in 1853. Here he installed his wife, whom he had married in Missouri three years earlier, and left her to bear four sons while he spent the rest of his life adventuring all over the West. After prospecting in Idaho and Montana (where he acquired the sobriquet "California Joe") Milner went to the southern plains in 1864 and to New Mexico in 1865. From 1866 to 1870 he scouted for the army, including Custer, in Kansas. Thereafter he again searched for gold, ran cattle in Nevada, and finally wound up as scout for the Dodge–Jenney Expedition to the Black Hills in the summer of 1875. He almost signed on again as a scout for Custer but instead, after spending the summer of 1876 in the Black Hills, scouted for General Crook. California Joe was shot and killed at Camp Robinson, Neb., in October 1876 by Tom Newcomb, as the result of a feud of several months duration. He was buried in the post cemetery with military honors. A romanticized biography is Joe E. Milner and Earle R. Forrest, *California Joe, Noted Scout and Indian Fighter* (Caldwell, Idaho: Caxton Press, 1935).

MOYLAN, MYLES. Moylan played a long and important part in the affairs of the 7th Cavalry. As adjutant from 1867 to 1870 and as captain of Troop A for almost two decades, he was one of the most outstanding figures in the early years of the regiment. With sandy mustache and blocky face and frame, he exuded an air of quiet and capable dependability.

Born in Massachusetts on Dec. 17, 1838, Moylan enlisted in the regular army in 1857 and worked his way up to first sergeant of a company of the 2d Dragoons. As an enlisted man he fought at Fort Donelson and Shiloh in 1862. In February 1863 he won a commission as second lieutenant in the 5th U.S. Cavalry. The first lieutenant of his company was George A. Custer. In this post Moylan fought at Beverly Ford, Gettysburg, and other engagements of the Army of the Potomac. In October 1863, however, he was charged with the seemingly trivial offense of visiting Washington without proper authority and dismissed from the army. He promptly enlisted in the 4th Massachusetts Cavalry under the name of Charles E. Thomas, worked his way quickly up to sergeant, and in January 1864 was commissioned first lieutenant. Promoted to captain in December 1864, he served on the staff of Maj. Gen. John Gibbon, participating in the Petersburg and Appomattox campaigns, until mustered out in August 1865.

Early in 1866 Moylan enlisted as a private in the regular army and in August was assigned to the 7th Cavalry, then organizing at Fort Riley. Custer promptly made him sergeant major of the regiment. In November Colonel Smith, Lieutenant Colonel Custer, Major Gibbs, and Captains Sheridan, West, and Keogh united in endorsing his application for a commission. The Secretary of War, learning the circumstances of the 1863 dismissal, set aside this disability and issued an appointment of first lieutenant in the 7th. But Moylan failed the examination. Custer then entered a plea for a second chance, writing to General Hunter, president of the examining board: "He is thoroughly conversant with the duties of a soldier and a subaltern, and in case his examination had been satisfactory he would have been the unanimous choice of the officers of this regiment as Adjutant. Being a young man [he was a year older than Custer] of extreme modesty and diffidence I cannot but feel assured that his failure to pass a satisfactory examination is attributable to this cause rather than incompetency." On the second try he passed.

In *Tenting on the Plains*, Mrs. Custer relates that, however enthusiastic about Moylan the top officers of the regiment may have been, some of the junior officers ostracized him because he had been an enlisted man and indeed withheld the customary invitation to join the bachelor officers' mess. Custer thereupon took Moylan into his personal family until the erring officers began to see how impolitic their actions were and relented. Moylan's ties to Custer became even closer when he married Charlotte Calhoun, sister of Lt. James Calhoun, husband of Custer's half-sister Margaret. Calhoun joined the 7th in 1871 and died at the Little Bighorn.

Moylan was promoted to captain in 1872 and commanded A Troop at the Little Bighorn, where he was with Major Reno in the valley fight and on the bluffs. At the Battle of Bear Paw Mountain with the Nez Percés in 1877 he received a severe wound. In 1890 a Medal of Honor and brevet of major for "most distinguished gallantry" recognized his conduct in this action. He also commanded his troop in the Battle of Wounded Knee in 1890. Promoted to major, 10th Cavalry, in 1892, he retired a year later, settled in San Diego, and died Dec. 11, 1909, of cancer.

MYERS, EDWARD.   Born in Germany in 1830, Myers emigrated to the United States and in 1857 enlisted in the 1st Dragoons, in which he rose to the rank of sergeant. This regiment became the 1st Cavalry in 1861, and in July 1862 Myers was commissioned second lieutenant. Promotion to first lieutenant came a year later. Brevets up to lieutenant colonel recognized his services at Todd's Tavern and Five Forks. In 1866 Myers received one of the captain's vacancies in the 7th Cavalry allotted to the regular army and commanded E Troop from 1866 to 1871. He seems to have been a somewhat dull-witted officer who also had a temper not always restrained by the requirements of military discipline. As Barnitz notes, Myers almost lost his commission. At Fort Wallace in August 1867 he had disobeyed certain orders of Major Elliott relating to quartermaster requisitions, then had refused to submit to arrest, then had broken arrest. Twice he had drawn a pistol on Lieutenant Robbins and once challenged him to a duel. And, taking issue with Dr. Coates's decision to release a sick man from duty, Myers called Coates a "God damn fool" and put the man back on duty. Tried by a court-martial at Fort Leavenworth in December 1867, Myers was sentenced to be cashiered. But the Judge Advocate General, on a showing of undue prejudice against the accused, disapproved the sentence in June 1868 and returned Myers to duty. For ten years he suffered declining health and finally, becoming very feeble, died at Spartanburg, S.C., where his troop was stationed, on July 11, 1871.

NOWLAN, HENRY J.   One of the 7th Cavalry's foreign contingent, Nowlan was born on Corfu on June 17, 1837. Graduated from the Royal Military Academy at Sandhurst in 1854, he served as an officer of H.M. 41st Regiment in the Crimean War and fought at the siege of Sevastopol. In 1862 he resigned his commission and came to the United States to aid the Union cause in the Civil War. He served as a first lieutenant in the 14th New York Cavalry from January to June 1863, when he fell captive to the Confederates at the siege of Port Hudson. For almost two years he endured the prison camp life of Andersonville and Charleston before escaping in February 1865 and joining up with General Sherman's army, which had just marched from Atlanta to the sea.

Mustered out of the volunteer service in May 1866, Nowlan promptly applied for a regular army commission and received an appointment as second lieutenant in the 7th Cavalry. He devoted the rest of his life to the regiment. Promotion to first lieutenant came in December 1866 and to captain in 1876. He served as regimental commissary of subsistence (1867–70) and regimental quartermaster (1872–76). He participated in the Little Bighorn campaign of 1876 but missed the battle because he was on detached service on General Terry's staff. For conduct at the Battle of Canyon Creek, in the Nez Percé campaign of 1877, he later received a brevet of major. He commanded Troop I at the Battle of Wounded Knee in 1890. Promoted to major, 7th Cavalry, in 1895, he died of a heart attack on Nov. 10, 1898, at Hot Springs, Ark., and was buried in the national cemetery at Little Rock.

PARSONS, CHARLES C.   Captain Parsons commanded the much-admired Light Battery B, 4th Artillery, at Fort Leavenworth during Barnitz's western tour and participated with it in the Hancock Expedition of 1867. An 1861 West Point graduate, he fought with his battery at Shiloh, Perryville, and Stones River. For almost two years (1863–64) he was on leave convalescing from surgery. During this period, while assigned to West Point, he was court-martialed for disobedience of orders but reinstated a month later after an appeal. With brevets up to lieutenant colonel, he became captain of his battery in July 1866. Parsons was a West Point classmate and close friend of Custer and served as his defense counsel in the 1867 court-martial. Religiously inclined, in 1870 he resigned his commission and became rector of an Episcopal congregation in Memphis, Tenn., where he died in a yellow fever epidemic on Sept. 7, 1878.

PAWNEE KILLER (Sioux).   Pawnee Killer was an accomplished war leader in the Oglala Sioux band of Little Wound. These Indians, together with the Brulés of Little Thunder and Spotted Tail, had drifted southeast from the main Sioux country beginning in the late 1850s and associated themselves with the Southern Cheyennes between the Platte and the Arkansas. They became known as Southern Oglalas and Southern Brulés. Pawnee Killer's tepees were among those burned by General Hancock on Pawnee Fork in April 1867. It was Pawnee Killer, also, who in June gave Custer his first lessons in Indian warfare and both outwitted and outgeneraled him. And it was Pawnee Killer who, at the same time, wiped out Lieutenant Kidder's detachment. Pawnee Killer fought at

Beecher's Island in September 1868. After Summit Springs, in July 1869, the 5th Cavalry operated against the Sioux of the Platte and twice struck and scattered the Southern Oglala camp. After 1869 Pawnee Killer slips into obscurity. His band ultimately settled at the Red Cloud Agency, where the chief, Little Wound, worked closely with Red Cloud to keep the peace without surrendering the old values.

ROBBINS, SAMUEL M.   Robbins was one of a number of 7th Cavalry officers who were good leaders when sober but increasingly fell under the influence of drink. Born in New York in 1832, he moved to Illinois in 1844 and to Colorado in 1860. As a captain of Colorado volunteers, he commanded a company of cavalry at the Battle of Apache Canyon, where in March 1862 the Confederate invasion of New Mexico was turned back, and subsequently served (1863–65) as chief of cavalry for the District of Colorado. Appointed a first lieutenant in the 7th Cavalry in 1866, he was promoted to captain as a result of Hamilton's death at the Washita. In 1871, in Kentucky, Robbins was brought before a court-martial for offenses involving repeated public drunkenness: he had openly cohabited with a woman in Louisville's Galt House, he had beaten Lt. A. E. Smith's horse and then Smith himself, and he had knocked down a quartermaster sergeant who declined to drink with him. The court decreed dismissal, but Colorado Territory's delegate in Congress interceded and Robbins was allowed to resign. Thereafter he sought, unsuccessfully, to win reinstatement through the same political influence. He died on Sept. 25, 1878.

ROMAN NOSE (Cheyenne).   Of Roman Nose, George Bent, who rode with the Cheyennes, has said: "At the time of the great wars of the 1860's he was known as a great warrior to all the Indians of the Plains, and his fame so spread to the whites that they credited him with being leader in all the fights where the Cheyennes were engaged"—including, as Barnitz supposed, the action at Fort Wallace in June 1867. Roman Nose was not a chief, however, or a Dog Soldier, but an eminent warrior of the Northern Cheyennes whose prowess attracted many followers in war expeditions. His name meant Hook Nose, which the whites translated Roman Nose. He is known to have been a principal leader in the Platte Bridge and Walker–Cole fights of 1865 on the northern plains. In the summer of 1866 he went south and in 1867–68 fought with the Southern Cheyennes. Roman Nose was widely known for his war bonnet, which trailed almost to the ground and, in combination with distinctive facial paintings, gave him protection against harm in battle. But before the Beecher's Island fight of September 1868 he broke a taboo against eating food that had been handled with metal implements. This nullified his medicine, and he was killed leading a charge against Forsyth's scouts on the first day of the fighting.

SATANK (Kiowa).   Born about 1810, Satank, or Sitting Bear, was the foremost chief and medicine man of the Kiowas in the 1860s. He signed the Treaty of Medicine Lodge, but after his son was killed in a Texas raid he became more militant. With Satanta and others, on May 10, 1871, he wiped out the Warren wagon train near Fort Richardson, Tex., and later boasted of the deed to the agent at Fort Sill. General Sherman, whose own party had narrowly missed the fate of the Warren train, was at Sill and ordered the arrest of Satank, Satanta, and Big Tree. En route to Texas for trial in the civil courts, Satank threw off his chains, sprang from the wagon, and was shot dead beside the road.

SATANTA (Kiowa).   For years the best-known Kiowa chieftain, Satanta was a warrior of outstanding prowess and accomplishment. Also, he was known as the "Orator of the Plains." Born about 1830, by the middle 1860s he was regarded by his people as second in stature only to old Satank and, later, Lone Wolf. In 1867 Satanta accepted General Hancock's gift of a major general's dress uniform, only to appear in it on a raid on the horse herd at Fort Dodge. After the Washita, Custer seized both Satanta and Lone Wolf as hostages for the surrender of the Kiowas, an act that was partly successful. In 1871 Satanta participated in the Warren wagon train massacre and, with Satank and Big Tree, was arrested at Fort Sill, tried in a Texas state court, and imprisoned. Released in 1873, he was returned to the penitentiary in 1875 following his participation in the Red River outbreak. Here he committed suicide on Oct. 11, 1878.

SHERIDAN, MICHAEL V.   Mike Sheridan's career advanced steadily under the patronage of his distinguished older brother. Born May 24, 1840, in Ohio, Mike served throughout the Civil War as an aide to his brother, participating with distinction in all the major battles in which General Sheridan fought. After the war Mike received a regular army appointment of second lieutenant in the 5th Cavalry in February 1866 and, after the expansion of the army, captain in the 7th Cavalry in December 1866. Brevets up to lieutenant colonel recognized his wartime attainments. Detailed for a time to the general's staff in 1867, he received a full staff appointment of lieutenant colonel in 1870, after his brother became lieutenant general. Thereafter he served on Sheridan's staff until his death in 1888. In the Spanish–American War Mike was a brigadier general of volunteers, and he retired in 1902 a regular brigadier. He died on Feb. 21, 1918.

SHERIDAN, PHILIP H.   After Grant and Sherman the nation's most honored war hero, "Little Phil" came to the Indian frontier in 1868 as Hancock's successor in command of the Department of the Missouri. An 1853 West Point graduate, he brought with him considerable experience in Indian fighting before the Civil War as well as a dedication to "total war" that matured on the battlefields of Virginia. A pugnacious little Irishman, stocky, bullet-headed, with black mustache and piercing eyes, Sheridan ruled over a large portion of the frontier army for the next decade and a half. He approached the Indians as he had the Confederates: so long as they were the enemy, they were to be ruthlessly crushed, and no price in blood and toil and treasure was too great to win the objective. A veritable demon on the battlefield, in social relations he was affable and witty although somewhat reticent. As the Barnitzes remark, he made a good impression on the officers of the 7th Cavalry.

Both Custer and Barnitz served under Sheridan in Virginia in 1864–65, when he commanded the Cavalry Corps, Army of the Potomac. During this period Custer became one of Sheridan's most trusted lieutenants, an aggressive and audacious fighter who shared his chief's theories of war. For the rest of his career Custer enjoyed Sheridan's favor, even in adversity. Sheridan helped him obtain the lieutenant colonelcy of the 7th Cavalry, and it is commonly supposed that he saw to it that the colonel of the regiment remained on detached service. For ten years, at any rate, the 7th Cavalry was Custer's regiment.

Upon Grant's inauguration as President in 1869, Sherman was summoned to Washington to become general-in-chief of the army, and Sheridan, promoted to lieutenant general, succeeded him as commander of the Military Division of the Missouri, a huge command extending from the Mississippi to the Rocky Mountains and from Mexico to Canada. Thus the final wars with the tribes of the Great Plains occurred under his overall command, including the great Sioux War of 1876, in which Custer fell. Sheridan held this post until 1883, when he succeeded Sherman as general-in-chief. He died in office, on Aug. 5, 1888, at the age of fifty-seven.

SHERMAN, WILLIAM T.   During the years Barnitz served with the 7th Cavalry, "Cump" Sherman was commanding general of the Division of the Missouri, with headquarters in St. Louis. Thus he was responsible for the entire Great Plains region. Subsequently, upon Grant's inauguration to the Presidency on March 4, 1869, Sherman reluctantly relinquished his command to Sheridan and, assuming four-star rank, went to

Washington as general-in-chief. In this post he served unhappily until his retirement in 1883.

Sherman brought to his postwar duties a place in public esteem second only to Grant's. He had fought as Grant's lieutenant at Shiloh, Vicksburg, and Chattanooga, but it was as supreme commander of the western armies, after Grant's summons to the East, that Sherman revealed his military genius. The Atlanta campaign and the March to the Sea proved decisive in crushing the Confederacy.

Intelligent, quick-minded, blunt and sometimes irascible, Sherman exuded an air of authority that few challenged. His stature, his command presence, his solicitude for the welfare of the line, and the veneration with which it was repaid gave him great influence over the postwar regular army. Even though the post of general-in-chief carried little real authority, the regiments of the line were distinctively "Sherman's Army." Moreover, his views on Indian warfare, shared by Sheridan, shaped the frontier army's approach to its mission. All Indians who resisted the westward movement, he believed, should be promptly and ruthlessly crushed by the methods of "total war" that he had applied so successfully in Georgia and the Carolinas. Most of the major postwar operations, however unsuccessful in execution, were planned and organized with Sherman's philosophy in mind.

Sherman's success came late. Born on Feb. 18, 1820, an 1840 West Point graduate, he resigned his commission in 1853 but did badly in banking and other business ventures. Then the war lifted him from failure and obscurity, and for the rest of his life he remained an honored national hero. He died at New York City on Feb. 14, 1891.

SMITH, ALGERNON E. "Fresh" Smith—Smithy—was a member of the Custer clique, as was "Mrs. Smithy," the wife whom Jennie found somewhat too common for her taste. Born in Newport, N.Y., on Sept. 17, 1842, Smith was mustered as a second lieutenant in the 117th New York Infantry in 1862 and emerged a captain three years later. Beginning in the fall of 1863 he served on the staffs of a succession of generals, including Ames, Ord, and Terry. He participated in the siege of Charleston, the attack on Fort Wagner, the siege of Petersburg and Richmond, the Battle of Cold Harbor, and finally the charge on Fort Fisher, N.C. In the last, serving on Terry's staff, he was severely wounded in the shoulder. After the war Smith was appointed a second lieutenant in the 7th Cavalry and received brevets of first lieutenant and captain for Drury's Farm and Fort Fisher. In 1870 he sought disability retirement because of his old wound, which caused frequent pain and limited the use of his arm, which he could not raise above the level of the shoulder. After undergoing treatment, however, he withdrew the application. In the same year Colonel Sturgis referred Smith to the Hancock Board as "wanting in integrity," but the board found him "not unfit for the service" and restored him to duty. In command of E Troop at the Little Bighorn, he fell on the slope below Custer.

SMITH, ANDREW JACKSON.   A veteran of almost thirty years' hard field service, "old A.J." received the appointment as the first colonel of the 7th Cavalry, to rank from July 28, 1866. Because of his assignment to detached service, however, the organization and command of the regiment fell to Lieutenant Colonel Custer. Even so, as commander of the District of the Upper Arkansas, Smith played an influential role in the early years of the 7th Cavalry.

Born in Bucks County, Pa., April 28, 1815, Smith was graduated from West Point in 1838, a year before Custer's birth. He served as a dragoon officer at frontier stations and in Indian campaigns all over the West, fought in the Mexican War, and in the Civil War rose to major general and corps commander in the Army of the Tennessee. His battle honors included Vicksburg and Nashville, but most remarkably he boasted the exclusive distinction among Union generals of having defeated the wily Confederate cavalryman Gen. Nathan Bedford Forrest—at the Battle of Tupelo, Miss., July 14, 1864. Regular army brevets up to major general honored his wartime achievements.

Able, distinguished, respected, and well liked, Smith was for many years one of the army's most prominent officers. One associate characterized him as "of small stature, with rather brusque, abrupt manners, sometimes verging on irascibility, yet was popular with his troops, and shunned none of the hardships to which they were subjected." "I do not remember that General Smith ever lost a day in the field from sickness," testified General Sherman in 1888; "and in California, in Oregon, on the plains, and throughout the Civil War had the reputation of being the hardest worker and hardest fighter in the Army." And newspaper correspondent Henry M. Stanley (who later "found" Livingstone in Africa) penned this in April 1867, when a snowstorm immobilized the Hancock Expedition at Fort Larned: "He has a grey head, but is as active as any young blood in the command. He is a tough old soldier; laughs at the 'dandified young bucks' who wear shoulder straps and are afraid of a little snow. During the wildest snowstorm that has visited this part for many a year, . . . the General was out on foot, stamping through the snow, performing duties with as much celerity as the youngest subaltern. Being of a kind and genial disposition, he has many friends and admirers."

On May 6, 1869, Smith resigned his commission and was appointed by his old comrade, now President, U. S. Grant to the office of postmaster of St. Louis. Later he served for many years as city auditor. In 1889, by a special act of Congress, he was restored to the regular army rolls and placed on the retired list as a colonel of cavalry. He died in St. Louis on Jan. 30, 1897, at the age of eighty-two.

SMITH, H. WALWORTH. "Salt" Smith was born in Groton, Conn., on Jan. 6, 1827. He went to California in the 1849 gold rush and thereafter took to the sea, spending time in the Caribbean, Peru, and Ecuador. In 1864–65 he served as a lieutenant and captain in the 4th Massachusetts Cavalry. Early in 1867 he received an appointment of second lieutenant in the 7th Cavalry but was in the West Indies and did not immediately accept. In August 1867 he was reappointed and in September 1869 advanced to first lieutenant. In 1871 Smith was charged with embezzling $1,200 and promptly deserting from camp near Fort Hays, Kan. But he had already been dropped from the rolls, and the court's findings of dismissal and imprisonment were overturned for lack of jurisdiction.

STERNBERG, GEORGE M. Good friend of the Barnitzes and the medical officer who treated the wounded Albert after the Battle of the Washita, Sternberg became a distinguished military surgeon. Born in Otsego County, N.Y., on June 8, 1838, he was graduated from Columbia College of Physicians and Surgeons in 1860 and entered the army medical service in May 1861. During the Civil War he served first with the Army of the Potomac and then in the Department of the Gulf. After the war he was stationed at various frontier posts and also wrote extensively on medical topics, including a textbook on bacteriology. In 1893 he was promoted to brigadier general and Surgeon General of the army, a post he held through the Spanish–American War until his retirement in 1903. Sternberg's first wife, close friend of Jennie Barnitz, had died at Fort Harker in 1867 and he had remarried in 1869. He died on Nov. 3, 1915.

STUMBLING BEAR (Kiowa). Cousin of Kicking Bird, Stumbling Bear figures conspicuously as a great warrior and leader in the chronicles of the Kiowas from the 1850s well into the reservation period. He is especially remembered for his bravery and daring at the Battle of Adobe Walls in 1864, when Col. Kit Carson attacked a Kiowa village in the Texas Panhandle. Stumbling Bear signed the Treaty of Little Arkansas in 1865 and the Treaty of Medicine Lodge in 1867. He was a member of a delegation of Comanches and Kiowas that journeyed to Washington in 1872.

SULLY, ALFRED.   Son of artist Thomas Sully, Alfred Sully was born in Philadelphia in 1821. Although artistically inclined himself, he went to West Point and was commissioned in the 2d Infantry in 1841. He fought in the Seminole War and the Mexican War and served in California in the 1850s. His paintings and letters (recently published by his grandson Langdon as *No Tears for the General: The Life of Alfred Sully, 1821–1879* [Palo Alto, Calif.: American West Publishing Co., 1974]) form an important record of military life in the mid-nineteenth century. Appointed colonel of the 1st Minnesota Infantry in March 1862, Sully was commissioned a brigadier general of volunteers in September. Of his conduct at Second Manassas Gen. Oliver O. Howard wrote: "I found Sully in action an admirable commander; cool, clear-headed, and full of expedients." Following the Sioux uprising in Minnesota, General Sully was sent to Dakota and led major campaigns against the Sioux of the upper Missouri in 1863, 1864, and 1865, in all of which he demonstrated skill and aggressiveness as an Indian fighter. With the close of the war, he reverted to a regular army rank of lieutenant colonel of the 3d Infantry with a brevet of brigadier general. Unaccountably, he also became a slow and excessively cautious officer. As commander of the District of the Upper Arkansas in 1868, he acquired a reputation as an ambulance general, and his conduct of the expedition south of the Arkansas in September 1868 reinforced the impression. In November General Sheridan retired him to a desk and substituted Custer as field commander. Promoted to colonel of the 21st Infantry in 1873, Sully died on April 27, 1879.

TALL BULL (Cheyenne).   Together with White Horse and Bull Bear, Tall Bull was a principal leader of the Cheyenne Dog Soldiers throughout the 1850s and 1860s. The Dog Soldiers, numbering about 500, had originated about 1837 as a warrior society such as was common in all the Plains tribes. Gradually, however, the Dog Soldiers transformed themselves into a separate Cheyenne band, renowned for its outstanding warriors and deeds of warfare. The Dog Soldiers usually resisted the efforts of the peace chiefs of the Cheyenne tribe to reach an accommodation with the whites. In 1867 Tall Bull, Bull Bear, and White Horse were persuaded to sign the Medicine Lodge treaty, but thereafter they spearheaded the resistance to its execution. Tall Bull led the raid on the Kaw Indians at Council Grove, Kan., in June 1868, that set in motion the events that resulted in the Cheyenne outbreak of August 1868. He also figured prominently in the Battle of Beecher's Island in September. After Custer's winter operations of 1868–69, Tall Bull's band decided to join the Sioux north of the Platte. En route they were overtaken by a cavalry command under Maj. Eugene A. Carr. In the Battle of Summit

Springs, July 11, 1869, Carr defeated the Cheyennes and destroyed their village. Tall Bull was shot and killed—possibly by "Buffalo Bill" Cody. Summit Springs broke the power of the Dog Soldiers. Thereafter they no longer presented a serious threat to the frontier. Custer described Tall Bull as "a fine, warlike looking chieftain."

TEN BEARS (Comanche). Once a renowned warrior, Ten Bears in the late 1860s spoke for peace and increasingly became alienated from the dominant sentiment of his people. His eloquent speech to the peace commissioners at Medicine Lodge in 1867 is often quoted. Ten Bears represented the Comanches in the delegation of chiefs that visited Washington in 1872 but upon his return suddenly sickened and died.

THOMPSON, WILLIAM. Thompson was the oldest officer of the 7th Cavalry—fifty-three when appointed captain in 1866. He had had a long and varied life. Born in Pennsylvania on Nov. 13, 1813, he read law in Mount Vernon, Ohio, and was admitted to the bar there in 1837. Two years later he moved to Iowa, locating in Mount Pleasant, and won a place in Democratic politics. In 1842–46 he was chief clerk of the territorial legislature. After serving as secretary of the convention that framed the state constitution in 1846, he was elected to the U.S. Congress as the first representative from the southern district. He occupied his seat for one and a half terms (1847–50). Thompson then practiced law in Iowa, surveyed public lands, and for five years edited the daily *Iowa State Gazette*. In 1861 he recruited a company of the 1st Iowa Cavalry and was elected captain. He served in Missouri and Arkansas and rose to colonel of the regiment. In 1865 he went with General Custer to Texas and in 1866 received a captaincy in Custer's 7th Cavalry with brevets of major and lieutenant colonel for the Battles of Prairie Grove and Bayou Metoe. In 1875 Thompson, now sixty-two, retired on disability and returned to Iowa to resume the editorship of the *Gazette*. He died on Oct. 6, 1897, at Tacoma, Wash., of "old age and debility."

WALLINGFORD, DAVID W. The record of this officer suggests why Barnitz and his associates disliked him. Born in Vermont in 1837, he migrated to Kansas and served for two years (1863–65) as a second lieutenant in the 15th Kansas Cavalry. In 1865 a court-martial convicted him of several acts of pillage upon civilians in Arkansas and Kansas, and he was dismissed. Amazingly, however, he applied for a regular army commission. A heavy array of Kansas political figures endorsed him, and, one supposes because of this influence, the War Department removed the impediment to reenter the service caused by his court-martial, which in effect gave him an honorable discharge. He failed the examination for a regular army commission the first time but passed it the second time and was appointed second lieutenant in the 7th Cavalry and promoted to first lieutenant in June 1867. Wallingford's mentor, Governor Samuel J. Crawford of Kansas, urged that he be brevetted major for gallantry at the Washita. Instead, he found himself before another court-martial, in September 1869, charged with publicly associating with enlisted men and "prostitutes and lewd women" and generally comporting himself in an unmilitary manner. The court found him guilty and decreed dismissal, but higher authority ruled otherwise. Even so, Wallingford's taste in companions finally brought him down, for almost immediately another court found his behavior with "a notorious prostitute or lewd woman" in the Perry House and American House hotels in Sheridan, Kan., an offense "to the scandal and disgrace of the military service," and he was dismissed from the army on May 10, 1870. He died on July 11, 1883—in the Kansas Penitentiary, according to Captain Benteen, where he was serving a sentence for horsestealing.

WEIR, THOMAS B.   Throughout the Custer regime, Weir was a loyal and enthusiastic supporter of the regimental commander in opposition to the anti-Custer faction. Born in Nashville, Ohio, on Nov. 28, 1838, he early removed to Michigan and attended the University of Michigan from 1858 to 1861. He enlisted in the 3d Michigan Cavalry in August 1861 and served throughout the war in the western theater, first as an enlisted man, then as an officer. He participated in the siege of Corinth, the campaigns against Forrest in Alabama, and the reduction of Mobile. For six months in 1862 he was a prisoner of the Confederates. As a major, Weir went to Texas with his regiment in 1865 and there served on the staffs, respectively, of Generals Gibbs and Custer. Appointed a first lieutenant in the 7th Cavalry in 1866, he was promoted to captain a year later and also received regular army brevets of major and lieutenant colonel for Civil War services. Upon the reduction of the army in 1869, Weir was one of the 7th Cavalry officers recommended by Colonel Sturgis for release: "intemperate," he wrote, "and when dissipating becomes dissolute and abusive." The charge was quashed by the Secretary of War, however, on the recommendation of the department commander, Brig. Gen. John Pope, and Weir remained the captain of D Troop. In this capacity he fought at the Little Bighorn, where he led an unauthorized and unsuccessful sortie from Reno's command in support of Custer. Assigned to a recruiting detail in New York City, Weir died less than six months later, on Dec. 9, 1876, of "congestion of the brain."

WEST, ROBERT M.   Chiefly because of his bitter conflict with Custer, West was one of the dominant figures of the 7th Cavalry in its formative years. He brought to his regular army appointment in November 1866 a long and distinguished military record. Born in Newton, N.J., Sept. 16,

1834, he had served as an enlisted man in the old Regiment of Mounted Riflemen in 1856–61 before entering the volunteer service at the outbreak of the Civil War. By the summer of 1862 he had risen to full colonel and commander of the 1st Pennsylvania Light Artillery, which in 1864 became the 5th Pennsylvania Cavalry. He led his regiment in some of the bloodiest battles of the Army of the Potomac and distinguished himself particularly in the Appomattox campaign, as attested by a string of regular army brevets up to colonel and a volunteer brevet of brigadier general.

As captain of Troop K, West was one of the ablest officers of the 7th Cavalry (at least when he was sober). Captain Benteen remembered him as a "distinguished man, but given at times to hellish periodical sprees." Custer wrote in September 1867 that West was drinking so heavily that he had delirium tremens. And Barnitz recorded that West was constantly so drunk during the Sully Expedition of September 1868 that he had to be hauled in a wagon.

West's feud with Custer seems to have begun at Fort Hays in May 1867, when Custer forced him, as officer of the day, to shave the heads of six men who had gone to the sutler's store without permission. Then in June, during the Republican River operations, two of the deserters shot on Custer's authority were members of West's troop. To the charges brought against Custer by Colonel Smith for absence without leave West brought supplementary charges related to the shooting of the deserters. Later, after Custer's court-martial, West was responsible for the murder indictment that landed Custer in the civil court at Leavenworth City. Custer, for his part, brought charges of drunkenness against West for which a court-martial at Fort Leavenworth early in 1868 convicted and suspended him for two months.

It is interesting to follow Barnitz's changing view of West: from "a thorough soldier and a polished gentleman—of the *reliable* type" (April 1867) to "crafty, scheming, envious, selfish, malicious" (June 1868), which may trace a decline related to his drinking problem.

According to Captain Benteen, after the Washita battle, West, "feeling that Custer would catch and salt him away surely," won a promise from General Sheridan of the sutlership at newly established Fort Sill, I.T. His fellow officers chipped in to help him buy the initial stock, and he resigned his commission effective March 1, 1869. How far he progressed with this plan is not known, but it never fully matured, for West died near Fort Arbuckle on Sept. 3, 1869.

WHITE HORSE (Cheyenne). White Horse was a foremost chief of the Cheyenne Dog Soldier band during the 1850s and 1860s (see also TALL BULL). He signed the Treaty of Medicine Lodge of 1867 but was prominent in the war of 1868–69. With Tall Bull, he led the Dog Soldiers in the Battle of Beecher's Island in September 1868. After Tall Bull's death at Summit Springs in July 1869, White Horse led his people north to live with the Northern Cheyennes in the Wind River country. Gradually, however, they drifted back to the reservation established for them in Indian Territory pursuant to the Treaty of Medicine Lodge. With other Cheyennes, Kiowas, Comanches, and Arapahos, White Horse's Dog Soldiers left their reservations in 1874 and fought in the Red River War. They were present at the Battle of Palo Duro Canyon in September and surrendered with the main Cheyenne body in January 1875.

WYNKOOP, EDWARD W. A man of ability and humanity, Wynkoop played a major role in the relations between the Southern Cheyennes and the whites from 1864 to 1868. As a major in the 1st Colorado Cavalry in 1864, he commanded the post of Fort Lyon when the tension began to build that led ultimately to the Sand Creek Massacre. Wynkoop came to have an understanding and sympathy for the Indians not shared by most Coloradoans and certainly not by his superior, Col. John M. Chivington. Wynkoop worked for peace in opposition to the war policies of Chivington. The latter of course prevailed, with Sand Creek the result. After the war, as Indian agent for the Cheyennes and Arapahos, Wynkoop worked hard from 1866 to 1868 to prevent hostilities. He vigorously championed the cause of his charges and defended them when accused of depredations. Often he was right but often, also, wrong, and he lost credibility with both army officers and frontier settlers. After the Cheyenne outbreak of 1868, he resigned in disillusion. His letter of resignation was a long and labored vindication of the Cheyennes, whom he pictured as innocent victims of blundering government policies. After the Battle of the Washita he publicly likened Custer to Chivington and the battle to Sand Creek.

Born in Philadelphia on June 19, 1836, Wynkoop emigrated to Kansas in the mid-1850s. In 1858 he joined the Pike's Peak gold rush and was one of the founders of Denver. With the outbreak of the Civil War, he was commissioned in the 1st Colorado Volunteers and in March 1862 fought as a company commander at Apache Canyon and Glorieta Pass, where the Confederate invasion of New Mexico was turned back.

After his resignation as Indian agent in 1868, Wynkoop returned to Pennsylvania and went into the iron-making business. Ruined by the Panic of 1873, he participated in the Black Hills gold rush and briefly fought Indians, in company with the "poet-scout" Capt. Jack Crawford, in a local ranger unit. Thereafter he wandered from one job to another, including Adjutant General of New Mexico and warden of the New Mexico Penitentiary. He died in Santa Fe on Sept. 11, 1891, and was buried in the national cemetery there. A biographical sketch by his son, Edward E. Wynkoop, appears in the *Kansas Historical Collections* 13 (1913–14): 71–79.

YATES, GEORGE W. Born in Albany, N.Y., on Feb. 26, 1843, Yates enlisted as a private in the 4th Michigan Infantry in 1861, at the age of eighteen. He fought at Manassas and the Seven Days, was commissioned first lieutenant and adjutant of the regiment, and fought at Antietam, Fredericksburg (where he was wounded), and Chancellorsville. As an aide-de-camp to Maj. Gen. Alfred Pleasanton, he participated in all the remaining actions of the Army of the Potomac in 1863 and then went to Missouri and campaigned against Confederate Gen. Sterling Price. In March 1866 Yates was appointed a second lieutenant in the 2d U.S. Cavalry and in August was commissioned a captain in the 7th Cavalry. Yates commanded F Troop (the "Band Box" troop) from 1866 to 1876, when he was killed with his troop, near Custer, at the Little Bighorn.

Appendix B

Forts Identified in the Text with an Asterisk

The typical frontier fort was not the bastioned log stockade dear to the imagination of movie script writers, and contrary to the popular image Indians rarely directly attacked a fort. All the posts associated with Barnitz's service in the West were simply a collection of stone, adobe, or frame buildings laid out neatly—or not so neatly—around a parade ground. Officers' quarters edged the quadrangle on one side, soldiers' barracks the other. Administrative, quartermaster, commissary, stables, hospital, and other functional buildings were scattered here and there at the two ends of the parade and elsewhere. Except for the parade ground and flagpole, little distinguished most forts in appearance from nearby civilian communities.

CAMP SUPPLY, I.T. Custer and Sully established Camp Supply in November 1868 as a base for Sheridan's winter campaign of 1868–69. It was located near the junction of Wolf Creek and the North Canadian River. From here Custer embarked on his march to the Washita, and here also he paraded in victory before General Sheridan. Although never considered a permanent installation, Camp Supply endured as an active post until abandoned in 1895. Troops from Camp Supply participated in the Red River War of 1874–75, and it helped watch over the Cheyenne–Arapaho Reservation established under the Treaty of Medicine Lodge.

FORT DODGE, KAN. Established by Wisconsin Volunteers in September 1865, Fort Dodge was located on the north bank of the Arkansas River and was designed to protect travelers on the Santa Fe Trail, which forded the Arkansas at the Cimarron Crossing twenty-five miles to the west. The post was named for Maj. Gen. Grenville M. Dodge, who selected the site in 1864. It served as the principal base for the Sully Expedition of September 1868 and, with Camp Supply, for Sheridan's winter operations of 1868–69. Again in the Red River War of 1874–75 it was a major supply base for troops operating in western Indian Territory and the Texas Panhandle. The cow town of Dodge City grew up adjacent to the fort. By the close of the 1870s, the frontier had moved on and Fort Dodge was abandoned in 1882.

FORT HARKER, KAN. Established in 1864 as Fort Ellsworth, Fort Harker was renamed in 1867 in honor of Brig. Gen. Charles G. Harker, killed at Kennesaw Mountain. Located on the Smoky Hill River at the crossing of the Santa Fe stage road, it gave protection also to the Smoky Hill Trail to Denver and, in 1867–68, to workers on the Kansas Pacific Railroad. It was General Hancock's base for the ill-starred expedition of April 1867. Completion of the railroad to Denver made Fort Harker of little use, and it was abandoned in 1872.

FORT HAYS, KAN. Named for Brig. Gen. Alexander Hays, who had been killed in the Wilderness in 1864, Fort Hays was established in October 1866 as one of a chain of posts to protect construction workers on the Kansas Pacific Railroad. It was first located near the mouth of Big Creek, but, after the flood of June 1867, it was moved to a new site, selected by Maj. Alfred Gibbs, fifteen miles upstream to the west, where the railroad crossed the creek. Fort Hays figured significantly in the Indian hostilities of 1867–70 but thereafter served primarily as a garrison for troops. It was abandoned in 1889. Surviving buildings are now preserved in a state park.

FORT LARNED, KAN. One of the most important posts on the central plains, Fort Larned was established on the Pawnee Fork fifteen miles from its confluence with the Arkansas River in October 1859. Named for Paymaster General Benjamin F. Larned, it was intended as a guardian of the Santa Fe Trail. It played a vital part in the Indian hostilities of 1864–65 and 1867–70, and from 1861 to 1868 it was the location of the agency for the Cheyennes and Arapahos. Abandoned in 1878, it is now a national historic site administered by the National Park Service.

FORT LEAVENWORTH, KAN. For more than half a century, Fort Leavenworth was a keystone of the western military system, significant first as an operational base, then as command center and quartermaster depot. It was named for its founder, Col. Henry Leavenworth, who began construction on the west bank of the Missouri River in 1827. A link in the chain of posts defining the so-called Permanent Indian Frontier, it was planned also as a base for protecting the Santa Fe Trail, the eastern terminus of which was nearby. Later it performed the same function for the eastern segment of the Oregon Trail. In the Mexican War Gen. Stephen Watts Kearny organized the Army of the West here for the march to New Mexico and California. During the 1850s it figured in the

Bleeding Kansas strife. With the advance of the frontier after the Civil War, the fort took on new significance as headquarters of the Department of the Missouri, which gave direction and logistical support to military operations against the Plains Indians until the end of hostilities in 1875. New Mexico also fell within its jurisdiction. Beginning in the 1880s, it became an important center for military education, a tradition carried on today by the Command and General Staff School. Still a major military installation, Fort Leavenworth is the oldest active post west of the Mississippi and one of the most historic in the nation.

FORT LYON, COLO. First named Fort Wise (in honor of Virginia Governor Henry A. Wise) upon its establishment in 1860, Fort Lyon was renamed in 1862 for Brig. Gen. Nathaniel Lyon, who had been killed at the Civil War Battle of Wilson's Creek. It was located on the north bank of the Arkansas River a mile above Bent's New Fort, a trading post, and was intended to protect traffic on the Mountain Branch of the Santa Fe Trail. Fort Lyon played a key part in the events surrounding the Sand Creek Massacre of 1864. In 1867, because of floods and other unhealthful conditions, the army moved Fort Lyon twenty miles upstream to a location two miles below the mouth of the Purgatoire River. It was the base for Maj. E. A. Carr's column in Sheridan's winter campaign of 1868–69. It was abandoned in 1889.

FORT MORGAN, COLO. Fort Morgan was a rude and short-lived sod-and-log post established in July 1865 on the south bank of the South Platte River where the Denver branch of the Overland Trail diverged from the main route. It afforded protection to stagecoaches and other traffic until completion of the Union Pacific Railroad in 1868, when it was abandoned.

FORT RILEY, KAN. Located at the confluence of the Republican and Smoky Hill rivers where they form the Kansas River, Fort Riley dates from May 1853. Named for Col. Bennett Riley, its purpose was to protect the Smoky Hill and Oregon trails. Throughout the 1850s, 1860s, and 1870s, troops garrisoned at Fort Riley participated in operations against the Plains tribes. Like Fort Leavenworth, Fort Riley has also been a center for military education, housing the Cavalry School until 1946, when it was abolished. The fort is still an active military installation.

FORT WALLACE, KAN. The westernmost post of the Smoky Hill defense system, Fort Wallace was established in 1865 at the junction of Pond Creek and the South Fork of the Smoky Hill River. It was named for Brig. Gen. William H. L. Wallace, mortally wounded at Shiloh. Fort Wallace figured importantly in the 7th Cavalry's operations during the summer of 1867 and in Maj. George A. Forsyth's campaign in 1868 that led to Beecher's Island. The post was abandoned in 1882.

FORT ZARAH, KAN. The fort was built in 1864 on Walnut Creek three miles above its junction with the Arkansas River. Its purpose was to protect the Santa Fe Trail, but Forts Harker and Larned met this need, and Zarah was abandoned in 1869.

Appendix C

Organization and Distribution of the 7th Cavalry

May 31, 1867

In camp near Fort Hays, Kan.
  Field and Staff
    Lt. Col. George A. Custer, commanding regiment
    Maj. Wickliffe Cooper
    Maj. Joel H. Elliott
    Assistant Surgeon Henry Lippincott
    1st Lt. Myles Moylan, adjutant
    2d Lt. Charles Brewster, acting quartermaster
    2d Lt. William W. Cooke, acting commissary

  Troop
    A   Capt. Louis Hamilton
    D   1st Lt. Samuel M. Robbins
    E   Capt. Edward Myers
    F   2d Lt. Henry J. Nowlan
    G   Capt. Albert Barnitz, 2d Lt. Henry Jackson
    H   1st Lt. Thomas W. Custer (detailed from A)
    K   Capt. Robert M. West
    M   1st Lt. Owen Hale, 2d Lt. James T. Leavy

Fort Dodge, Kan.
    B   Capt. William Thompson

Fort Wallace, Kan.
    I   Capt. Myles W. Keogh, 2d Lt. James M. Bell

Fort Lyon, Colo.
    C   1st Lt. Matthew Berry

Fort Morgan, Colo.
    L   Capt. Michael V. Sheridan, 1st Lt. Lee P. Gillette, 2d Lt. Henry
        H. Abell
Detached service: Col. A. J. Smith, Capt. Frederick W. Benteen, 1st Lt.
        Thomas B. Weir
In arrest: Capt. William P. Robeson

288

October 31, 1867

Fort Harker, Kan.
  Field and Staff
    Maj. Alfred Gibbs, commanding regiment and post
    1st Lt. Myles Moylan, adjutant
    1st Lt. Charles Brewster, acting quartermaster (at Fort Hays)

  Troop
    A Capt. Louis M. Hamilton, 1st Lt. Thomas W. Custer, 1st Lt.
       James T. Leavy (temporarily assigned from G), 2d Lt. John M.
       Johnson
    D 1st Lt. Samuel M. Robbins, 2d Lt. H. Walworth Smith, 2d Lt.
       Donald McIntosh (temporarily assigned from M)

Fort Hays, Kan.
    E Capt. Edward Myers
    H Capt. Frederick W. Benteen, 1st Lt. William W. Cooke, 2d Lt.
       Frank Y. Commagere (temporarily assigned from K)
    K Capt. Robert M. West, 2d Lt. Edward Law

Fort Wallace, Kan.
    F 1st Lt. Henry J. Nowlan, 2d Lt. William B. Clark
    I Capt. Myles W. Keogh, 2d Lt. James M. Bell

Fort Larned, Kan.
              Indian Peace Commission Escort
    Maj. Joel H. Elliott, commanding
    1st Lt. Henry Jackson, adjutant
    Assistant Surgeon Henry Lippincott
    G Capt. Albert Barnitz, 2d Lt. Edward S. Godfrey
    M 1st Lt. Owen Hale, 2d Lt. Bradford L. Bassett

Fort Dodge, Kan.
    B Capt. William Thompson, 1st Lt. David W. Wallingford

Fort Lyon, Colo.
    C 1st Lt. Matthew Berry, 2d Lt. John F. Weston

Fort Reynolds, Colo.
    L Capt. Lee P. Gillette (commanding temporarily in absence of
       Captain Sheridan), 1st Lt. Henry H. Abell, 2d Lt. J. Henry
       Shellaberger
Detached service: Col. A. J. Smith, Capt. Thomas B. Weir, Capt. Michael
       V. Sheridan
In arrest: Lt. Col. George A. Custer

March 31, 1868

Fort Leavenworth, Kan.
  Field and Staff
    Maj. Alfred Gibbs, commanding regiment
    1st Lt. Myles Moylan, adjutant
    1st Lt. James M. Bell, quartermaster
    1st Lt. Henry J. Nowlan, commissary

  Troop
  A Capt. Louis M. Hamilton, 1st Lt. Thomas W. Custer, 2d Lt.
     Francis M. Gibson
  D 1st Lt. Samuel M. Robbins, 2d Lt. H. Walworth Smith
  E 2d Lt. Algernon E. Smith
  F Capt. George W. Yates
  G Capt. Albert Barnitz
  K 2d Lt. Edward S. Godfrey (temporarily assigned from G), 2d Lt.
     Edward Law

Fort Harker, Kan.
    Maj. Joel H. Elliott, commanding post and squadron
  H Capt. Frederick W. Benteen, 1st Lt. William W. Cooke
  M 2d Lt. Donald McIntosh

Fort Dodge, Kan.
  B Capt. William Thompson, 2d Lt. Bradford S. Bassett

Fort Wallace, Kan.
  I   2d Lt. Edward G. Mathey

Fort Lyon, Colo.
  C Capt. Lee P. Gillette, 2d Lt. John F. Weston (with detachment at
     Trinidad, Colo.)

Fort Reynolds, Colo.
  L No officer present
Detached service: Col. A. J. Smith, Capt. Thomas B. Weir, Capt. Michael
     V. Sheridan, Capt. Lewis M. Dayton, 1st Lt. Henry Jackson, 1st
     Lt. Matthew Berry, 1st Lt. John M. Johnson, 1st Lt. Henry W.
     Abell, 2d Lt. Oliver W. Longan, 2d Lt. J. Henry Shellaberger
Leave of absence: Capt. Myles W. Keogh, 1st Lt. David H. Wallingford,
     1st Lt. James T. Leavy
In arrest: Capt. Edward Myers, 2d Lt. William B. Clark
Undergoing GCM sentence: Lt. Col. George A. Custer, Capt. Robert M.
     West

October 31, 1868

Camp Sandy Forsyth, Kan.
  Field and Staff
    Lt. Col. George A. Custer, commanding regiment
    Maj. Joel H. Elliott
    1st Lt. Myles Moylan, adjutant
    1st Lt. James M. Bell, quartermaster
    1st Lt. Henry J. Nowlan, commissary
    1st Lt. Samuel M. Robbins, engineer officer
    Assistant Surgeon Henry Lippincott (attached)
    Acting Assistant Surgeon William C. Rennick (attached)

  Troop
    A   Capt. Louis M. Hamilton, 1st Lt. Thomas W. Custer
    B   Capt. William Thompson
    C   Capt. Lee P. Gillette
    D   Capt. Thomas B. Weir, 2d Lt. H. Walworth Smith
    E   Capt. Edward Myers, 1st Lt. John M. Johnson
    F   Capt. George W. Yates, 2d Lt. Francis M. Gibson (temporarily
        assigned from A)
    H   1st Lt. William W. Cooke
    I   1st Lt. Charles Brewster
    K   1st Lt. Edward S. Godfrey, 2d Lt. Edward Law
    M   1st Lt. Owen Hale

Camp near Fort Dodge, Kan.
    G   Capt. Albert Barnitz, 2d Lt. Thomas J. March

Fort Lyon, Colo.
    L   1st Lt. Henry W. Abell, 2d Lt. J. Henry Shellaberger
Detached service: Col. A. J. Smith, Maj. Alfred Gibbs, Capt. Michael
        V. Sheridan, Capt. Myles W. Keogh, Capt. Lewis M. Dayton, 1st
        Lt. David W. Wallingford, 1st Lt. Henry Jackson, 2d Lt. John F.
        Weston, 2d Lt. Oliver W. Longan, 2d Lt. Edward G. Mathey
        (joined in time for Washita).
Sick: 2d Lt. Donald McIntosh
Leave of Absence: Maj. James G. Tilford, Capt. Frederick W. Benteen
        (joined in time for Washita), Capt. Robert M. West, 1st Lt.
        Matthew Berry (joined in time for Washita), 1st Lt. Bradford S.
        Bassett
Undergoing GCM sentence: 2d Lt. William B. Clark

Bibliography

BELL, WILLIAM A. *New Tracks in North America*. London, 1869. Reprint. Albuquerque, N.M.: University of New Mexico Press, 1965.

BERTHRONG, DONALD J. *The Southern Cheyennes*. Norman: University of Oklahoma Press, 1963.

CARRIKER, ROBERT C. *Fort Supply, Indian Territory: Frontier Outpost on the Plains*. Norman: University of Oklahoma Press, 1970.

CARROLL, JOHN M., ed. *The Benteen–Goldin Letters on Custer and his Last Battle*. New York: Liveright, 1974.

CHANDLER, MELBOURNE C. *Of Garryown in Glory: The History of the 7th U.S. Cavalry*. Privately published, 1960.

CRAWFORD, SAMUEL J. *Kansas in the Sixties*. Chicago, 1911.

CUSTER, ELIZABETH B. *Boots and Saddles, or, Life in Dakota with General Custer*. New York, 1885. Reprint. Ed. Jane R. Stewart. Norman: University of Oklahoma Press, 1961.

———. *Following the Guidon*. New York, 1890.

———. *Tenting on the Plains: General Custer in Kansas and Texas*. New York, 1887. Reprint. Ed. Jane R. Stewart. Norman: University of Oklahoma Press, 1971.

CUSTER, GEORGE A. *My Life on the Plains, or, Personal Experiences with the Indians*. Norman: University of Oklahoma Press, 1962.

DAVIS, THEODORE. "A Summer on the Plains." *Harper's New Monthly Magazine* 36 (February 1868): 292–307.

FOUGERA, KATHARINE GIBSON. *With Custer's Cavalry*. Caldwell, Idaho: Caxton Press, 1940.

FRAZER, ROBERT W. *Forts of the West*. Norman: University of Oklahoma Press, 1965.

FROST, LAWRENCE A. *The Court-Martial of General George Armstrong Custer*. Norman: University of Oklahoma Press, 1968.

GODFREY, EDWARD S. "Some Reminiscences, Including an Account of General Sully's Expedition against the Southern Plains Indians, 1868." *Cavalry Journal* 36 (July 1927): 417–25.

———. "Some Reminiscences, including the Washita Battle, November 27, 1868." *Cavalry Journal* 37 (October 1928): 481–500.

GRINNELL, GEORGE B. *The Fighting Cheyennes*. 2d ed. Norman: University of Oklahoma Press, 1956.

HAMMER, KENNETH. *Men with Custer: Biographies of the 76th Cavalry, 25 June 1876*. Fort Collins, Colo: Old Army Press, 1972.

HYDE, GEORGE E. *Life of George Bent, Written from his Letters*. Ed. Savoie Lottinville. Norman: University of Oklahoma Press, 1967.

JONES, DOUGLAS C. *The Treaty of Medicine Lodge: The Story of the Great Treaty Council as Told by Eyewitnesses*. Norman: University of Oklahoma Press, 1966.

KEIM, DeB. Randolph. *Sheridan's Troopers on the Borders: A Winter Campaign on the Plains*. Philadelphia, David McKay, 1891.

LECKIE, WILLIAM H. *The Military Conquest of the Southern Plains*. Norman: University of Oklahoma Press, 1963.

MERINGTON, MARGUERITE, ed. *The Custer Story: The Life and Intimate Letters of General Custer and His Wife Elizabeth*. New York: Devin-Adair, 1950.

MONAGHAN, JAY. *Custer: The Life of General George Armstrong Custer*. Boston and Toronto: Little, Brown, 1959.

MILLBROOK, MINNIE DUBBS. "Custer's First Scout in the West." *Kansas Historical Quarterly* 39 (Spring 1973): 75–95.

———, ed. "Mrs. General Custer at Fort Riley, 1866." *Kansas Historical Quarterly* 40 (Spring 1974): 63–71.

———. "The West Breaks in General Custer." *Kansas Historical Quarterly* 36 (Summer 1970): 113–48.

NATIONAL ARCHIVES. Regimental Muster Rolls, 7th U.S. Cavalry, 1867–68, and officer personnel records in Appointments-Commissions-Promotions files, Record Group 94.

NYE, WILBUR S. *Carbine and Lance: The Story of Old Fort Sill*. Norman: University of Oklahoma Press, 1937.

———. *Plains Indian Raiders: The Final Phases of Warfare from the Arkansas to the Red River*. Norman: University of Oklahoma Press, 1968.

PRUCHA, FRANCIS PAUL. *Guide to the Military Posts of the United States*. Madison: University of Wisconsin Press, 1964.

SPOTTS, DAVID L., AND EARL A. BRININSTOOL. *Campaigning with Custer and the Nineteenth Kansas Volunteer Cavalry*. Los Angeles: Wetzel, 1928.

STANLEY, HENRY M. *My Early Travels and Adventures in America and Asia*. 2 vols. New York: Scribners, 1905.

UTLEY, ROBERT M. *Frontier Regulars: The United States Army and the Indian, 1866–91*. New York: Macmillan, 1973.

Index

295